The 386 PC Companion

Allen Brown

SIGMA

d Kingdom

First published in 1990 by

Sigma Press, 1 South Oak Lane, Wilmslow, Cheshire SK9 6AR, England.

British Library Cataloguing in Publication Data

A CIP catalogue record for this book is available from the British Library.

ISBN: 1-85058-209-2

Typesetting and design by

Sigma Hi-Tech Services Ltd

Printed in Malta by

Interprint Ltd.

Distributed by

John Wiley & Sons Ltd., Baffins Lane, Chichester, West Sussex, England.

Acknowledgement of copyright

Within this book, various proprietary trade names and names protected by copyright are mentioned for descriptive purposes. Full acknowledgment is hereby made of all such protection.

Figures 2.3, 2.4, 2.6, 3.1, 5.2 and 7.2 are the copyright of Intel and reproduced with their permission and our thanks.

Preface

The Personal Computer (PC) has become the basic tool in all areas of Information Technology. The need for the effective processing of information became well established in the eighties in areas such as data evaluation, information archiving, mathematical modelling and information presentation. The most economical means by which this can be achieved is with the Personal Computer and it has subsequently become an indispensable part of modern business and commercial practice. As successive generations of PC systems emerge, they are accompanied by enhanced facilities and improved performance. The third generation of PCs, based on the Intel 32-bit 80386 microprocessor (386 PCs), is experiencing a substantial market growth by creating new application opportunities and by displacing the second generation of IBM AT personal computers. Although personal computers are appearing based on the Intel 80486 and Intel i860, with their Reduced Instruction Set Computer (RISC) architecture, the 386 PC still represents the most economically priced system for a high-performance computer.

This book has a four-fold purpose: firstly it is intended for readers who wish to familiarise themselves with the major aspects of 386 PC technology. Many first time users of 386 PCs may not have used a PC before and much of the material provided in the text should lighten the effect of being confronted by a high-performance computer. The second aim is to enable the reader to gain an appreciation of what can be expected from a 386 PC. Thirdly the contents should be helpful to potential buyers of a 386 PC by arming them with sufficient knowledge to assess the qualities and deficiencies of a particular make. The final aim is to acquaint the reader with the large variety of peripheral services for the 386 PC. One of the key features of the 386 PC is the option of adding peripherals to enable the user to customise the computer for a specific application or a range of shared, multi-user services.

At the beginning of some sections the material is of an introductory nature aimed at providing an overview of the material within the rest of the section without going into any detail. The text following each overview will cover the subject matter in greater depth and provide information of a more specific nature.

An important aspect in the discussion of applications for 386 PCs is a review of some commercially available products. Although several are cited in the course of the book,

In all specialist areas, be it technology, commerce, law, accountancy, medicine or engineering, a jargon-oriented language evolves which, although it appears confusing to the layman, is essential in order to promote communication between individuals. Computer technology is no exception and it has its own terminology which evolves as fast as the technology itself. Although the rationale behind the adoption of new phraseology is somewhat obscure it does form an important element in the understanding and education of computer technology. This book should therefore serve as a glossary for much of the current terminology used in the field of personal computing. Although it cannot serve as a complete lexicon it will go some way towards understanding the current language.

I would like to express my sincere gratitude to Mr Neal Hutchingson of the Microcomputer Unit for patiently reading the manuscript and making many useful and constructive suggestions.

Allen Brown

Contents

Chapter Eight: Networking and Multi-user Systems

1

Introduction

During the 1980s personal computers have come of age and these affordable low-cost systems have opened up a variety of computer functions, such as financial planning, data processing and text management to a wider range of users. The explosive growth and acceptance of desktop computers has resulted in widespread applications and hardly any office can be found without a PC. It has now become an integral part of information processing and the growth of office systems based on the PC will continue with the same momentum.

As each new model reaches the marketplace, there is a greater expectation of performance with a lower price tag. Today, significant emphasis is placed upon reliability, not only in software but also in machine hardware. High-performance PCs are expected to cope with large amounts of data and low levels of reliability can lead to substantial losses which are quite unacceptable. The high degree of competition in the marketplace has therefore led to elevated levels of quality at reasonable prices.

The engine in the personal computer is the microprocessor and the vast majority of PCs employ microprocessors made by the American chip manufacturer Intel. Successive generations of PCs have followed Intel's development of bigger and faster microprocessors. Intel, with the release of its 32-bit 80386 microprocessor in 1984, ushered in the dawn of the third generation of personal computer and today, in the market, there are many PCs based on the Intel 80386 microprocessor.

The first generation of PCs was based on the Intel 8088 8-bit microprocessor. The number of bits represent the actual width of the data bus on the processor. It is useful to think of an 8-bit bus as a country road, a 16-bit bus as a dual carriageway and a 32-bit bus a motorway. The greater the bus width the faster the information flow and larger the volume of data (traffic). The speed of a microprocessor is governed by the crystal oscillator (the clock) which drives and synchronises the microprocessor's operations. The crystal frequency is measured in MHz (MegaHertz or millions of cycles per second). Low-performance PCs have clock speeds of 4.77 MHz whereas in high-performance 386 PCs the clock frequency reaches 33 MHz.

Paramount in the function of a personal computer is the software operating system (Section 5.1) which is best thought of as a working environment with its own conditions for controlling the disk units, the screen, the keyboard and the other peripherals attached to the PC. An application program (or software package) is said to run under the operating system. The comprehensive design of the Intel 80386 microprocessor allows a number of operating systems to run concurrently or in a near simultaneous fashion on the 386 PC.

Multi-tasking

The major attribute of a PC based on the 80386 microprocessor is its ability to run several application programs concurrently and this is known as multi-tasking. As an example, a user may have a word processor application program running and may want to input some information from a spreadsheet. In a multi-tasking PC, a spreadsheet application program can be called up in parallel with the word processor and the user switches his attention to the spreadsheet. Once the calculations in the spreadsheet have been completed, the user can switch back to the word processor and import the results into the text display. Both application programs can therefore be kept loaded side by side. To enable a multi-tasking facility, a suitable software environment is required and this is covered in greater detail in Chapter 5.

1.1 First and Second Generation PCs

International Business Machines (IBM) adopted the Intel 8-bit 8088 microprocessor (running at 4.77 MHz) for its first design of personal computer in the early eighties. Referred to as the IBM PC it gained considerable success and soon became the industry standard. The operating system for the PC was written by Microsoft for IBM and was called PC-DOS (Personal Computer Disk Operating System). Microsoft also brought out its own operating system MS-DOS which is basically the same as PC-DOS and has now become the recognised standard.

Updated versions of the PC, which included hard discs with greater memory capacity, followed with the release of the IBM XT version with corresponding modification in DOS to manage the addition facilities. The IBM PC had a number of annoying features including the poor screen refresh mechanism with its monochrome display adapter (MDA). IBM's first attempt at a graphics format resulted in the very poor Color Graphics Adapter standard (CGA). However the reputation of IBM was sufficient to thrust and maintain its PCs to the forefront of the market where it remains the dominant leader.

Intel, continuing with its design of microprocessors, issued the 80286 16 bit microprocessor and this was adopted by IBM for the AT version of its PCs. This represented faster processing time and the choice of alternative operating systems such as UNIX (Section 5.4). In response to the criticism levelled at the first generation of PCs with their poor screen display, IBM introduced the Enhanced Graphics Adapter (EGA – Section 4.3.2) which has a cleaner screen refresh and provides high-quality colour graphics.

After the mid eighties the clone manufacturers were active and a plethora of IBM compatible machines, both XT and AT appeared in direct competition with IBM. Many of these clone manufacturers have become respectable computer manufacturers in their own right and this has resulted in the affordable, but more importantly, usable computer systems for the man in the street.

Another feature which has secured the IBM standard, is the wealth of software which will run under DOS on any IBM compatible PC (clone). Almost all software written for the IBM PC/XT/AT is upwardly compatible and will run (faster) on a 386 PC, thus protecting any software investment when the hardware is upgraded.

1.2 Third Generation PCs

Technology, not standing still, saw the emergence of the next microprocessor generation in the form of the Intel 32-bit 80386 which as expected has greater speed and performance breadth than the previous models. However at this point in the evolution of personal computers there was a change in direction by the market leader IBM. Having watched the clone manufacturers muscle in on its product IBM introduced the Personal System/2 (PS/2 – Section 3.8) range with its Micro Channel Architecture (MCA – Section 3.8.1) with the intended purpose of stopping the clone makers in their tracks. History will judge whether this has been successful. The PS/2 with its Operating System (OS/2 – Section 5.6), written by Microsoft and IBM, has been designed with the Intel 80286 16-bit in mind. However there is a version available for the 386 PC, known as OS/2-2, which exploits several of the special features of the 80386 central processing unit.

Meanwhile many other PC manufacturers have introduced their own personal computer based on the Intel 80386 microprocessor. Although IBM has used the 80386 in its PS/2 Models 70 and 80 machines (Section 3.8), the contents of this book will be applicable to all types of personal computer based on the 80386 microprocessor.

The 386 PC has become well established in the PC marketplace and there are many different manufacturers and designs. However most of them share common features, the distinguishing characteristics being: high computational speed and breadth of performance, enormous memory capacity, graphics-orientated displays, good networking potential and a low price.

These characteristics will be discussed in greater depth in the appropriate sections where emphasis will be placed on methods for realising the potential of the 386 PC.

An indication of the performance of a 386 PC is given by its clock speed, and there are four; 16, 20, 25 and 33 MHz. A 16-MHz 80386 microprocessor with its coprocessor is capable of performing 5 million floating point calculations per second (see insert) and this represents a considerable improvement over 8-bit PCs which could only manage several hundred. Only a few years ago a computer with a performance comparable to that of a 386 PC would have cost in excess of £60,000. It is this pricing feature which marks the revolution in personal computing.

In addition to these features is the availability of vast amounts of low-cost data storage in the form of hard disk drives. Hard disk storage is now purchasable with ever-increasing limits, well in excess of 300 MBytes. Paramount in the design of a high-density hard disk is a fast access time and figures around 23 msecs are now commonplace – quite acceptable for 386 PC applications. The reliability of hard disk drives has improved with each new design and this is of considerable importance. The unexpected loss of 200 MBytes of data is no easy plight to recover from.

The current generation of 386 PCs exploits the advantages of the highly visual displays based on Windows, Icons, Mouse and Pull-down menus (WIMPS). The speed of 386 PCs permits rapid screen refresh rates which allow the screen to become a powerful user interface. Another attractive feature of most 386 PCs is the hardware and software compatibility with earlier generations of PCs. Software which runs on an IBM XT or AT PC will, in general, run on a 386 PC. The bewildering array of peripherals built for 8088 and 80286 based PCs by third party manufacturers are also upwardly compatible with the 386 PC.

There are various methods for determining the performance of personal computers and one which has reached prominence is the Landmark CPU Speed Test, a software product from Landmark Software of Sunnyvale, California. This can be used to measure the computational rate of a 386 PC and is often quoted in the manufacturer's literature. The Landmark Test provides two figures: the first is the relative performance of the 386 PC compared with an IBM-XT running at 4.77 MHz. The second is a clock speed at which an IBM-AT (16-bit based PC) would have to run to achieve the same performance as the 386 PC. As a broad indication, for a 20 MHz 386 PC the Landmark speed should comfortably exceed 25 MHz.

A question frequently asked by the new user is: What has the 386 PC got to offer over and above its predecessor apart from speed? There is a variety of features of immediate interest to the new user several of which will be briefly covered here. This information will serve as a gentle introduction to the many features offered by the 386 PC, but more details can be found in the sections referenced after each item where a more complete description is given.

386SX PC

Many 386 PCs operate with a scaled-down bus version of the 80386 central processing unit (CPU) – the 80386SX (Section 2.2.5), and they usually carry the 386SX label. These machines are generally cheaper than a machine hosting the full 80386 CPU (80386DX) and at present all software which runs on 80386 based PC will also run on a 386SX PC, albeit somewhat slower. A 386SX PC will have a clock speed of 16 or 20 MHz. However it is not just the clock speed which will render the machine slower than an equivalent 386 PC; the data bus on the 80386SX CPU is 16 bits as opposed to 32 bits on the 80386. For DOS (Section 5.5) programs, the reduced data bus width will not make any significant difference. DOS code normally uses 8 bits only, but there are some DOS application programs which use 16. Both types of code will run on a 386SX PC. The width of the address bus on the 80386SX has been reduced to 24 bits and this provides a maximum on-board memory of 16 MBytes. Again this is not likely to affect the operation of the majority of application programs running under DOS. To accompany the 80386SX there is a 80387SX maths coprocessor (Section 3.1.2).

Clock Speed

In general, the higher the clock speed the more expensive the 386 PC. This is due in part to the fast dynamic RAM (Section 2.3.1) which is required by the 80386 CPU and this goes up in price with clock speed. There is also the additional cost arising from fast digital circuitry and tighter design tolerances on the motherboard circuit layout. At present there are four clock speeds for the 80386: 16, 20, 25, and 33 MHz and competitive priced machines start with the 20 MHz clock speed. Unfortunately the clock speed does not necessarily reflect the true speed of the 386 PC. If the on-board memory is slow, the 80386 may run at the specified clock speed but still has to wait for the memory to respond.

On-board RAM

When an application program is to be run on a computer, a copy of the program, which is on disk, is loaded into the on-board memory and executed from this memory. All 386 PCs will have a base or conventional memory of 640K bytes, however many DOS application programs now run more efficiently with additional memory installed in the 386 PC.

Extra memory is available as either Expanded (Section 2.3.3) or Extended (Section 2.3.4) and in general a 386 PC should have a minimum of two MBytes of on-board memory. A software utility, known as an Extended Memory Manager, will probably be required to reconfigure the memory to the user's needs. However several application programs reconfigure the on-board memory automatically.

Cache Memory

Several 386 PC manufacturers have enhanced the performance of their machines by including a cache memory (Section 2.3.2) which is resident between the 80386 CPU and the main memory. Cache memory is much faster than normal on-board memory and allows the CPU to run at its full operating speed. Every time the CPU reads part of a program from the on-board memory, a copy of it is made in the cache memory. The next time the CPU runs the same part of the program, it will do so from the cache memory which runs much faster. Cache memory normally comes in one of two sizes: 32K or 64K. A 386 PC with cache memory will have a faster performance than one without it. The majority of 25-MHz machines will have this facility.

DOS and other Operating Systems

The majority of 386 PCs come with DOS Version 3.3 (Section 5.3). However the most recent edition of DOS is Version 4 (Section 5.3.2) which has a few additional features to DOS 3.3 including the provision for larger hard disk partitions (Section 2.5.1). The majority of 386 PCs operate quite adequately under DOS 3.3 and this has the facilities for coping with a number of network requirements (Section 8.4.1). If a number of 386 PCs are to be networked it is essential to have the same version of DOS on each machine or incompatibility problems will occur. One of the attractive features of the 386 PC is its ability to host a UNIX operating system (Section 5.4). However the user must be warned that UNIX is an expensive ball game and running software under UNIX still tends to be a costly exercise.

Graphics Options

One feature which is of prime importance on a 386 PC is the quality of the screen display. For general purpose 386 PCs the graphics options are Hercules (Section 4.3.1.), EGA (Section 4.3.2.) and VGA mono or colour (Section 4.3.3). Experienced users have tended to move towards the VGA option which complements the high performance of the 80386 CPU and this is becoming a standard feature on 386 PCs. VGA colour offers high image resolution and a large variety of colours. Alternatively, VGA mono offers the same image quality and a minimum of 16 shades of grey which is most appealing for desktop publishing applications.

Floppy Disk Drives

There are two choices for floppy disk drives on a 386 PC: the quad density 1.2-MByte 5.25 inch drive (Section 2.4) or the 1.44-MByte 3.5 inch drive. Although the 3.5 inch drives are becoming very popular, many application programs are still only available on 5.25 inch floppy discs. Having both types of drive on a 386 PC is an unnecessary expense and at present the 5.25 inch drive will probably suffice for the majority of users. Normally buying application programs on 3.5 inch discs costs more than the usual quad density 5.25 inch discs. If necessary a 3.5 inch drive can always be added at a later date.

Coprocessors

A 80387 coprocessor (Section 3.1) will greatly enhance the performance of a 386 PC if an application program involves numerically intensive operations. It is specifically designed to speed up the 80386 CPU by performing mathematical tasks instead of the CPU. When the CPU encounters a maths instruction, it passes the instruction to the coprocessor which is able to perform it in a fraction of the time it would take the CPU. Several of the early 386 PCs only had a socket for the 16-bit 80287 coprocessor (Section 3.1.1). But today, virtually all 386 PCs have a socket for accommodating a 80387 coprocessor. Coprocessors are available in four clock speeds: 16, 20, 25 and 33 MHz to match the 80386 CPU. Never run a coprocessor faster than its specified clock rate; it can however run slower. A 25-MHz 80387 coprocessor can run with a 20-MHz 80386 CPU without any problems.

Expansion Bus

On removing the cover from the 386 PC unit, the expansion slots of the card cage will be revealed at the rear of the unit (Section 7.3). There are currently a number of standards for the interface connection for the cards which fit into the PC. The expansion slots will probably be in three sizes, short (8-bit), medium (16-bit) and long (32-bit). There are standards for the short and medium connectors (MCA and EISA – Section 7.3), but not for the long connector which is strictly for additional memory of the manufacturer's design. Since 8-bit expansion cards will fit into the 16-bit (medium) connectors it can be questioned why there should be any 8-bit connectors in a 386 PC.

Hard Disk Drive

Every 386 PC should have a hard disk drive (HDD – Section 2.5) since it is an essential component in its normal operation. The minimum memory capacity of a HDD must not be smaller than 44 MBytes. Many of today's application programs take up a significant amount of hard disk space. As new releases of standard application programs come onto the market, they will invariably require more hard disk space than their predecessor. In addition the HDD should have an access time not exceeding 28 msecs. This will be the average time taken for the CPU to access data on the HDD.

33 MHz 386 PCs

The top of the range 386 PCs will feature a 80386 CPU operating at 33 MHz. 386 PCs in this category are more expensive due to the additional cost of the fast digital chips and tighter tolerance in the printed circuit board of the motherboard layout design.

When specifying a 33 MHz machine, it should come with a fast access time hard disk drive (less than 20 msec) with suitable disk caching software (Section 2.7) to optimise data transfer. Every 33-MHz 386 PC will have a hardware cache facility of at least 32K as this is necessary to maximise its performance. 33-MHz 386 PCs are well matched to the requirements of a multi-user system where there is likely to be heavy demands on the CPU processing time.

1.3 Buying a 386 PC

There are many 386 PCs on the market today with numerous accessories and options. It will be no easy task to match your requirements to a particular 386 PC and its options. The clock speed will be the first indication of cost with 16-MHz machines offering the lowest price tags. The 25-MHz and 33-Mhz 386 PCs will not only have faster memory (with its own high cost) but there are likely to be additional hardware features (cache controller circuitry) to maximise the speed.

The first deciding factor will be your budget ceiling, which in many respects will determine the complexity of your system. If you have a general requirement for a high-speed PC then your task of choosing the most appropriate model will be a difficult one. If your need is for a high-quality screen display you will probably also need to obtain comparable high-quality hard copies of it, and your budget must reflect this.

As an example, on the opposite page are six possible requirements that can be adequately accommodated by a 386 PC with suitable options and the sections where more information can be found are referenced. The emphasis will be placed only on the hardware options and possible software solutions, and does not infer a recommendation for those products.

1.4 Minimum 386 PC Configuration

On the market at present there is a plethora of 386 PCs and there is an obvious desire to get value for money without finishing up, at the end of the day, with a white elephant. Several dealers tend to use the pick and mix principle with each 386 PC component coming from a different source – a graphics card from one manufacturer, the monitor from another and the hard disk drive from yet another. In principle this method of configuring a 386 PC is quite acceptable providing the manufacturing standards are adhered to. This does not always occur and you should not be too surprised if you find the occasional software package which is incompatible with a composite 386 PC configuration.

Task 1: A large amount of data processing with fast throughput and large areas for data storage.

Solution: 20-MHz 386 PC with large capacity hard disk drive(s) (2.5), tape streamer back up (3.7), possible coprocessor (3.1.2), Lotus 1-2-3 Version 3 (Protect).

Task 2: A requirement for archiving information which will be cross referenced with frequent amendments.

Solution: 20-MHz 386 PC with large hard disk drive (2.5), possible read/write optical disk drive (MO 7.4.3), database application program – dBase IV or FoxBase.

Task 3: A need for large number crunching operations (heavy computation loads), computer modelling and solving equations.

Solution: 25 or 33-MHz 386 PC, 80387 coprocessor (3.1.2) or Weitek 3167 (3.1.3), FORTRAN compiler (9.1.1).

Task 4: A requirement for a computer-aided design system with high-quality, rapid-response graphics.

Solution: 25-MHz 386 PC with 60-MByte hard disk drive (2.5), AutoCAD/386 (9.3.2) or VersaCAD/386 (9.3.3), very high resolution graphics (4.3.4), coprocessor (3.1.2) quality vector plotter (6.6).

Task 5: A requirement for a desktop publishing system with good quality text and graphic processing with fast screen writing.

Solution: High-resolution graphics VGA monitor (4.3.3), laser printer (6.1.2), image scanner (6.2), possible plotter (6.3), possible image setter for very high-quality photographic production (9.2.4), Ventura (9.2.1), PageMaker (9.2.2).

Task 6: A requirement for a multi-user system for data processing and spreadsheet analysis.

Solution: Networked multi-user system with fast large memory 386 PC acting as a terminal server or a stand-alone file server (8.5.4), network versions of dBase IV for data processing and Lotus 1-2-3 Release 3 (Protect) for spreadsheet analysis.

As a preliminary guide, a minimum 386 PC configuration should have at least the following components (section references are in parentheses):

❑ A VGA monochrome monitor (4.3.3)

❑ A half-height 44-MByte hard disk (2.5)

❑ Two MBytes of RAM (2.3)

❑ Two RS-232 interface ports (3.3.2) on the motherboard

❑ One parallel (Centronics) interface (3.3.1)

❑ At least five free slots in the card cage (3.2.1)

❑ A 1.22-MByte 5.25 inch floppy disk drive (2.4)

❑ A slot for a 80387 or 80287 coprocessor on motherboard (3.1.2)

❑ A real-time clock/calendar

❑ A 102-key AT-style keyboard (3.4)

❑ On a 25-MHz machine there should be a cache memory of at least 32K (2.3.2)

❑ A 160-watt power supply for supporting additional plug-in expansion boards (3.6)

❑ A mouse, with either serial interface or a dedicated mouse port (3.5)

❑ DOS Version 3.3 or higher (5.3)

❑ Extended Memory Manager software (2.3.4)

In addition to the specific discussions on the various aspects of 386 PCs, the following chapters will also provide enough advice to guide the user through the many unknowns of 386 PC technology.

Before buying, carefully read the product specification and try to identify the areas where the manufacturers have neglected to mention certain aspects of their design. They all claim that their 386 PC is among the fastest on the market, but I have yet to meet any who will openly admit that their machine is one of the slowest.

Publications of interest:

PC Magazine: (Monthly), Reed Business Publishing, Quadrant House, The Quadrant, Sutton, Surrey.

BYTE: (Monthly), McGraw-Hill Publications, McGraw-Hill House, Maidenhead, Berkshire.

What's New in Computing: (Monthly), Morgan Grampian, Calderwood Street, London SE18.

Micro Technology: (Monthly), Hanover Press, 80 Highgate Road, London NW5 1PB.

2

Standard 386 PC Hardware

There are many 386-based personal computers (386 PCs) on the market and the majority of them have standard hardware features. A 386 PC will consist of at least three physically separate components: the monitor, the keyboard and the computer unit. A number also have a mouse (Section 6.2) as standard but this is by no means general although it can be argued that a mouse is an essential 386 PC peripheral. In this chapter we shall be discussing the components within the computer unit and their overall role in the operation of the 386 PC. An awareness of their function is of considerable value when assessing the performance and operation of the 386 PC. The material covered here will also be helpful when evaluating the specifications of a 386 PC and should provide enough information to judge the limitations of a particular make.

2.1 The Motherboard

As a result of modern manufacturing techniques, most of the electronics for a 386 PC can be encompassed on a single printed circuit board (PCB) which is referred to as the motherboard. The complexity of its design usually requires multilayer (several layers of tracking) PCBs. A single board minimises the cost, improves the reliability and eliminates the problems which arise when electronic signals pass from board to board. For a high-speed 386 PC design it is essential to have the fast integrated circuits geometrically close to minimise electronic signal propagation delays.

On occasions the user of a 386 PC will need to remove the cover from the machine. However on looking inside the unit, only a small portion of the mother board will normally be visible since it lies at the base of the unit. Sometimes the 80386 central processing unit (CPU) is visible – one of the large integrated circuits, measuring 1.4 by 1.4 inches. The socket for the coprocessor should also be clearly visible and accessible.

A typical motherboard will have a number of the system features, as shown in Figure 2.1: the CPU, expansion slots for input/output (I/O) expansion plug-in cards, some memory chips, the ROM BIOS (the integrated circuits with windows) and other obligatory support integrated circuits which may include a proprietary chip set. It is commonplace to find **Programmed Array Logic** (PAL) chips on the motherboard where the internal logic is configured by the board designer.

The synchronism of the digital electronics is maintained by the master clock which is connected directly to the 80386 and its coprocessor. The master clock (which is a quartz crystal oscillator) for a 386 PC will operate at either 16, 20, 25 or 33 MHz. On every motherboard there are a number of jumpers and it may be necessary, on occasions, for the user to reconfigure the jumper settings. This is especially true if extra internal features are added. The jumpers allow control to be exercised over the type of display monitor, the presence of the coprocessor and sometimes the partitioning of the memory.

Figure 2.1 An example of a 386 motherboard. (Photo: Courtesy of Intel)

Normally some information is given in the user manual for the PC regarding the setting of these jumpers. However most user manuals are very badly written and can quite easily be misunderstood. It is therefore very important to read the instructions carefully before attempting to make any changes to the jumper settings. If in doubt, contact your dealer, as incongruous jumper settings can cause hardware damage to your PC.

To allow the design of the motherboard to be compact, a significant reduction in chip count can be achieved with the inclusion of a dedicated **chip set.** Much of the support logic on the motherboard can be replaced by the dedicated chips which leads to a simplification in the wiring layout of the board. Intel manusfactures chip sets for the 80386DX and the 80386SX microprocessors. Referred to as the 82340D(S)X family, the consist of the following devices:

❑ 82343 System controller for the 80386SX

❑ 82346 System controller for the 80386DX

❑ 82385 32-bit Cache controller for the 80386DX

❑ 82385SX Cache controller for the 80386SX

❑ 82344 Industry Standard Architecture (ISA) bus controller

❑ 82345 PC/AT data buffer for the 80386DX

❑ 82077 Floppy disk controller

❑ 82341 High integration peripheral controller for keyboard, serial ports and so on.

To help the manufacturers of 386 PCs to evaluate the performance of the 82240 chip set Intel also provides evaluation boards which can be used to good effect as testing grounds for future layout designs. Intel is not the only company to manufacture chip sets to support the 80386 and among the other proprietary chip sets is the TACT83000 product range from Texas Instruments.

The TACT83000 family consists of eight chips which support the full 32-bit bus architecture of the 80386DX, the 80486 as well as the reduced bus architecture of the 80386SX. The introduction of chip sets in the design of the 386 PC has lead to smaller size units (footprints) and heightened reliability since much of the circuitry is highly integrated.

2.2 Intel 80386 Microprocessor

At the heart of every 386 PC system there is a high performance 32-bit Intel 80386 microprocessor, also known as the **central processing unit** (CPU). This microprocessor is especially suitable for advanced desktop computer systems and work stations for specific computer-aided design (CAD) or engineering (CAE). The 80386 has an enhanced high speed architecture and this enables the processor to switch between programs even when running under different operating systems – this is the so-called multi-tasking facility. It is fabricated in CHMOS-IV 1.5 micron geometry technology and is supplied in a pin grid array package (Figure 2.2 overleaf). When running at a clock rate of 16 MHz the 80386 can execute between three and four million machine instructions per second.

The architecture of the 80386 is based on a pipeline design which allows the operation of the functional units to overlap. By pipelining the functional units, the 80386 can overlap the execution of different parts of each program instruction. Therefore at any one time, several instructions can be in various stages of completion. As an example the processor can decode and execute one instruction while at the same time it can address and fetch the next. Each of the processor's instructions takes on average 4.5 machine cycles to complete, (duration of machine cycle = 1 clock frequency) and the pipeline design allows different parts of successive instructions to be executed simultaneously. It is equivalent to staggering the execution of the processor's instructions.

Figure 2.2 Pin Grid Array (PGA) package of the 80386. (Photo: Courtesy of Intel)

As part of a deliberate policy, Intel has ensured that code written for other Intel microprocessors is upwardly compatible with the 80386; it is said to be **binary compatible.** This means that code written for the Intel 8088, 8086, 80186 and the 80286 microprocessors can also run, unmodified, on the 80386 thereby protecting earlier software investments.

As part of its general design and in order for the processor to be compatible with the previous Intel microprocessors, the 80386 can operate in a number of different modes. The various modes represent the flexible features of the 80386 which make it suitable for running old DOS application programs as well as future programs running under either DOS or other operating systems.

The internal architecture of the 80386 is divided into six functional units (Figure 2.3):

❑ Bus Interface Unit (BIU)

❑ Code Prefetch Unit (CPfU)

❑ Execution Unit (EU)

❑ Segmentation Unit (SU)

❑ Paging Unit (PU)

❑ Instruction Decode Unit (IDU).

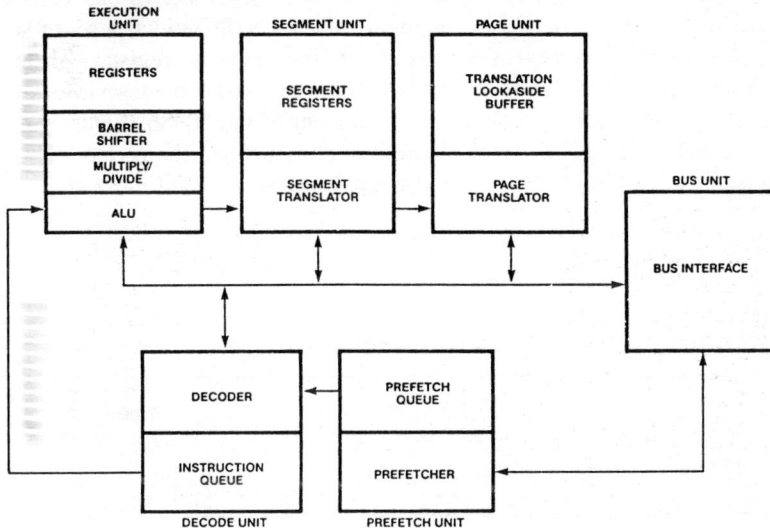

Figure 2.3 The six functional units of the 80386

These units can operate in an autonomous fashion and are connected by an array of 32-bit wide internal buses. Working collectively, they fetch program instructions (or code) from memory and execute them, and they are designed to optimise this operation. The BIU is responsible for data transfer in and out of the processor and accepts requests to fetch program code from the CPfU and the EU. It also performs the necessary bus timing signals for the external buses. The CPfU on the other hand is responsible for issuing code addresses before the code is actually required. This function is known as **Lookahead.** When the BIU is not involved with the execution of an instruction, the CPfU issues requests to the BIU to fetch sequential instructions in anticipation and these are stored in a **Code Queue** ready for the IDU. Its function is simply to translate the fetched code instructions into microcode which are then stored in an **Instruction Queue.** The EU then executes the instructions by converting them into control operations. The Segmentation Unit and the Paging unit collectively form the **Memory Management Unit** which is discussed in Section 2.2.4.

Part of the Execution Unit of the 80386 is the multiply/divide unit which can perform 32-bit multiplications which take between 9 and 41 clock cycles. A similar length of time is taken for performing 32-bit division calculations. Binary shift operations are performed in the function unit called the barrel shifter and this can perform a 1 to 64-bit right or left shift in a single clock cycle.

The mechanism by which the 80386 generates memory addresses is known as **segmentation**. The logical address range – as seen by the assembly language programmer – for the 80386 CPU, consists of 48-bits. These 48-bits consist of a 16-bit **segment selector** and a 32-bit **segment offset.** The 80386 has a set of **segment registers** which hold segment selectors. With the segment registers there is an associated table of **descriptor registers** which contain **segment descriptors** relating to addressing information for each memory segment of the 80386 (Figure 2.4). Each segment descriptor carries the segment address, its range and the access rights to the memory segment. Access rights are fundamental to the protected mode design of the 80386.

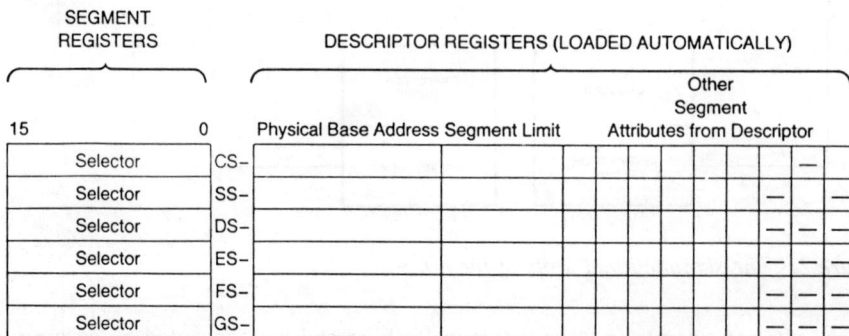

Figure 2.4 The 80386 segment registers and associated descriptor registers

Each segment descriptor, contained within a descriptor register, will determine whether its memory segment is read only, read/write or privileged. Privileged memory areas, which can be reserved for operating systems, can therefore be protected from entry by the users. The segment selector is used to index the table of descriptor registers and by this means the 48-bit original address is transformed into a 32-bit **linear address** by adding the segment offset to the 32-bit physical base address value held in the descriptor register (Figure 2.5). The segment registers are accessible by the programmer and contain values identifying the currently addressable memory segments.

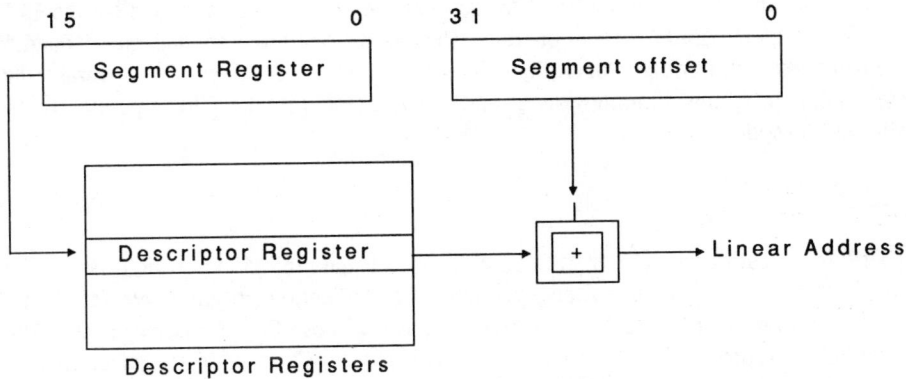

Descriptor Registers

Figure 2.5 To generate a linear address the segment register indexes the appropriate descriptor register and the segment offset is added to the base address in the descriptor register

At any one time the current addressable memory segments are partitioned into six areas which are defined by the contents of the segment registers. These are:

❑ Code Segment (CS) relating to the program area

❑ Stack Segment (SS) relating to the stack area used by the current task

❑ Data Segments (DS, ES, FS and GS) current data areas.

When multi-tasking, the 80386 switches from task to task and the segment registers are updated with the new task parameters. When this happens the descriptor registers automatically update for the new task. The updated descriptor registers will contain the base addresses and the memory attributes (access rights) allocated to the new and current task.

2.2.1 Real 80386 Mode

When the 80386 CPU is first powered up (or when reset from the front panel of the 386 PC) it enters its Real Mode of operation. The option of the Real Mode is to ensure that a PC based on the 80386 microprocessor can execute code in the same manner as the Intel 8086 microprocessor except faster. In this mode the 80386 therefore behaves the same as the 8086 except it has a 32-bit performance and operates at the much higher clock speed.

When using a 386 PC under MS-DOS without multi-tasking, the 80386 will operate in its Real Mode. The addressable memory is restricted to one Mbyte, the same as the Intel 8086, however it is able to execute program code at maximum speed. It achieves this because the CPU is free of the overheads normally imposed from the intervention of the operating system. In the Real Mode, a single program can monopolise the CPU thus ensuring maximum execution rate. The 80386 operating in this mode handles interrupts and input/output operations in the way the 8086 does. For several 8086 application programs running concurrently (multi-tasking), the CPU operates in the Virtual 86 Mode.

2.2.2 Virtual 86 Mode

There is a feature on the 80386, known as Virtual 86 Mode, which is able to construct protected operational environments for application programs written for the first generation of IBM PC/XT personal computers. These PCs are based on the 8086 or 8088 microprocessor which can only have a one Mbyte address space. In each operational environment, the 80386 emulates the operation of the Intel 8086 (or 8088) microprocessor. In this mode the 386 PC is often referred to as running 8086 engines or **Virtual Machines** (VMs).

When the 80386 is switched into the Virtual 86 Mode the VM86 flag in the CPU's internal Flag Register is set, the CPU acts as an 8086 or an 80386 depending on the setting of the VM86 flag. One multi-tasking feature of the Intel 80386 is its operation in this mode and this enables several 8086 programs to run concurrently – that is, several VMs. Each 8086 environment can have its own DOS and an applications program running while confined within its own one Mbyte address space.

Although there could be several VMs operating concurrently, there is only one set of peripherals which have to be shared by the VMs. It is therefore necessary for the Virtual 86 Mode to accommodate system calls from each VM which require the use of the peripherals. System calls are common operations, such as writing to the screen or responding to the keyboard. Whenever a VM generates a system call, the 80368 passes from the localised Virtual 86 Mode into the Protected Mode and services the requested peripheral. On completion of the call it then switches back to the Virtual 86 Mode and continues operating the VMs. To achieve this response, the operating system is supplemented with a **Virtual Machine Monitor** (VMM) which is a software interface between the Virtual 86 task and the operating system running on the 80386 (Figure 2.6 opposite). This ensures that the full resources of the 80386 are not compromised when executing 8086 code.

To further emphasis the power of the 80386, the Virtual 86 Mode is actually a subset of the Protected Mode and can operate simultaneously with other Protected Mode operating systems executing programs in a different part of memory. Although the 80386, in its Virtual 86 Mode, should be able to run all 8086 programs, you may

80386
TASK

80386
TASK

80386
TASK

80386
OPERATING
SYSTEM

VIRTUAL MACHINE MONITOR

VM86
TASK

VM86
TASK

VM86
TASK

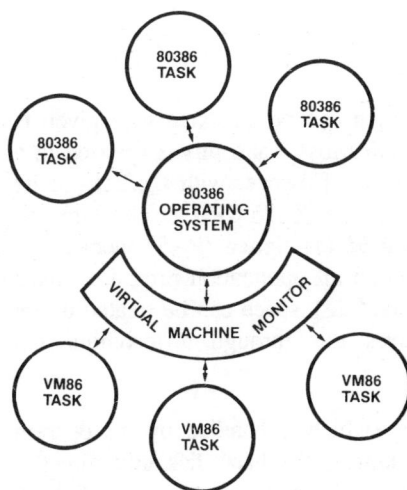

Figure 2.6 The Virtual Machine Monitor forms a software interface

experience problems if the program involves by-passes the BIOS (Section 2.8). An example of this is bit-mapping control over the screen display. This sometimes occurs when attempting to run graphic intensive applications under Windows/386 (Section 5.5.1).

2.2.3 Protected 80386 Mode

When operating in the Protected Mode, the full facilities of the 80386 can be accessed. One of the elegant design features of the 80386 is the depth of protection it offers programmers and system designers. If the 80386 is used for multi-tasking purposes, then protection is necessary in order to prevent concurrently operating application programs from interfering with each other; for example, ensuring that each program remains within a designated area of memory when an error is encountered in the software. Protection is also important for maintaining the integrity of the operating system. The memory allocated to the operating system remains out of bounds of the applications programs.

The 80386 has up to four levels of protection and the current operating system (Section 5.1) occupies the highest priority. In consequence the 80386 CPU is able to provide memory protection by confining the operation of an application within a defined address space of memory – a form of damage limitation management. If the processor is executing several application programs concurrently (multi-tasking) and one should crash, it can only inflict minimal damage to the collective operation of the processor. In the Protected Mode, a multi-tasking environment can be supported which has up to 16 Mbytes of addressable memory for each application program.

2.2.4 The Memory Management Unit

The maximum memory which can be allocated to a given task by the 80386 is 64 Tbytes (Terabyte = 1,000,000 Mbyte) and this is referred to as the **Logical Address Space** (LAS) for the processor. However with the help of its Memory Management Unit (MMU), which is part of the 80386 CPU architecture, the LAS can be translated or mapped into **Physical Address Space** (PAS) memory which can, in principle, reside in disk space. Although all application programs manage with memory areas much less than this limit, hard disk space can be treated by the 80386 CPU as if it is on-board RAM. It achieves this through a technique called **Virtual Memory Addressing.**

Virtual memory addressing, which is handled by the operating system, permits the 80386 microprocessor to address the hard disk unit directly as if it were physical RAM. A very large program, which exceeds the size of the on-board memory space of the PC, would rely on **overlays** which are fetched from disk memory as required by the program. During its development, the program would be partitioned into segments of size not exceeding the common working area of available RAM on the PC. As each segment of the program is required, it is transferred from disk and overlayed onto the common working area in RAM and then executed.

However with a virtual memory facility, the size and address range of the program is limited only by the available disk space. The address range of the application program extends far beyond the PAS of the computer. However, only a small portion of the application program is ever resident in RAM at any one time. During its execution, when the program reaches an address outside the physical address area of the RAM, the processing is momentarily suspended and the virtual memory process comes into operation.

Virtual memory access occurs through the operating system and is transparent to the user apart from the hard disk light illuminating from time to time. In the context of the operating system, when an instruction from within the application program addresses an area outside the present page, the 80386 CPU automatically traps from the program to the operating system. By using the **demand paging** facility of the integral MMU, the MMU fetches from disk the required program segment (or page) and transfers it to the working RAM area. The MMU then translates the address to the start of the RAM working area which now contains the new page. The instruction is re-executed and the program continues normally.

To speed up the virtual memory addressing there is an on-board cache called the **Translation Lookaside Buffer** (TLB) which contains mapping information for the 32 most recently accessed memory pages. The TLB allows the 80386 to quickly generate the appropriate virtual memory address without having to access the disk page table. The execution of large application programs can therefore be realised without the need for partitioning them into overlays. The advantage of this technique lies in the cost of the respective memory – RAM is far more expensive than disk memory and requires more complex design.

Although DOS does not normally use virtual memory, OS/2 (Section 5.6) and UNIX (Section 5.4) both use it since it is essential for large-scale multi-tasking systems.

2.2.5 Intel 80386SX

Intel also manufactures a scaled down version of the 80386DS, called the 80386SX, which has an internal 32-bit architecture identical to the 80386 but the external data bus is only 16 bits wide with a reduced address bus of 24 bits.

The 80386SX has the same instruction set as the 80386 and can operate in the three modes, however the maximum clock rate is 20 Mhz. It has been intentionally fixed at this level to prevent it from been adopted into systems which would normally use the full architecture of the 80386DS. Pitched at 16 Mhz or 20 Mhz, the 80386SX offers a minimum competition to the 80386 as an alternative processor.

Despite its limited external bus features, any 386 PC based on the 80386SX will operate within all multi-tasking software environments. With the reduced data bus and the low clock rate the 80386SX will invariably be slower than the 80386, but its performance will still be superior to 80286-based PCs for multi-tasking functions. The 24-bit address bus means that the 80386SX has a logical address space limited to 16 Mbytes of RAM. However this should not pose any problem in the specification of high performance 386 PCs.

There are currently many models of 386 PC based on the 80386SX including the Compaq Deskpro 386S, the Apricot Xen-S 250 and the ALR FlexCache SX-386Z. The appearance of IBM's PS/2 Models 55SX and 65SX (Section 3.8), based on the 80386SX, clearly sanctions the 80386SX as a viable processor which will in time probably replace the 16-bit 80286.

Many low-cost 386 PCs will be built around the 80386SX CPU and these will emerge onto the market in growing numbers. The 80386SX is particularly attractive for the manufacturers of high performance Lap-top 386 PCs since the scaled down architecture lends itself to simplified circuit board design with fewer support chips.

To accompany the 80386SX Intel also manufactured a scaled down coprocessor, the 80387SX, which has the same internal architecture and performance as the 80387 but with a reduced data bus of 16 bits.

2.3 Random Access Memory

The random access memory (RAM) on a 386 PC will either be resident on the mother board or as plug-in modules. The data and address buses of the 80386 CPU are connected directly to the RAM. When the user chooses to run an application program on the 386 PC then all or part of the program is loaded into the 386 PC's RAM and executed from there. The RAM must therefore provide space for the program and any data space which may be required. RAM for a 386 PC can be configured in several ways and this easily leads to confusion. It is therefore worthwhile discussing some of its common features.

2.3.1 Base Memory

Many application programs for the 386 PC will run under the DOS operating system (5.3) and a constraint of DOS 3.3 and lower versions is the amount of memory directly accessible by the CPU. This arose from the first CPU used by IBM, the Intel 8088, which only has an address space of one Mbyte. This remnant of the early design is still present with today's 386 PCs and only 640K of the one Mbyte is accessible to the user for application programs. Most of the remaining 384K is reserved for system use. The first 640K of memory is referred to as the base or conventional memory. All 386 PCs have 640K of on-board RAM as standard. Most medium scale application programs can run within the base memory limit and do not normally present too many problems. DOS version 4 has extended this 640k barrier (Section 5.1.2), but requires a specific RAM, configured according to the LIM standard (Section 2.3.3).

Many application programs running under DOS are confined to the base memory, but one of the appealing features of the 386 PC is the ability to run several application programs, known as multi-tasking, in different blocks of 640K. However suitable software environments are required to enable multi-tasking and this is covered in Chapter 5. When the 386 PC is first powered up in DOS, the DOS software is loaded into the base memory and resides at the top of the memory (Figure 2.7 opposite).

There is a class of other software utilities which can also reside permanently within the base memory, known as Terminate and Stay Resident (TSR). Examples of TSRs are device drivers, network drivers and disk cacheing programs (Section 2.7). These encroach on the limited base memory space and remain in place until removed with suitable software tools or during a system reset. Some large application programs require the maximum available space in the base memory and the problem of installing TSRs can be solved by using a product such as 386Max Professional Memory Manager distributed by First National Sales. Once the TSRs are installed, 386Max moves them to a memory address above the base memory boundary, thereby freeing the base memory for large application programs.

The characteristics of the available memory chips are also worth considering when specifying RAM. Two types of memory chips are used – **Static Random Access Memory** (SRAM) and **Dynamic Random Access Memory** (DRAM). SRAM is characterised by its fast access time (the time it takes to address it and perform a read or write operation). This can be as low as 0.02 micro seconds. The higher the clock frequency of the system the greater the demands on the SRAM which means shorter access times. SRAM is expensive and generally, the shorter the access time the greater the cost. There are methods of using slow SRAM with a fast CPU and one method involves the CPU taking two or more clock cycles (known as wait states) to access the SRAM. Including wait states is not a desirable feature as the overall CPU performance is compromised, but it does keep the cost of the system down. The designers of the 80386 were well aware of the problems of fast memory addressing and made allowances in its design.

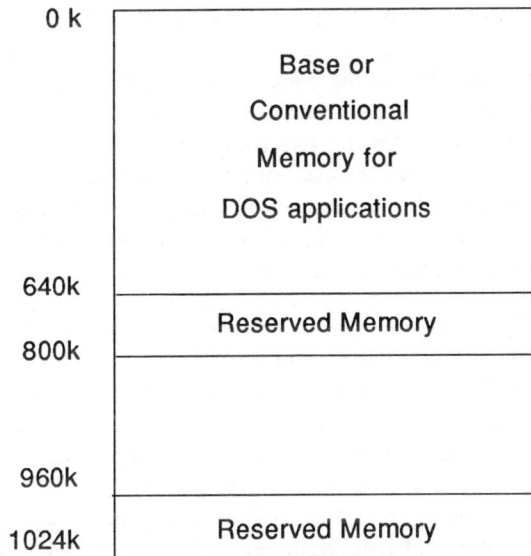

0 k	Base or Conventional Memory for DOS applications
640k	
800k	Reserved Memory
960k	
1024k	Reserved Memory

Figure 2.7 Simplified memory map of the Intel 8088. The address space has a maximum value of 1024K and DOS application programs use the first 640K

DRAM on the other hand is much cheaper than SRAM, but has much longer access times. Due to the design of DRAM it requires a refresh every 10 msec to maintain its memory contents, which takes on the form of localised electric charge. Additional circuitry and time is required to enable this refresh cycle. When accessing DRAM it is sometimes necessary for the 80386 CPU, with its pipelining facility, to add wait states (extra clock cycles) to allow the DRAM to keep pace with the CPU. The price difference between the 20 Mhz, 25 Mhz and 33 Mhz 386 PC is partially due to the cost of faster DRAM.

2.3.2 Cache Memory

An interesting design feature of the 80386 microprocessor system is the cache memory control. The CPU will run faster if it can use SRAM without any wait states and many 386 PCs have a special reserve of cache memory for permitting this option. During the execution of an application program, the program's code is normally stored in the motherboard DRAM. Each time the CPU accesses a segment of the code a copy of the segment is made and stored in cache memory. Cache memory resides between the main 640K and the 80386 processor. The next time the CPU executes the same segment of code, it accesses the copy in the cache memory which it can execute faster since it does not have any wait states. The cache memory therefore keeps lots of code segment copies and the CPU, before accessing the motherboard DRAM, first checks the cache table to see if a copy of the code is resident in cache.

As new code segments are copied into cache memory old copies are discarded and there are a number of algorithms for determining whether a code segment should be retained. One such algorithm is the **Least Recently Used** (LRU). The greater the amount of cache memory the higher the probability the CPU will find a required code segment in cache, referred to as the **Hit Rate.** Cache memory is very effective for applications which require considerable, but repetitive computation. The addressing of the cache is also simplified by having a cyclic behaviour which does not require the CPU's address bus and this allows each CPU instruction to be executed in only two clock cycles, providing there are no overhead operations to perform.

Depending on how the 80386 is configured it can operate two types of bus cycles – non-pipelined and pipelined. The operation of the cache memory depends on the non-pipelined mode. Executing instructions outside the cache memory relies on the slower pipelined mode which permits lower costing DRAM to be used. External hardware to the 80386 can dynamically enable the pipelining option by controlling the /NA pin on the 80386. This hardware may include the Intel 82385 32-bit cache controller which implements the cache control functions by storing a copy of the frequently accessed code and data from the main DRAM into the zero wait state SRAM cache memory. The 82385 cache controller permits the 80386 processor to operate at its full potential.

The rationale behind the use of the 82385 depends on the **principle of locality** which relies on the assumption that if a memory location is addressed it's probable that it will be addressed again in the near future. Once a segment of code has been accessed in DRAM the next time round it will be accessed from its copy in the fast cache memory. The way the cache controller does this is to compare the address on the 80386 address bus with its own list of recently accessed address tags. If there is a match the address and data buses are directed towards the cache memory otherwise a normal address read occurs. When the latter case happens the cache memory is updated during the read operation.

Due to its dual bus architecture, the 82385 cache controller can allow different devices to access the other resources in the system while the 80386 is operating locally out of the cache memory. By using different types of memory, a mix can therefore be realised which allows extra tuning to the system cost. However not all 386 PCs employ a cache facility and it is worth enquiring whether cache memory is on the mother board. It is preferable to have a cache controller as a hardware design feature on the board which operates without any software overheads. Cache memory is normally available in 32K or 64K depending on the manufacturer and the model.

2.3.3 Expanded Memory

The first generation of IBM personal computers were based on the 8-bit Intel 8088 microprocessor which could only address one Mbyte of memory. However 384K of this memory was reserved for special applications – disk controllers, the BIOS (Section 2.7) and terminal emulation devices. This left 640K for DOS application programs and data storage which is known as the DOS barrier. One method of overcoming the limitations of the 640K DOS boundary was introduced by Lotus, Intel and Microsoft in 1985 and was referred to as the Lotus/Intel/Microsoft Expanded Memory Specification (version 3.2) or LIM-EMS for short. This allows DOS application programs to access a further eight Mbytes of RAM. Since the address space of the Intel 8088 was limited to one Mbyte, the expanded memory was accessed through a technique known as bank switching. To effect this technique assembly language instructions are required to switch a bank or block of memory into the logical address space (LAS) of the processor. There can be several banks of memory but only one bank can be switched into the address space at any one time.

Once Expanded Memory has been installed in a PC a 64K block of reserved address becomes an 'access window' for the Expanded Memory (Figure 2.8 overleaf) and this is addressed as 64K pages. This additional memory can only be accessed by software packages specifically designed to conform to the LIM-EMS standard. Many of these packages recognise the presence of Expanded Memory and adjust their operational limits accordingly. Lotus 1-2-3 and MathCad are two such packages and they use the Expanded Memory for data storage. With LIM-EMS version 3.2 program code cannot run directly from Expanded Memory, it can only be used for data storage and for storing program overlays.

The introduction of personal computers with Intel 80386 microprocessors brought further problems for Expanded Memory. These devices, when operating in the Protected Modes, can address memory areas far greater than the eight Mbytes limit set by the LIM-EMS standard. The remedial measure of manufacturer AST was to introduce an Enhanced Expanded Memory Specification (EEMS). The EEMS supported all the functions of the LIM-EMS standard with extra benefits which were exploited by Desqview/386 (Section 5.5.2) from Quarterdeck and Concurrent DOS/386 from Digital Research. The LIM-EMS standard was updated in 1987 with the release of Version 4.0 which allowed up to 32 Mbytes of Expanded Memory to be addressed. In addition, not only can data program code be resident but the programs can be run from within Expanded Memory. Examples of software packages which use the LIM-EMS Version 4 are Lotus 1-2-3 Version 3 and Microsoft's Excel.

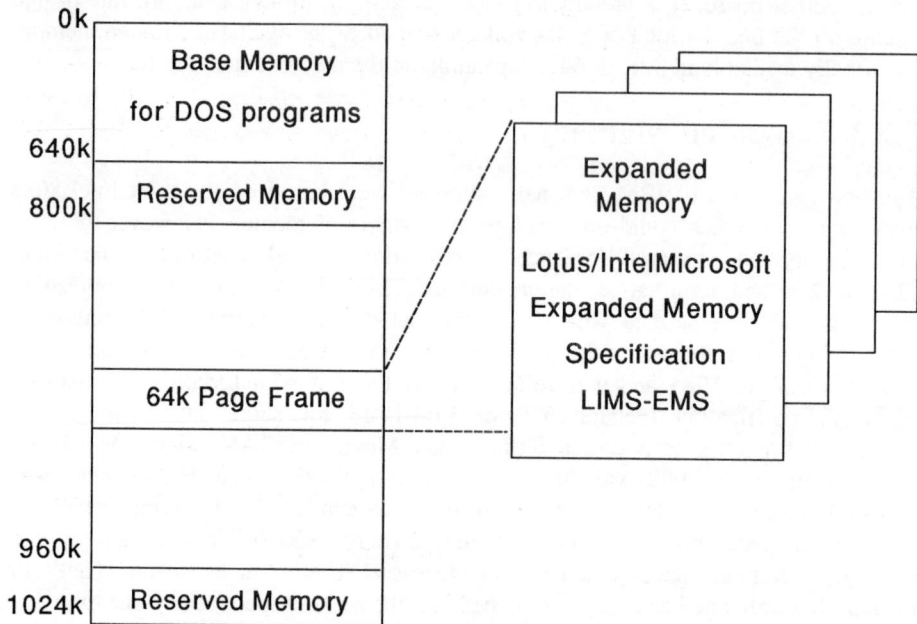

Figure 2.8 64K pages of Expanded Memory can be mapped into the 64K page frame

To make efficient use of Expanded Memory an Expanded Memory Manager (EMM) driver is normally installed (within the CONFIG.SYS file) when the 386 PC is booted up. This apportions the memory to the user's choice of Expanded and/or Extended memory and the details of its installation can be found in the user manual. Expanded Memory is available in units of 2, 4, 8, 16 or 32 Mbytes. Additional Expanded Memory for a 386 PC can be bought in two forms, either as plug-in cards which occupy the 32-bit slots in the card cage (Section 3.2.1) or as **Single Inline Memory Modules** (SIMMs) which slot directly into the mother board. When buying additional memory it is important to establish whether the memory is Expanded or Extended and on some boards the memory can be configured as either (through software or by a jumper setting). The difference between the two types is confusing and care should be exercised when specifying the product. By and large Expanded Memory is useful for specific commercial DOS application programs and more packages are now recognising it. However some software will recognise Extended Memory as Expanded memory, Windows/386 (Section 5.5.1) being one example.

2.3.4 Extended Memory

The physical addresss space of the primary DOS microprocessor, the Intel 8088, is one Mbyte and the available working space for DOS applications programs is 640K (the DOS boundary). However since the physical address space of the 80386 is four Gbytes it is not surprising to learn that the 640K base memory can be augmented with RAM and this is referred to as Extended Memory. It can be extended up to 32 Mbytes provided the RAM conforms to the LIM-SPEC 4.0. However to use this memory effectively, one of a range of software utilities must be used. These have now become known as Extended Memory Managers and an example is QEMM-386 from Quarterdeck.

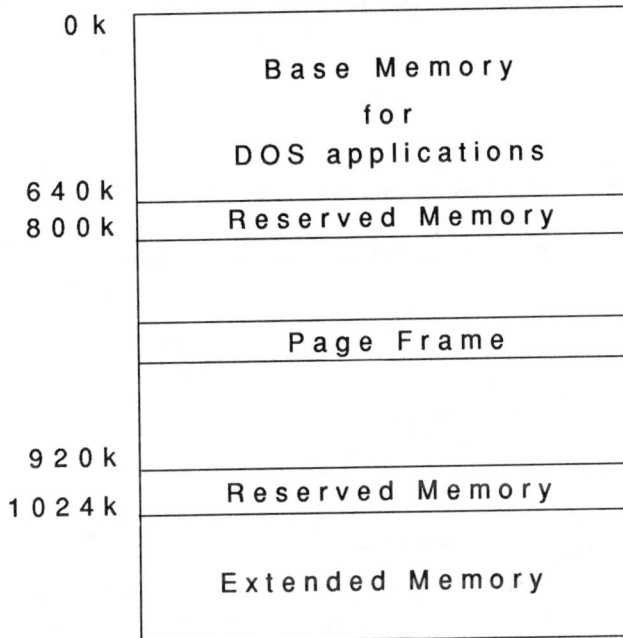

```
  0 k   ┌─────────────────────────────┐
        │                             │
        │      Base  Memory           │
        │          for                │
        │    DOS  applications        │
640 k   │                             │
800 k   ├─────────────────────────────┤
        │    Reserved  Memory         │
        ├─────────────────────────────┤
        │                             │
        │       Page  Frame           │
        │                             │
920 k   ├─────────────────────────────┤
1024 k  │    Reserved  Memory         │
        ├─────────────────────────────┤
        │                             │
        │    Extended  Memory         │
        │                             │
        └─────────────────────────────┘
```

Figure 2.9 Extended Memory occupies the address space beyond the 1024K boundary

Extended Memory cannot be used directly as program space if a DOS version lower than 4.0 is operating on the 386 PC. However if the 80386 microprocessor is operating in its Protected Mode then it can accommodate a number of multi-user operating systems and they can make use of Extended Memory. Figure 2.9 shows the memory map of a 386 PC with Extended Memory. Extended Memory can also be used to accommodate **Terminate and Stay Resident** (TSR) programs – for example, print spoolers (6.1) and RAMDISK (Section 2.6) – and it is preferable to store these in Extended Memory than dedicating any of the 640K base memory for their storage.

There are several application programs which need Extended Memory and these employ an appropriate DOS Extender – for example, AutoShade for AutoCAD and Lotus 1-2-3 Release 3 (Protect Mode). There are two well known DOS Extenders; the 16 Mbytes Extender from Rational Systems and the Phar Lap 386|VMM (virtual memory manager) which conforms to the Phar Lap virtual Control Program Interface Specification (VCPI). When the 80386 CPU is operating in its protected mode, it is able to access memory areas beyond the 640K limit.

To enable a DOS application program to run with the CPU in its protected mode, the source program is compiled with the appropriate software switches. The compiled code is then linked with the Extender software to produce an executable application program. Application programs produced with the Phar Lap 386|VMM can also use demand page virtual memory access thus enabling very large programs to run within a DOS environment.

2.3.5 Direct Memory Access (DMA)

On occasions there is a requirement for a rapid transfer of data to or from the RAM in the 386 PC. The data can be channelled through the 80386, which acts as a controller. However there is another technique which allows data from a peripheral to be loaded directly into system RAM and employs a technique known as **Direct Memory Access**. Data can be transferred directly to RAM, by-passing the 80386.

DMA Channel	Function	Input/Output Address
0	Spare	0087
1	SDLC	0083
2	Disk Unit	0081
3	Spare	0082
5	Spare	008B
6	Spare	0089
7	Spare	008A

Table 2.1 Addresses and functions of DMA channels

Intel manufactures a special purpose IC which is compatible with the 80386 for performing this task in a very efficient manner, the **Intel 82380 DMA controller.** It can support up to eight channels of 32-bit DMA and provide interrupt control, wait state generation for DRAM refresh control and system reset. DMA is a frequent requirement for I/O expansion plug-in boards for fast data acquisition (Section 9.4.1) and can operate concurrently with other processor operations.

To effect a DMA transfer it is normal to use assembly language routines which can be linked to main program modules and these are normally supplied by the manufacturers of the expansion plug-in boards. Data transferred via the DMA should be located in RAM which is not occupied by a concurrent program. If DMA data does overflow into a concurrent program space, then a crash can be expected. To avoid this the limiting parameters for the DMA have to be carefully set up.

The number of DMA channels on a 386 PC can be as large as seven where the first three channels (0 to 2) transfer data between an 8-bit or 16-bit adapter and system memory in 64K blocks. Channels 5 to 7 can perform 16-bit data transfer in blocks of 128K. When additional expansion plug-in card are fitted into the card cage it is sometimes necessary to have knowledge of the available DMA input and output addresses and these are given in Table 2.1 opposite.

2.4 Floppy Disk Drives

The majority of 386 PCs are equipped with at least one floppy disk drive and this serves as the most convenient method for externally loading application programs or data into the 386 PC. There are two designs of floppy disk drive to accommodate the quad density 5.25 inch and 3.5 inch floppy disks. The more common, high-density 5.25 inch drive is favoured at present because the majority of commercial software is available in this format.

There is a trend towards the 3.5 inch disks because of their reliability, compactness and hard cover and they have been adopted by IBM for its PS/2 range of PCs. The 5.25 inch disk drive on 386 PCs accommodates the high-density disks which hold up to 1.2 Mbytes of data. Fortunately these disk drives can also read the lower density floppy disks (360 Kbyte double density). Low-density drives cannot read high-density 5.25 inch disks or format them. However, high-density drives can format low-density disks provided the switch /4 is used during the FORMAT instruction, but this is not always reliable. The access time for floppy disks is not of major importance, but the high-density disk drives are significantly faster. When buying a 386 PC there is no point in having more than one 5.25 inch drive since it is only likely to have two functions: firstly for the initial loading of software into the 386 PC and secondly for the possible long term storage (back-up) if a tape streamer is not available.

The 3.5 inch disk drive is growing in popularity and a number of manufacturers include both sizes of drive in their 386 PCs. However this increases the cost of the basic 386 PC and the second drive should only be added as an option. 3.5 inch floppy disks are also available in high and low-density formats, but only the high-density variety are normally used in 386 PCs. These can hold up to 2.44 Mbytes of data. As with 5.25 inch disks, low-density disks can be read with high-density drives. Unlike 5.25 disk drives a 3.5 inch disk drive requires a device driver which may not be resident in the BIOS ROM. If this is the case, the driver will normally be included on the support software accompanying the 386 PC and must form part of the boot up.

In DOS the floppy drives are allocated logical drives :A and :B or just :A if only one drive is present. Formatting floppy disks is a straightforward operation and the DOS manual will provide greater details:

format a:	format disk in drive A
format a: /v	format disk in drive A and add label
format a: /v /s	format disk in drive A, add label and place DOS operating system on the disk.

2.5 Hard Disk Drives

A hard disk is an essential feature of a 386 PC and is normally supplied as standard. They are available in varying sizes ranging from 44 Mbytes to 600 Mbytes. Improved manufacturing techniques, driven by enormous market demands, have resulted in low-cost, high-quality hard disk products. Once known as Winchester Drives, they have improved in leaps and bounds over the past few years and the notorious head crash is a comparatively rare event for a well treated system. Hard disk drives (HDDs) are sealed units to prevent dust from entering the delicate mechanism. They are available in two sizes, full height or half height, and compartments are allocated for them at the front of the 386 PC unit.

As the density of hard disk drives has increased, greater demands have been on the magnetic reading head alignment and it travels within a few microns of the disk surface. HDDs normally have a stack of disks or platters with several reading heads which scan the surface. Disk crashes (when the heads collide with the disk surface) can occur if the unit is suddenly moved or jerked while the disk is being accessed. It is always advisable to have the 386 PC on a firm table where it is not likely to be knocked. As a precaution, before the 386 PC is switched off the heads on the hard disk should always be parked. When the heads are parked, using the DOS utility FXPARK, they are situated over an unused area of the disk referred to as the **Landing Zone.** In some designs this is done when the power is disconnected and on other 386 PCs a disk-park program is available for this purpose.

With HDDs having large memory capacities it will be necessary to have a form of HDD management especially if there are several users accessing the same 386 PC. One problem which can arise is fragmentation which leaves gaps on the HDD. For example, suppose there are three data files in consecutive memory locations on the HDD. If the second data file is appended then it may be too large to reside between the other two. It is then stored somewhere else leaving a gap between the other two files. Fragmentation has the effect of increasing the access time. However it can be cleared up by using the Norton Utilities which is an excellent software product for HDD management. It can also be used to recover 'erased files'. During the erasure of a file the contents remain intact provided nothing else has been written to the HDD. The Norton Utilities will help to recover the data from the erased file.

2.5.1 Hard Disk Configuration

The internal design of a HDD – also known as the fixed disk – is structured as a stack of platters or disks (Figure 2.10) and the data on each disk is enscribed in circular tracks on a platter. During the low-level formatting (Section 2.5.5) of the HDD under DOS, each of the tracks is divided into 17 **sectors** which hold, typically, 512 bytes of data. The tracks which occupy the same relative position on the platters form a **cylinder** and this can be thought of as a concentric tube. During the high-level format the HDD is divided into **partitions** and up to four can exist on any one HDD.

Figure 2.10 The Seagate ST1144N hard disk drive showing reading heads and platters. (Photo: Courtesy of Seagate)

Every position on a partition is defined by three parameters (a 3-D coordinate): the cylinder number, the sector number and the reading head number. On the system HDD, the first few sectors on the first cylinder is a reserved area which contain the BOOT code and information known as the **BIOS Parameter Block (BPB).**

When the 386 PC is powered up and after the completion of initial tests, the first legend to appear on the screen emerges from the BIOS ROM (Section 2.8). This is followed by the loading of the BOOT code from the HDD into the 386 PC system RAM. This enables the 386 PC system to load the DOS device drivers from the HDD, IBMBIO.COM, and the operating system kernel IBMDOS.COM. Next the command process, COMMAND.COM is loaded which enables the 386 PC to function in the DOS environment.

There are three other sections in addition to the reserved section on the HDD: the **File Allocation Table** (FAT), the **root directory** and the **file storage area**. The file storage area accounts for most of the disk space and will contain subdirectories and files of data and application programs. When files are created on the HDD they are allocated contiguous sectors referred to as **clusters** and the cluster size is determined during the format operation (typical four sectors per cluster). Among other things the FAT is a map and holds information on how the storage area on the HDD is used. Each file on the HDD has an entry in the directory and each directory contains a pointer to a location in the FAT. This holds information on the position of each cluster (and file) on the partition.

In the IBM operating system – OS/2 (Section 5.6) – the user has the option of an alternative file system – the **High Performance File System** (HPFS). The HPFS is intended to encompass the requirements of many types of data storage systems, for example CD-ROMs (Section 7.4) and WORMs (Section 7.4.2). An attractive feature of the HPFS is its flexibility; a hard disk drive may have HPFS and FAT partitions with HPFS file names extending up to 254 characters. Under HPFS each file is stamped with the time and date of the last access plus additional information contained within an Extended Attribute (EA). The purpose of the EA is to carry information relating to the nature of the file. There are nine field types used in the format of the EA, referred to as the **Standard Extended Attributes** (SEAs) (see Figure 2.11 opposite).

The HPFS scores well for hard disk intensive applications which are typically found among local area network file server applications (Section 8.5). Access information, regarding the address of a file, is stored as a balanced tree whereby the search path for the file system is a minimum. The tree has nodes which give rise to several branches on which files are 'attached'. By balancing the growth, the path to each file is of the same length. In the HPFS scheme, data files are contained within bands on the hard disk and each file has an fnode maintained physically close to its respective file. Fnodes contain information relating to the amount of disk space that a file has been allocated and a bitmap area, which resides outside the band, points to the address of the fnodes. The bitmaps are strategically placed relative to the bands to minimise the movement of the reading heads. They are organised as:

Band 1	Bitmap 1	Bitmap 2	Band 2	Band 3	Bitmap 3	Bitmap ... 4

At the centre of the HPFS partition is the directory band which points to the bitmaps which in turn point to the fnodes. This design forms part of the balanced tree structure. To get to the directory there is an area at the start of the disk called the **Super Block** which has the address of the directory band. On reading the directory, much of its contents are 'disk cached' (Section 2.7) in order to minimise the number of directory accesses. As far as possible files are kept in contiguous sectors and this leads to a reduction in file fragmentation which occurs with the FAT method.

HDDs are classified as types, which gives an indication of the number of cylinders, heads and memory capacity. A table of HDD types and their characteristic are is given in Appendix 2A. Before a HDD can be installed its type number will be required by the installation software and this should be noted. There are three important aspects to consider when selecting a hard disk drive unit for a 386 PC: its **storage capacity,** the **average access time** and the **maximum data transfer rate.**

TYPE	Type of file: application program, executable code, text document
KEYPHRASES	Recognition information – groups or categories
SUBJECT	Subject of file
COMMENTS	Additional comments may be included
HISTORY	List of dates of file changes and file originator
VERSION	Version number of file
ICON	Bitmap date required by file for use in screen window
ASSOCTABLE	Information used by applications, concerning data files
CODEPAGE	Signifies whether Codepage is needed for the file

Figure 2.11 Standard Extended Attributes

The storage capacity should be a minimum of 44 Mbytes. The average access time is a measure of two processes: the time taken for the read/write head to locate the data and that taken to read or write the data. This is dependent upon the head actuator design, which for fast drives, employs a closed loop servo system to maximise the response time. A good figure to aim for is a maximum of 28 msecs; certainly no longer otherwise a sluggish performance will occur for software which involves frequent hard disk access. The data transfer rate is an indication of how fast data can be transferred to (from) the HDD from (to) the CPU or its memory and is measured as either MegaHertz (Mhz), which in this context is equivalent to million bits per second (MBPS). For fast HDDs operating within a 386 PC, this value is close to, or possibly in excess of, 10 Mhz, but is only realised with a process using direct memory access (Section 2.3.5).

2.5.2 Interleaving

When the hard disk is formatted, each platter is divided into sectors (Figure 2.12) and as the disk rotates the sectors pass under the magnetic reading heads. In the access mechanism of the HDD, a head must access a sector and the disk controller must verify that the data on the sector is valid before the next sector passes under the head. However it may be impossible to access consecutive sectors, therefore some sectors pass under the head before it is ready to access another sector. This is referred to as interleaving and the number of sectors which pass under the head between each access is the interleave ratio. Ideally one should expect an interleave ratio of 1:1 which means that no sectors are skipped and consecutive sectors are used.

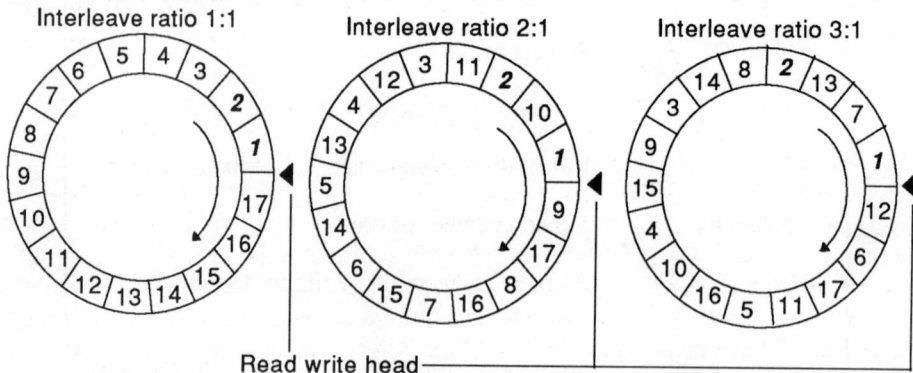

Figure 2.12 Marking of sectors on a hard disk drive platter

In the case of an interleave ratio of 1:1, the sectors (17 per track) are marked consecutively. If the read/write operation is too slow the platter will have to make a complete rotation before the operation can be completed. In this case interleaving would be preferable. In the event of an interleaving ratio other than 1:1 the sectors are marked according to the ratio. Since there are 17 sectors per track, none of the sectors are wasted and they are all used.

Interleaving is time wasting and in the specifications for the hard disk, it should be stated if interleaving is present. Some control can be exercised over the interleave ratio when the HDD is formatted (see FDISK) to give optimum performance, but in general for a single user the lower the interleave ratio the quicker the HDD will be in moving data to and from the CPU. Having said this, IBM's OS/2 usually works with a 2:1 interleave ratio to allow the PC to respond more effectively to the needs of multi-tasking.

2.5.3 Hard Disk Drive Density

With its high performance, there will be great demands upon the storage capacity of the 386 PC. To support a number of operating systems and several commercial application programs a large HDD will be required. The minimum HDD storage capacity for a 386 PC should be 44 Mbytes and if it is to be used in a multi-user environment where the 386 PC may act as a file server (Section 8.5.4) a minimum 70 Mbytes should be sought. If there is an occasion to increase the number of HDDs, particular attention will have to be paid to the system requirements. Each HDD unit will require a disk controller. This can either be integrated into the HDD unit itself or on an expansion card which will occupy one of the slots in the card cage. When choosing a HDD which requires a separate controller card, it may be possible to support it on the existing controller card. However, in general each additional HDD will require another card controller. It is therefore wise to estimate, before buying a 386 PC, how much memory will be required as in the long term a low capacity HDD will not prove to be economical.

The device driver for a HDD is present in the BIOS ROM, and DOS versions 3.3 and 4 provide the necessary links for communicating with the unit. However one of the drawbacks of DOS version 3.3 (Section 5.3.2) is the limited size of a hard disk (32 Mbytes) which can be allocated to each logical drive. In DOS Version 4 this limit has been extended and is less restrictive. If you are working under DOS 3.3, the HDD, with a capacity greater than 32 Mbytes, can have DOS extended partitions which are assigned to logical drives D:, E: and so on, and this partitioning is accomplished during the formatting of the disk. There are exceptional versions of DOS that will support HDDs larger than 32 Mbytes and an example of this is used in DR DOS (Section 5.3.3).

2.5.4 Disk Controllers

The hardware that interfaces the 386 PC motherboard to the disk drives is known as the host disk adaptor or controller card which can occupy one of the expansion slots in the card cage. The only time the user has to worry about the controller card is during an upgrade of the hard disk drive capacity of the 386 PC. There are three interface standards for controller cards: ST-506, introduced by Seagate in 1980; ESDI, Enhanced Small Disk Interface; and SCSI, Small Computer System Interface (Section 7.3.3).

The majority of controller cards on 286-based personal computers are based on the Seagate ST-506 and several 386 PC manufacturers use this standard for their host adaptors. Its low cost has sustained its popularity for HDDs up to 140 Mbytes capacity. Alternatively the **Enhanced Small Disk Interface** (ESDI) is growing in popularity for 386 PCs and is similar to the ST-506. In the ESDI design, the data transmission is serial and generally the seek mechanism is faster than the ST-506. An interesting feature of the ESDI design is the provision for mapping bad tracks of hard disk drives and storing the map on the disk for use by the controller during data writes.

On a hard disk drive which conforms to ESDI, the data separator is resident on the disk drive unit itself not the controller card. The data exchanged between the disk unit and the controller card is a proper digital format. The coding mechanism for ESDI is referred to as **Not Returned to Zero** (NRZ). In the operation of the ST-506 design in order to transfer data to or from a disk drive a coding method must be used. There are three types of data coding methods: **Modified Frequency Modulation** (MFM), **Run Length Limited** (RLL) and **Advanced Run Length Limited** (ARLL). Within the MFM process period, a magnetic flux change in the disk writing head signifies a digital 1 and a no magnetic flux change signifies a digital 0. However, to reduce the chance of an error a flux change is always placed between two successive 0s. MFM operates on a single bit level and the controller card only processes or codes one bit at a time. The MFM method can support data transfer rates up to a maximum of five Mbits/sec (MBPS).

An alternative to this is to code a group of bits into a pattern of flux changes – the RLL. In the RLL coding technique each byte of data (eight bits) is allocated a code pattern of 16 flux changes, which is in effect equivalent to doubling the number of bits required. This involves increasing the number of flux changes on the disk writing head during a process period, which has the effect of increasing the capacity of the disk.

What about the possible errors this may introduce? Since the information capacity of a 16-bit word is much greater than a single byte only a small number of 16-bit flux change patterns are required to represent all possible byte values. Some flux change patterns are easier to perform on the disk than others and it is these patterns which are used to represent the byte values. A binary 1, represented by a flux change, is easier to effect that a binary 0, no flux change.

In the standard format of RLL successive binary 1s must be separated by a number of 0s and this can range from 2 to 7. The standard format is therefore given the label 2,7 RLL. Although this coding method doubles the number of bytes required to represent a segment data, each binary 1 has between it 2 and 7 binary 0s and they can be compressed into a smaller area of the disk surface. The improvement over the MFM in storage density is 50% without decreasing the physical separation between flux changes. There is a corresponding improvement in disk access time with this coding method. The ARLL, also known as the 3,9 RLL is another variation of RLL except the number of binary 0s between each binary 1 can range from 3 to 9. The overall effect of this is to increase the storage capacity by another 50%.

However a disk drive which uses MFM coding is not compatible with a RLL controller card despite the fact that they may appear to work. This only prevails in the short term until disk read errors begin to occur with increasing frequency. A hard disk drive which uses the RLL coding method is made to a higher mechanical specification than the conventional MFM drives and is able to respond to the higher data transfer rates. RLL controllers require magnetic field strengths (coercivity) on the heads to be between 600 and 700 Oersted and a motor speed tolerance within 1% of 3,600 revs/min. The head positioning must also be more accurate with a working distance between 8 and 12 microns from the platter surface. To add to the possible confusion the connector plugs on a MFM disk system are the same for a RLL system but they still remain incompatible.

The controller card and the disk drive must use the same coding method. However the ST-506 can support up to four compatible disk drives. Part of the circuitry on the ST-506 controller card, referred to as the data separator, is responsible for distinguishing between the disk location addressing and the actual data stored on the disk. Although the ST-506 has been widely used by disk manufacturers the data transfer rate is limited to 5 Mhz. The specification for controlling the head movement and the disk spin are limited and this leads to long access times.

2.5.5 Formatting a Hard Disk

Operations involving the formatting or similar functions of HDDs can lead to the loss of the information on the unit, therefore existing files on the HDD should always be backed up. The process of formatting a HDD involves a procedure for dividing up the tracks on the platters into sectors and establishing the file allocation table (FAT), the root directory and the file area on the HDD. From time to time it may be necessary to format or reformat your hard disk(s). You may want to change, augment or even update your operating system. You may even choose to install an additional hard disk drive in your 386 PC.

When choosing an additional HDD consideration must be given to capacity (size in Mbytes) and access time. It is a difficult task trying to match projected needs to the most appropriate disk size and a rough guide is to choose a disk with 50% more capacity than you estimate your requirement to be. The disk type number relating to its capacity (Table 2A in Appendix A2) might be required during the formatting procedure, so keep a note of it. If buying a new HDD, enquire whether it has already been formatted and the DOS version on it. To avoid problems the DOS version should be the same as your existing system.

The hardware installation procedure is usually laid out in the user manual. It cannot be stressed enough how important it is to carefully read these instructions. On the assumption that the HDD and its card (if it has one) has been installed, you are now ready to go ahead and format the unit. Formatting a HDD is not as easy as formatting a floppy disk and it must be remembered that any previous information on the HDD will be lost. It may even be prudent to consider commercially available HDD set-up software. Examples of these are Disk Manager from Ontrack or SpeedStar from Storage Dimension.

There may be four or more procedures you may have to follow to accomplish a successful format. These are:

❑ Select the hard disk type during set-up

❑ Preformat (low-level format) the hard disk drive

❑ Execute FDISK from MS-DOS

❑ Execute FORMAT (high-level format) from MS-DOS.

Your 386 PC may have a set-up procedure for choosing the appropriate HDD installed. If the 386 PC was bought with the HDD already installed then it will almost certainly have been set up properly. If however you are installing a new or additional unit the disk type number (relating to its capacity) will probably be required during the set-up procedure. The procedure of the set-up may be in the form of a menu-driven option. The set-up procedures will also refer to other options in the 386 PC: screen type, on-board RAM and so on. It is customary for new HDDs to be already preformatted. Should this not be the case it is necessary to run a program which will perform this task. For the preformat operation a program called FXPREP is required and should be supplied with the system software. One of the important functions of the preformatting procedure is to determine the number and location (by marking) of bad tracks on the HDD. You normally have the option of entering the bad tracks yourself (if you have performed this procedure before and it can save time) or allow the program to scan the HDD for the bad tracks. The second option is usually preferable as any new bad tracks will be marked.

It will be surprising if there are no bad tracks, but for a new unit these should not exceed a few kbytes. It is the operation of preformatting that divides the tracks up into sectors and tests each sector individually and subsequently marks any bad sectors. An option will probably be available to allow the disk interleave factor to be adjusted. On a good quality HDD there should be no need to have interleaving so this should be set to 1. Preformatting can take up to several minutes to complete depending on the size of the HDD. However there should be a display revealing information on the progress of the process. Once this task is complete move onto stage three – FDISK.

2.5.6 FDISK

FDISK is an MS-DOS program (found on the system software supplied with the 386 PC) for configuring the HDD for individual needs. HDDs can be partitioned into up to four sections which can contain a different operating system if required. FDISK will enable a number of operations to be performed on the HDD unit.

There is an option to create the primary DOS partition and to make it the active partition. This should be chosen to enable DOS to be installed on the HDD and to boot up from it. If required, only one partition can be created, however this will have a maximum size of 32 Mbytes for DOS 3.3. Up to four partitions can be configured on a HDD and these can be used to hold other operating systems if required.

There is however another type of DOS partition to choose from apart from the primary and this is the extended partition. A DOS primary partition must be present on the HDD before the extended version can be created. The primary DOS partition will be the first partition and will contain the DOS operating system which is loaded when the PC is powered up, and will probably be assigned the logical drive C:. If the other partitions are configured as extended DOS partitions you will be allowed to assign logical drive letters to them (D: to Z:) and they can be accessed as if they are separate hard disk drives. If there are other HDDs in the system you have the option, during the FDISK exercise, of moving to the next and making similar modifications.

Once FDISK is completed the DOS operating system can be transferred from the floppy disk in A: to the HDD by using FORMAT.COM. This will take the form:

```
A > format C: /S
```

and completes the operation of formatting the hard disk drive(s).

2.5.7 Removable Hard Disk Drives

A hard disk storage medium, which is increasing in popularity as a convenient method of transporting data, is the removable hard disk (RHD). It has a cartridge type format and is loaded into a cradle which occupies a disk drive compartment of the 386 PC. It is particularly attractive for the secure storage of large amounts of data and the RHDs can be easily removed and stored or transported for safe keeping. Their internal design ensures that the heads remain fixed and the platters remain free from potentially damaging mechanical components. They can even survive being dropped. Typical memory capacity is 40 Mbytes with access times close to 28 msecs which makes them quite acceptable as mass storage devices for 386 PCs.

An example of a RHD is the Passport from the Plus Development Corp (Figure 2.13). This has a 40 Mbytes capacity with an access time of 28 msecs and an interleave ratio of 1:1. It has an impressive mean time before failure (MTBF) of 60,000 hours and only requires 7 seconds to load and 12 seconds to unload.

Figure 2.13 The Passport from Plus Development Corporation – a removable mass storage device. The 20 amd 40Mb versions slot into internal or external housings. (Photo: Courtesy of Computer Marketing)

2.6 RAM Disk

A RAM disk is a very useful software device and when installed makes a part of the RAM memory simulate disk memory with a FAT, a root directory and a logical drive (the next available letter). If required, it can be treated, to all intents and purposes as a proper disk drive with sub-directories if required. RAM disk, also known as virtual disk, has the advantage over a proper disk drive of enabling very rapid read and write access. However it can only be used for temporary storage, when the 386 PC is switched off the contents of the RAM disk are lost.

RAM disk is installed as a device driver in the CONFIG.SYS file and comes in the form of a software routine, sometimes labelled VDISK.SYS. Since it is a device driver it is loaded into the 386 PC system during the boot up phase. When installed the driver, like all other drivers, can occupy part of the base memory. However there are a number of options allowable during the installation of RAM disk, it can be placed in the base memory or in Expanded Memory (satisfying the LIM-EMS) or even in Extended Memory assuming either is installed. The amount of memory allocated to RAM disk is also adjustable and the instruction in the CONFIG.SYS file is:

```
DEVICE=VDISK.SYS [<disk size>] [<sector size>] [<entries>] /x
```

where <disk size> is a value in kbytes and defaults to 64K, <sector size> is the disk sector size (128, 256, 512 and 1024) in kbytes with a default value of 128K and <entries> specifies the number of entries in the root directories with a default of 64. There are three options for the switch /x. In the default the RAM disk is installed in the base memory. If however, it is set as /e the RAM disk is placed in the Extended Memory beyond the one Mbyte boundary or if /a is used the RAM disk is located in the Expanded Memory. Only one switch is allowed.

2.7 Disk Cache

One method for improving the speed of an application program which makes heavy use of disk drives is to use a disk cacheing utility. A disk cache is designed to speed up disk access by making copies of most recently accessed disk data and storing it in RAM. Subsequent accesses to the data is made to the RAM copy and not to the disk drive. Accessing RAM is much faster than accessing disk drives and this results in a marked improvement in performance. For a hard disk, this can be as large as 10 times and possibly up to 50 times for a floppy disk drive.

During the normal operation of an application program, a call may made to access data stored on a disk. The operating system performs this task by making calls through the BIOS to the disk drive and passes the acquired data on to the application program. It is during this process that the disk cache makes its copy of the accessed data and stores it in a reserved area of memory (storage buffer). The disk cache keeps a catalogue (cache directory) of its stored data and steps in every time the application program makes a disk access via the operating system. The disk cache checks its directory for the requested data and if it is present in its storage buffer it is passed to the operating system which in turn passes it to the application program. In the event of the requested data not being in the cache storage buffer the operating system accesses the disk as normal. A flow diagram to illustrate is shown in Figure 2.13.

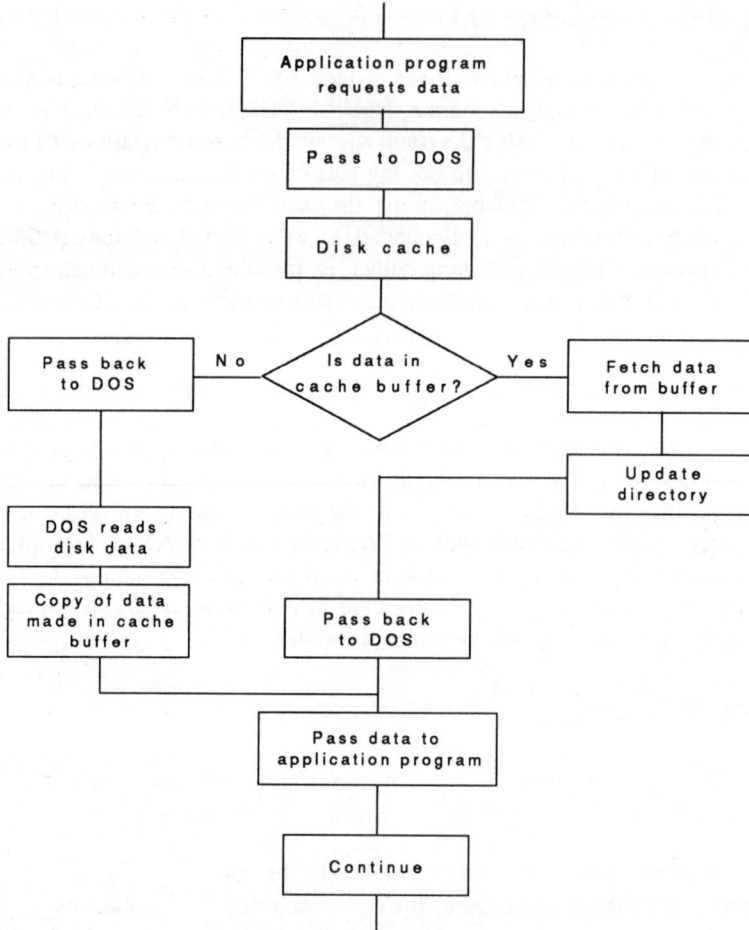

Figuure 2.13 Flow chart to illustrate disk cacheing

It is not unusual to find some disk cache software reading more data from the disk than the amount of data requested by the application program. For example if the application program asks for 64 bytes the cache will copy 512 bytes from the accessed sector. It is possible it may also copy the contents of the remaining 16 sectors in that track. The rational behind this lies in the belief that if data from a certain file is required then there is a high probability that more data from the same file will be required. This in effect should minimise the amount of time the operating system has to access the disk and results in a faster system operation.

In a 386 PC the cache buffer would occupy either expanded or extended memory and the data in the cache buffer is updated as the application program progresses. When the buffer is full there are at least two algorithms which are used to decide what data should be discarded to make way for new data. These are the **Least Recently Run** (LRR) and the **Least Frequently Used** (LFU) algorithms. They make use of the cache directory which keeps track of how often stored data is required and when it was last used by the application program. Two methods therefore determine whether a data segment is retained by the cache buffer. The LRR algorithm looks at the history of a data segment and the LFU looks at the frequency of calling. A compromise is reached; it is therefore quite possible for a data segment to have a low LRR rating yet remain in the buffer because of its high LFU rating. Some data segments can remain permanently resident in the cache buffer and an example is the file allocation table (FAT) which contains information on the data file positions on the disk which is normally read every time a disk access occurs.

The disk cache not only plays a role in reading data from the disk but also writing data to the disk. There are several schemes by which the disk cache can improve the system performance through disk writing. On an elementary level, the disk cache can make a copy of the data segment written to a disk. In the event of a rewrite of the data segment a comparison is made with the cache copy. If there is a match the disk write is cancelled thus saving an unnecessary disk access. However most disk cache write operations involve a degree of queueing and sorting so that when data is written to the disk it is accomplished in a minimum number of disk rotations and head movements. Advanced disk cache techniques involve temporary data storage for deferred writing until the 386 PC enters a low-duty cycle. This is an effective method for optimising the resources and is attractive for semi real-time applications.

There are however a number of potential problem areas with disk cacheing which the user must be aware of to avoid data loss or corruption. Most disk cacheing routines operating a deferred write process can detect if a floppy disk has been removed or changed. However the same cannot be said for removable hard disk units and in this case it is advised not to use deferred cache writing. Problems can also arise if a memory manage is used to install terminate and stay resident (TSR) programs in areas outside extended memory areas. Caution must also be exercised if there is a separate controller for the disk drives. However for most 386 PCs there is a single controller card for the hard disk and floppy disk drives.

There are several disk cacheing routines available: PC-Cache which is part of PC-Tools Delux from Central Point Software, PolyBoost II from Polytron and Mace Utilities. With Windows/386, there is a disk cache routine Smartdrive which is well matched to the requirements of a window environment. It is loaded from the CONFIG.SYS file and is only effective for fixed disk drives.

2.8 BIOS ROM

On the motherboard of a 386 PC there will be a set of ROMs which contain the code necessary to allow the 80386 CPU to communicate with the system peripherals, the screen, the printer, the keyboard, the disk units and the expansion ports. This is referred to as the Basic Input/Output ROM or BIOS ROM for short. Whenever the 386 PC is on, the BIOS is active and holds the control programs for servicing the computer's peripherals and therefore basically lies between the CPU and outside world. The code held in the BIOS is a library of service routines which can be executed by the CPU. For example if a program is running and requests an update of the screen then the CPU is armed with an interrupt number and a service number makes a call on the BIOS software and executes the appropriate code. Also, if a key is pressed then an interrupt to the CPU is generated via the BIOS which also provides the code for servicing the interrupt by reading the keyboard. The BIOS software itself is copyright protected and there are at least three versions that are currently available; these have been issued by the Phoenix Corporation, American Megatrends Incorporated (AMI) and Award Software Inc (ASI).

One attractive feature of the BIOS is that it is readily accessible to the system programmer and the software codes held in the BIOS can be called by the programmer. IBM has gone to some lengths to design well defined techniques for directing peripheral control operations through the BIOS ROM and this aspect has contributed, in part, to the concept of IBM PC compatibility.

The BIOS ROM service routines, which are activated by CPU interrupts, can be categorised into five service classes. The first is for specific peripheral device services which has six interrupts: video display, floppy disk drive, communications ports, PC system, keyboard and printer. The second class has two interrupts for the computer's equipment and the memory size. The third class deals with the time and date which have one interrupt. This leaves the last two which cope with the print screen (one interrupt), active ROM BASIC language and the active boot start-up code.

2.8.1 Shadow BIOS ROM

A problem which sometimes arises with the 386 PC is the access time constraint placed upon the actual chip(s) housing the BIOS ROM. If the access time is long, in excess of 0.8 micro sec for a 16 Mhz CPU, the CPU has to generate wait states for addressing the ROM. Subsequently the operational speed of the 386 PC peripherals is significantly impaired. This clearly shows itself in the performance of VGA graphics images which can be painfully slow if the CPU has to work directly through the slow BIOS ROM. To overcome this problem, it is common practice to copy the contents of the BIOS ROM in system RAM which has a far faster access time. This is referred to Shadow ROM. Many 386 PCs have a program utility for performing this function.

Shadowing ROM makes use of the mapping ability of the 80386 CPU to map the logical address (actual address) of the BIOS ROM to the physical address of the BIOS copy in RAM. The mapping of the BIOS ROM's logical address to the BIOS RAM physical address allows the video BIOS to execute at the system clock speed (16, 20, 25 or 33 Mhz) instead of the 8 Mhz of the 8-bit video adaptor connector.

There are however two problems with this method: firstly the BIOS RAM copy may occupy a part of the 640K base memory and secondly the software routines in the BIOS ROM are copywrite protected and making a copy of them, even temporarily, is breach of copyright. However many 386 PC manufacturers have licensing agreements with the BIOS ROM manufacturers to allow legitimate copying of their ROMs.

Further Reading:

The Intel 80386 Microprocessor
1. The Intel 80386 – Architectural and Implementation, K A El-Ayat & R K Agarwal, Electronic Design 17 October 1985.

2. Intel's 32-bit Wonder: The 80386 Microprocessor, C Petzold, PC Magazine 25 Nov. 1986.

3. Peripherals enhance 80386 design options, V S Kumar, Computer Design 1 March 1987.

4. 80386 High Performance 32-Bit CHMOS Microprocessor with Integrated Memory Management, Intel Information 231630-003 November 1986.

5. 80386 Technical Reference, E Struss, Prentice Hall (1987).

6. 80386 A Programming & Design Handbook, P Brumm & D Brumm, Tab Professional & Reference Books.

7. The 80386 Book, Ross Nelson, Microsoft (1988).

8. 80386/387 Architecture, P S Morse, Wiley (1987).

9. Intel 80386 Hardware Reference Manual, Intel (1986).

10. 80386 Microprocessor, C Pappas & W Murry, McGraw-Hill (1987).

Cache Memory
1. 80386 Cache Design, G Shires, Solutions Nov/Dec 1985.

2. Cacheing in the Chips, I Wilson, Electronics & Wireless World Jan. 1989 p75.

Direct Memory Access (DMA)

1. 82380 High Performance DMA Controller with Integrated System Support Peripherals, Intel information 290128-001 January 1987.

Hard Disk Drives

1. Guide to Hard Disk Management, Van Wolverton, Microsoft Press (1988).

2. Hard Disk Tips, Tools and Techniques, A Balfe, Sigma Press (1989).

3. The Hard Disk Companion, P Norton & R Jourdain, Brady.

4. Understanding Hard Disk Management, J Kamin, Sybex.

BIOS ROM

1. The New Peter Norton Programmer's Guide to the IBM PC & PS/2, P Norton & R Wilton, Microsoft Press (1988).

2. IO ROM BIOS, R Duncan, Microsoft Press (1988).

Appendix 2A: Table of Hard Disk Drive Type parameters

Type	Cylinders	No. of heads	Capacity in Mbytes
1	306	4	10
2	615	4	21
3	615	6	32
4	940	8	65
5	940	6	49
6	615	4	21
7	462	8	32
8	733	5	32
9	900	15	117
10	820	3	21
11	855	5	37
12	855	7	52
13	306	8	21
14	733	7	52
16	612	4	21
17	977	5	42
18	977	7	59
19	1024	7	62
20	733	5	32
21	733	7	44
22	733	5	32
23	306	4	10
24	612	4	21
25	306	4	10
26	612	4	21
27*	698	7	85
28*	976	5	85
29	306	4	10
30*	611	4	42
31*	732	7	89
32*	1023	5	89
33	1024	5	44
34	612	2	10
35	1024	9	80
36	1024	8	71
37	615	8	42
38	987	3	25
39	987	7	60
40	820	6	42
41	977	5	42
42	981	5	42
43	830	7	50
44	830	10	72
45	917	15	115
46	0	0	0

*The ST-506 controller using MFM coding will have a sector density of 17 sectors per cylinder. Types marked * based on a ESDI controller will have 34 sectors*

3

386 PC System Utilities

Expanding the functionality of the 386 PC may be desirable for a number of reasons. The initial task for which the 386 PC was bought may have been completed and there is a need to upgrade it for a quite different purpose. Alternatively, with experience a greater appreciation of the 386 PC's potential may have been gained. This may lead the user to explore the many exciting possibilities the 386 PC has to offer. Its functionality can be expanded in a variety of ways with the addition of enhancements and peripherals. These can be loosely categorised into devices which are situated internally or externally to the main 386 PC unit. This chapter will cover the former category of enhancements. The versatile and general design of the 386 PC motherboard will allow the inclusion of new peripheral features, and by installing additional hardware the user can effectively customise the 386 PC for a specific task. During the installation of any hardware, great care must be taken and a thorough reading of the installation procedures, which accompany the hardware, is recommended. In the case of expansion plug-in cards, particular attention should be paid to any jumper settings or DIP switches which may be adjustment to prevent contention with other expansion cards.

3.1 Numerical Coprocessors

One of impressive features of a 386 PC is the speed and breadth of its computational power. There are many applications where this aspect needs to be to enhanced especially if the 386 PC is used for numerically intensive functions such as computer-aided design (CAD) and other engineering design functions. This can be achieved by the addition of a mathematics coprocessor which is an integrated circuit chip working in parallel with the 80386 microprocessor and can significantly speed up the 386 PC. The coprocessor is designed specifically for performing floating point calculations (Appendix 3A) which maximise precision and numerical accuracy. On the motherboard of the 386 PC there will be one or possibly two sockets for a numerical coprocessor. However some machines may require the coprocessor to be mounted on an adapter card to be accommodated in the card cage. If, for numerically intensive work, you are appraising a 386 PC which has this feature, it should be rejected on the grounds of being a poor design.

There are many application programs which expect a numerical coprocessor to be present and the trend in current software development for engineering and scientific purposes reinforces this. To run an application program which requires a coprocessor on a 386 PC which does not have one, it may be possible to configure the 386 PC to force the application program to use floating point emulation software.

When the high-level language code of the application program was linked it may have contained a library which has the floating point emulation subroutine software. So instead of the CPU passing parameters to the coprocessor, it passes them to the emulation subroutines. The accuracy of the outcome will depend on the quality of the subroutines, but at least the application may run. The 386 PC may be configured to execute the emulation subroutines by using the SET instruction from MS-DOS as follows:

```
SET NO87 = 8087 Suppressed
```

If however the emulation library was not present during the code linking state then this technique will not work. In general, if a 386 PC is to be acquired specifically for serious engineering or scientific tasks it should have a numerical coprocessor fitted as standard.

3.1.1 Intel 80287

Intel manufactures a coprocessor chip to accompany its 80286, 16-bit microprocessor which was adopted by IBM in its AT machines and the clone manufacturers in their 286-based PCs. In the early 386 PCs it was a common design feature to find a socket only for the 16-bit Intel 80287 coprocessor. This was, in part, due to three reasons: firstly very few software packages required the full facility of the more advanced 32-bit 80387 coprocessor, secondly the prohibitively high cost of the 80387 (up to 60% of the cost of the machine) and thirdly the paucity of the chips. However, the cost of 80387 coprocessors is now more competitive and the majority of 386 PCs have sockets for one. If you are in possession of an older 386 PC then an 80287 coprocessor is better than none at all. Some makes of 16-MHz 386 PCs can accommodate either the 80287 or 80387 coprocessor (not both). However the faster 20MHz and 25MHz 386 PCs can only support the 80387 coprocessor.

3.1.2 Intel 80387

The 80387 numerical coprocessor effectively expands the architecture of the 80386

CPU by forming a close coupled pair and thereby speeding up high precision calculations. Together they form a unified system as the 80387 augments the resources of the 80386 central processing unit. The principal feature of the 80387 coprocessor is its ability to perform high-precision floating point calculations (Appendix 3A). With the presence of the 80387 coprocessor, the assembly language instruction set of the 80386 is expanded with over 70 additional instructions which are executed on the 80387 coprocessor. A high-level language compiler will therefore make use of these additional instructions provided the appropriate software switches are set before compiling and linking.

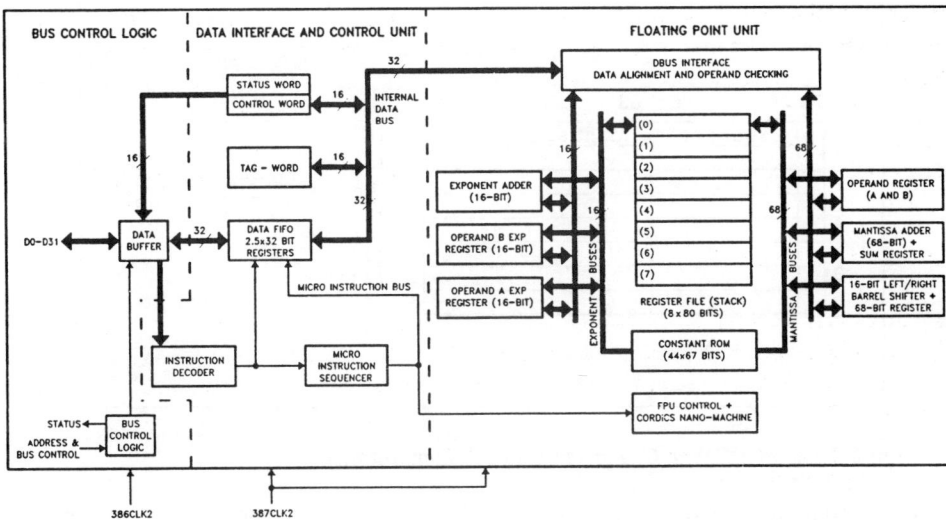

Figure 3.1 Block diagram of the 80387

Another attractive feature with the Intel design is that the object code for the Intel 8088/8087 and 80286/80287 pairs is upward compatible with the 80386/80387 since the instruction sets for the 8-bit and 16-bit processors are subsets of the 32-bit 80386/80387 pair. Whether the 80386 is operating in its virtual mode (8086/8087 compatible), its real address mode (80286/80287 compatible) or in its protected mode (total compatibility), the 80387 coprocessor acts directly on the instructions and data passed to it by the 80386 and is not dependent upon the processing of the 80386. The Intel 80387 coprocessor is packaged in a 68-pin grid array (PGA) and care must taken when inserting the device into its socket, not to bend any of the pins as once bent they can easily break off.

The block diagram for the 80387 (Figure 3.1) shows three functional elements which can operate in parallel to maximise the system's performance. As an example the **Bus**

Control Logic can be receiving commands and data from the 80386 for the next instruction while simultaneously the **Floating Point Unit** is performing the current instruction. The Floating Point Unit performs the numerical operations of the 80387. These include normal arithmetic and logical operations as well as transcendental (trigonometric and logarithmic) functions. The **Data Interface and Control Unit** has a four-fold task: it directs data into/out of the floating point unit, targets data into/out of the control registers, receives and decodes instructions and sequences the micro-coded instructions. The Bus Control Logic on the other hand is responsible for bus tracking and synchronous interfacing with the 80386.

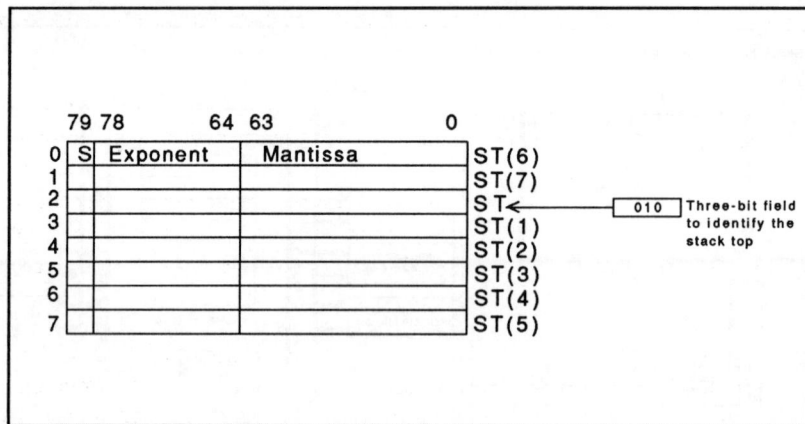

```
     79 78        64 63              0
  0 [S| Exponent  |  Mantissa  ]    ST(6)
  1 [           |             ]    ST(7)
  2 [           |             ]    ST <----- [010]  Three-bit field
  3 [           |             ]    ST(1)            to identify the
  4 [           |             ]    ST(2)            stack top
  5 [           |             ]    ST(3)
  6 [           |             ]    ST(4)
  7 [           |             ]    ST(5)
```

Figure 3.2 The 80387 Stack Register Set of Accumulators

Programming the 80387 is accomplished by using an extended set of assembly language instructions which work with the instruction set for the 80386. The assembly language programmer therefore not only sees the register set for the 80386 but also the eight extended floating point registers for the 80387 (Figure 3.2). In fact, floating point instructions treat the registers as a stack of accumulators where the top of the stack is denoted by ST, which incidentally can be anywhere in the stack. The current stack register in use is held in a three-bit field called TOP containing the absolute register number which is the current accumulator, ie top of the accumulator stack.

The other registers are labelled ST(i) where i represents the position relative to ST. The design of the stack allows the use of PUSH and POP type instructions to be used. So that every time the stack is PUSHed, the TOP is decremented and every time the stack is POPped, TOP is incremented. All instructions relating to the 80387 coprocessor are suffixed by F. For example if a number in memory location mem32 is to be passed to the 80387 and PUSHed onto the accumulator stack the instruction *FLD mem32* would be used.

If the value of TOP was 2 before the instruction, it would be decremented to 1 after the instruction was executed. After the instruction a copy of mem32 will be in ST. To multiply this number by the contents of ST(3), for example, the instruction *FMUL ST, ST(3)* would be used and the result is deposited in ST. To retrieve the result and store it in memory location mem32, you would use *FSTP mem34*.

Since this is a POP type instruction, the TOP would be incremented from 1 to 2 after the execution of the instruction. The 80387 instruction set not only has instructions for numerical operations but also for control functions. These are required for when the 80386 CPU performs a task switch (context switch); the register contents in the 80387 can be saved for when the 80386 returns to the task and carries on from where it left off.

An interesting question is often asked: What happens if a 16MHz 80387 is used in a 20MHz system? There is a remote chance that it will work properly, however it is more likely that, initially it will produce wrong answers to mathematical operations. There is also a great danger of the coprocessor drawing more current than it can cope with, which in turn leads to excessive power dissipation and eventual burn out. It is therefore not a recommended practice. A chip can usually run at a slower clock speed than it's specified for, but not faster.

A variation on the Intel 80387 coprocessor is the FasMath 83D87 from the Cyrix Corp, supplied in the UK by Micro Call Solution. The 83D87 is pin compatible with the 80387 which means that it can be inserted into the 80387 socket on the 386 PC motherboard. By having its coprocessor instructions embedded or hardwired into the silicon substrate, it can perform significantly faster than the 80387. It performs all 117 assembly language instructions of the 80387 and maintains the IEEE-754 floating point format. The 83D87 is available in four clock speeds: 16, 20, 25 and 33 MHz. Another compatible coprocessor is the ITT-3C87 from Integrated Information Technology and distributed by Dram Electronics. It is able to perform coprocessor instructions in a shorter time (fewer clock cycles) than the 80387 which gives it a 50% improvement. With its enlarged register set, it can execute instructions which are not available for the 80387. It is available in three clock speeds: 16, 20 and 25 MHz.

3.1.3 Weitek 3167 Floating Point Coprocessor

An alternative coprocessor to the Intel 80387 is the Weitek WTL 3167, which is a very high-performance single-chip coprocessor and can provide an improvement of three to four times over the 80387. It has been specially designed to work in parallel with the Intel 80386 and when operating under MS-DOS takes advantage of an anomaly in the real-mode addressing of the 80386 MCU. This allows an additional 65K of memory space to be addressed which is sufficient to accommodate the WTL 3176. The WLT 3176 requires a special 121-pin socket, defined as the **Extended Maths Coprocessor** socket (EMC), which is a superset of the Intel 80387 coprocessor. A daughter-board is available which accommodates the WTL 3167 and the Intel 80387. Not all 386 PCs have the pin superset and before buying you should enquire whether the facility is available.

Only software which has been compiled with the WTL 3167 assembly language instruction set, used as a subset of the Intel 80386 CPU, will benefit from its high numerical performance. However the WTL 3167 is supported by UNIX (Version V release 3.0) and MS-DOS protected mode operating systems. There are several C, Pascal and FORTRAN compilers available from Green Hills Software, Microway, Silicon Valley Software and Salford University. The WTL 3167 performs the normal arithmetic operations, in floating point, and the transcendental functions (trigonometric and logarithmic operations) are supported by run-time libraries which are linked into the program during the linking phase of the program development. The WTL 3167 conforms to the IEEE 754-1986 floating point standard.

3.2 Card Cage for Expansion Cards

The card cage is an area within the 386 PC which can accommodate plug-in expansion cards made to the IBM card standard with the connecting strip pins protruding at the base of the card. Expansion plug-in cards come in two lengths: half card and full-length card, the latter extending over the full width of the card cage and requiring a support guide. Through the use of plug-in cards the 386 PC can be customised to the user's specific needs and this feature above all else has lead to the widespread growth of the personal computer. On the market today there many different cards which perform a bewildering variety of functions. It is difficult to categorise the immense range , but they can be broadly grouped into three categories:

❑ Cards which expand the internal functionality of the 386 PC, for example Extended memory cards (Section 2.3.4) and intelligent graphics cards (Section 4.3.4)

❑ Cards which act as an interface between the 386 PC and peripheral(s), for example local area network Ethernet cards (Section 8.7.1)

❑ Accelerator cards which are purpose built for performing specific computational functions.

On removing the lid from the 386 PC (following the instructions in the user manual) the card cage becomes readily accessible and the bus expansion connectors are clearly visible. Some cards may already be present in the cage, for example the graphics card and disk controller. When removing or inserting cards from the cage always ensure that the power is off – it is good practice to disconnect the cable from the mains supply.

When inserting a card it may be necessary to exert a degree of pressure to ensure that the strip connector is secure in the bus expansion connector. For full-length expansion cards there will be additional guides to support the ends. The card should reside in a slot without bowing: if there is bowing due to length discrepancy ensure the card does not touch a neighbouring card. You may have to move the cards around to avoid this.

3.2.1 Bus widths

On the 386 PC there can be a variety of bus expansion connectors. For example, if the 386 PC is an IBM Model 55SX, 70 or 80 (Section 3.8) then the connectors will be of the Micro Channel Architecture (MCA) design. For a recently designed 386 PC there may be a Extended Industrial Standard Architecture expansion bus (EISA – Section 7.3.4) which is characterised by two closely spaced connectors – one short one long. Alternatively for the majority of 386 PCs the connectors conform to the Industry Standard Architecture (ISA) to cater for 8-bit and 16-bit cards.

How these connectors are distributed will vary from machine to machine. If fast memory expansion (Expanded or Extended) is required then it is highly probable that one 32-bit connector will be required. The 16-bit connectors are often referred to as AT slots which are congruous with the design to be found in the 16-bit 80286-based IBM AT personal computer. In reality 8-bit connectors are not required in a 386 PC since the 16-bit connectors can perform all the functions of an 8-bit connector which means that 8-bit cards can be slotted into 16-bit connectors.

3.3 Communication Ports

Peripherals play an important role in the 386 PC system and the transfer of information between the PC and the addition of new peripherals must be conducted in a standard, well ordered fashion. This is frequently achieved by using the communication ports which are a standard feature on 386 PCs.

There will be at least one parallel port and two serial interface ports which are the normal channels for communicating with printers and other external peripherals. On some 386 PCs there may be a games port, for interfacing to a joystick, and a port specifically for a mouse. The details of the mouse port will be covered by the accompanying 386 PC handbook.

3.3.1 Parallel Port

The least troublesome of the ports on the 386 PC is the parallel interface based on the Centronics standard. Normally only one Centronics interface is standard on a 386 PC, but there may be a second one featured on an asynchronous communications adapter plug-in card (Section 3.3.2). The parallel interface is a DB 25-pin female connector (with holes not pins) situated on the rear of the 386 PC and is ideally suited for printers. The settings on the parallel interfaces are almost always fixed and very few problems are ever experienced with this interface.

In MS-DOS the first parallel interface port will be assigned the label of LPT1. If there is a second then this will be labelled LPT2. The cable required to link the PC to a printer will require a DB 25-pin connector (male with pins and two affixing screws) on 386 PC end and the characteristic Centronics plug with its support clips on the other. There is limit of two metres of length for this cable.

3.3.2 RS-232 Serial Interface

The serial interface will be based on the RS-232 standard and can at times cause problems if it is not configured properly. The problems can arise from variations in the cable configuration and the hardware and software switch settings. If problems occur then careful attention must be paid to the pin wiring and switch settings. The RS-232 connector(s) on the rear of the PC may be either a DB 9- or 25-pin, both referred to as male connectors (with pins). IBM chose the 9-pin version as the standard on its AT range of personal computers.

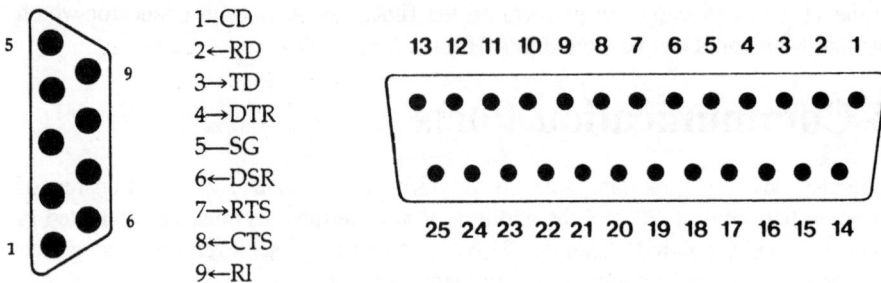

```
1–CD
2←RD
3→TD
4→DTR
5—SG
6←DSR
7→RTS
8←CTS
9←RI
```

Figure 3.3 IBM standard male RS-232 9- and 24-pin layouts

The RS-232 interface may form part of the 386 PC motherboard or occupy one of the expansion slots in the card cage. Not all the pins are used and Figure 3.3 shows the IBM standard pin layout for the two types of male connectors. The original RS-232 interface was designed to allow communication between a terminal and computer via an open communication link such as a telephone line.

The same interface is now used to allow the 386 PC to communicate with peripherals. Not all the lines are used but it is important to realise that certain conditions have to be satisfied before communication can be successful. The description of each line function is given in Table 3.1 opposite.

Frame Ground (GND)	Ground pin set at 0 volts.
Signal Ground (SG)	The signal earth for the interface, sometimes strapped to GND.
Transmit Data (TxD)	Data from the 386 PC flows out of this line to the data communication equipment. With no data transfer this is high.
Request To Send (RTS)	A signal sent to the peripheral to indicate that the PC is ready to transmit data (high).
Clear To Send (CTS)	A signal sent by the peripheral to indicate to the 386 PC that it is ready to receive and transmit data (high). Before the PC sends its RTS, the CTS must be high. When this is low it indicates to the PC that the peripheral is not ready to receive.
Carrier Detect (CD)	Normally used with a modem to indicate to the PC that the transmission carrier frequency has been detected (high).
Receive Data (RxD)	Serial data is received along this line.
Data Set Ready (DSR)	This serves to indicate to the PC that the peripheral is set up ready for data transfer.
Data Terminal Ready (DTR)	Indicates to the peripheral that the PC is set up for the transfer of data (high).
Ring Indicator (RI)	Normally used on modems to indicate to the 386 PC that the ringing tone has been detected by the modem.

Table 3.1 Line functions on the RS-232 interface relative to the 386 PC

The RS-232 interface is an asynchronous serial communication channel between **Data Terminal Equipment** (DTE), which is played by the 386 PC in this context, and **Data Communication Equipment** (DCE), the peripheral.

Table 3.2, overleaf, shows the pin layout for the 9- and 25-pin male connectors. In the 9-pin version pins 2 and 3 are required for the data transfer, pins 7 (RTS) and 8 (CTS) are required if the RTS/CTS handshaking is enabled. Pins 6 (DSR) and 8 (CTS) indicate if the PC and the peripheral are ready to exchange data and pin 4 (DTR) is needed to establish the link between the 386 PC and the peripheral.

RS-232 Handshaking

Handshaking is necessary in order to synchronise the flow of data between the 386 PC and the peripherals which are connected on the serial ports. The 386 PC and the peripheral will have memory buffers which temporary store the data which is transferred. When the buffer is full, the receiving device needs to indicate to the transmitting device that a buffer overflow is close. It achieves this through one of three types of handshaking procedure possible in the RS-232 standard:

❑ Hardware using of RTS/CTS lines

❑ Hardware using the DTR line

❑ Software using control characters XON/XOFF

Pin Number		Pin Label	
(9)	*(25)*		
1	8	CD	Carrier Detect
2	3	RxD	Receive Data
3	2	TxD	Transmit Data
4	20	DTR	Data Terminal Ready
5	7	SG	Signal Ground
6	6	DSR	Data Set Ready
7	4	RTS	Ready To Send
8	5	CTS	Clear To Send
9	22	RI	Ring Indicator

Table 3.2 RS-232 Pin format

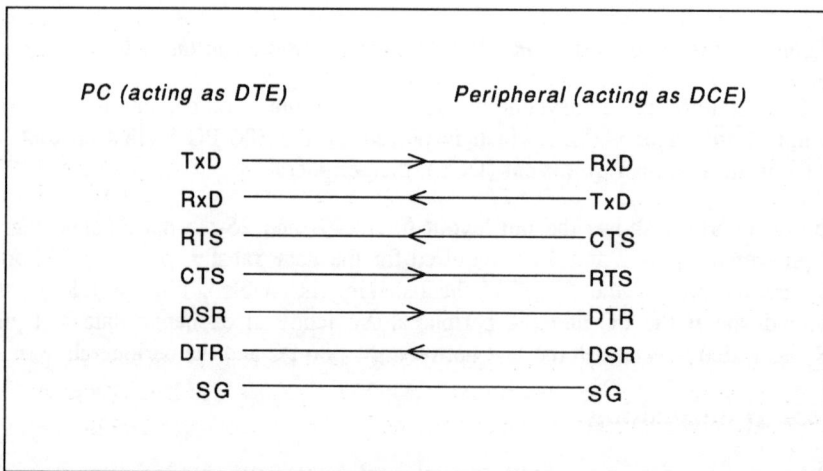

PC (acting as DTE)	Peripheral (acting as DCE)
TxD ————————→	RxD
RxD ←————————	TxD
RTS ←————————	CTS
CTS ————————→	RTS
DSR ————————→	DTR
DTR ←————————	DSR
SG ————————	SG

Table 3.3 Typical connections of PC when acting as a DTE

The most efficient data transfer is achieved using the RTS/CTS option where the polarity change on these lines indicates the current receiver status of each device. When the DTR line is used, it is taken low by the receiving device to temporarily halt data transmission. Once the buffer is empty the DTR line is asserted high.

In the RS-232 standard each character transferred is a member of the **American Standard Code for Information Interchange** (ASCII) character set and two of the ASCII characters are used for the software handshake. If the buffer on the receiving device is reaching overflow its sends the ASCII character DC1 (XOFF) to pause data transmission and DC3 (XON) to restart the transmission.

RS-232 Character Format

During transmission each character occupies up to 11 bits and in each 11 bits the following information is transmitted: the start bit(s), the character itself, the stop bit(s) and an error check (parity bit). The division of the bits is adjustable and a number of options are available. For baseband transmission (Section 8.1.2), which uses digital serial signals, the rate at which the bits are transmitted is referred to as the **Baud rate** and can have one of the values 300, 600, 1200, 2400, 4800, 9600 or 19200 bits per second. The widely used baud rate for 386 PCs and its peripherals is 9600. The character bits are either 7 or 8 depending on whether extended ASCII characters are used (values larger than 127). The stop bits are either one or two and the parity is either EVEN, ODD, MARK, SPACE or NONE (no checking).

With ODD parity a 1 is placed in the parity bit if the number of 1s in the ASCII character is even and a 0 if the number of 1s is odd. In EVEN parity checking the parity bit is set to 0 if the number of 1s in the ASCII character is even and 1 if the number is odd. When the parity is set to MARK the parity bit is always 1 and when set to SPACE it is always set to 0. The example shown in Figure 3.4 uses eight character bits, one stop bit, one start bit with EVEN parity.

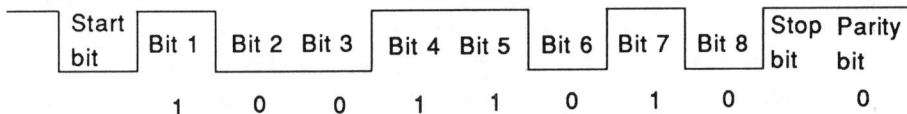

Start bit	Bit 1	Bit 2	Bit 3	Bit 4	Bit 5	Bit 6	Bit 7	Bit 8	Stop bit	Parity bit
	1	0	0	1	1	0	1	0		0

Figure 3.4 RS-232 Serial transmission data frame

In MS-DOS 3.3 the MODE instruction can be used for setting up an RS-232 port. For example if the second RS-232 port is to set up for a printer with a baud rate of 9600, EVEN parity, eight character bits and one stop bit the instruction would be:

```
mode COM2: 9600,E,8,1,p
```

For two way communication the *p* should not be included. The MODE instruction can also be used to re-direct data normally transferred through LPT1. This instruction is:

```
MODE LPT1:=COMx
```

where x can range from 1 to 6 depending on the required RS-232 – MS-DOS 3.3 can support up to six RS-232 interfaces (COM1 to COM6). The software handshake, if enabled, operates through the use of two ASCII characters, 17 DC1 (XON) and 19 DC3 (XOFF). When transmitting data via the serial port the RS-232 logic will read in characters on the RxD line from the peripheral. If an XON is read the PC continues to send data; if an XOFF is read the port ceases transmission until another XON is read whereupon data transmission is continued.

The advantage of this handshake technique is the interface only needs three wires, TxD, RxD and signal ground. There are many RS-232 links which are based on optic fibre technology and it is commonplace for them to use the XON/XOFF handshake since the link can be implemented with only two fibres (TxD and RxD).

RS-232 Troubleshooting

RS-232 problems can arise from three sources: the pin connections, the switch settings and/or the handshake procedure. Pin connections can be checked using a RS-232 tester or circuit breaker which is placed between the PC and its peripheral. It indicates the activity on the important lines and using it you can swap lines around, change the polarity on any line and set-up the handshake lines for their proper operations.

Each peripheral with an RS-232 interface will have an accessible DIP switch and by referring to the user manual the appropriate setting of baud rate, parity, character length and stop bits can be adjusted. The RS-232 setting on the peripheral must match the RS-232C port on the PC otherwise the communication will not be wholly satisfactory.

The third problem that may arise is through inadequate handshaking. This can lead to data being transferred to the peripheral faster than it can cope with, the result being buffer overflow and loss of data. If this should happen refer to the peripheral's user manual and ensure that the same handshake procedure is used by the PC and the peripheral.

If there is uncertainty, the RS-232 tester will indicate if a hardware handshake is in effect. If a software handshake is being used then this should be evident from the RxD LED on the tester. If on the other hand a hardware handshake is employed this should also be evident from the RTS and CTS LEDs.

Multi RS-232 Interfaces

If there is a requirement to connect the 386 PC to a number of peripherals with RS-232 interfaces then a plug-in board with several RS-232 connectors can be considered. An example of such a board is the Digiboard COMM/8i shown in Figure 3.5. It is built around the 10 MHz Intel 80188 microprocessor with 256K of RAM and it contains its own BIOS. The accompanying software will allow up to eight RS-232 devices to be interfaced to a 386 PC. If the 386 PC is to be used as a multi-user server there are a number of propriety products are compatible with multiple RS-232 expansion boards. This is covered in greater detail in Section 8.8.

Figure 3.5 Digiboard COMM/8i eight channel RS-232 interface board. (Photo: Courtesy of KPG Comm Net)

3.4 Keyboards

The majority of 386 PCs are issued with the standard 102-key QWERTY keyboard, with function keys F1 to F12 and a numeric key pad on the right-hand side for rapid number entry, which also doubles-up for cursor control. In spite of the advances in other data input devices, the keyboard is still the major method for entering data into a PC for word processors, databases and spreadsheets. To aid rapid data entry there is a nodule on the 5 key of the numerical key pad which acts as finger guide for the skilled user.

The majority of keyboards are manufactured according to the low-profile DIN ergonomic standard which ensures optimum ease of use. The switching mechanisms on keyboards can be broadly grouped into two categories: mechanical switching action and solid state switching.

The former group is made up of designs which use hard contact, reed, membrane or elastomerdome. The solid state switches use either optical, capacitive or the magnet Hall effect, but these have fallen out of favour due to the development in the mechanical types. Therefore most keyboards use the mechanisms of the mechanical variety.

The hard contact design relies on gold coated make or break contacts and are more subject to environment conditions, for example dampness. The reed contact switch on the other hand is hermetically sealed and free from contamination. The make or break action is effected by the keypress causing the movement of a small magnet which makes the reed move. The overall lifetime of the reed design is about 100 million presses compared with about 10 million for the hard contact.

One type of membrane switch design is made from surface printed contacts on two plastic sheets, separated by an insulating layer with holes which correspond with the key positions. With a keypress the membrane is depressed and contact is made. With this design the keyboard can be sealed to give added protection and extra lifetime. The elastomerdome mechanism relies on a small conductive dome attached to the key which completes the circuit between two gold coated contacts on a printed circuit board. This design is more environmentally stable than the others and has high reliability.

When buying a 386 PC the user should ensure that it is available with a keyboard of the appropriate nationality. In DOS 3.3 the keyboard can be configured according to letters of the language and country of usage. To achieve this under DOS, a keyboard driver, KEYB, can be loaded and entered from within the AUTOEXEC.BAT file. It uses the format:

```
KEYB xx,yyy, [drive:\ <path>],/N
```

where *xx* is a two letter country code (UK for Britain) and *yyy* is the code page for characters appropriate to the specific language (437 for the UK) or either the multilingual code 850. The *N* refers to the number of keys on the keyboard.

Some 386 PCs still use the older keyboard design and 84 keys with the function keys forming two rows down the left-hand side. The only advantage of this keyboard design is when the 386 PC is to be used in a confined area where the working space is limited.

The 386 PC will have a keyboard buffer which stores keystrokes. In the normal operation of the 386 PC when a key is pressed, the keyboard generates a interrupt to the 80386 CPU. If the CPU is busy performing another task, such as moving data to a disk, then the keyboard has to wait. Meanwhile the buffer is catching the other keys being pressed. When the buffer becomes full the 386 PC will issue a beep to indicate this condition and any more keypresses are lost until the buffer is emptied.

If there is a requirement for the 386 PC to act as terminal for an IBM Mainframe computer then two additional features should be considered: an IBM 3270 keyboard which is characterised by an extra row of function keys (F13 to F24) and a suitable interface card such as IRMA 3270 emulation expansion card. An example of a 3270 keyboard is the KB3270/PC from Keytronic which is directly compatible with the 386 PCs.

3.5 The Mouse

A mouse is an essential peripheral of a 386 PC and offers an ergonomic advantage when it is used with the left hand. Its function is to act as a controllable cursor for the user. Given that so many applications programs draw heavily on pull-down or drop-down menus and function within a window environment, the mouse becomes quite indispensable. For any task which is strongly screen-oriented the importance of the mouse is on equal par with that of the keyboard.

Many 386 PC manufacturers supply a mouse as standard and some 386 PCs (Compaq and Opus VII for instance) have dedicated mouse ports. However on most 386 PCs the mouse is interfaced through one of the RS-232 ports and normally works without modifications to the RS-232 connector.

In the design of the mouse, some manufacturers have extensively used optical techniques. Light from a light emitting diode (LED), embedded in the mouse module, illuminates a pad made with highly reflective perpendicular strips. As the mouse moves over the pad, the reflected light from the strips generates a stream of pulses which is scaled into the appropriate cursor movement.

Very small movements, .005 inch, can be detected using an optically based mouse and this is useful in computer-aided design (CAD) for which precision movement is required. Very little maintenance is needed with this mouse design since there are no moving parts. Alternative mouse designs rely on a ball which has contact with a hard rubber surface. The movement of the ball is either sensed through an opto-mechanical means or just through a set of mechanical gears.

Some software for the mouse control employs a technique known as **dynamic acceleration.** The mouse software responds not only to the positional change of the mouse but also to its acceleration (rate of movement). This provides the user with variable movement resolution depending on how fast the mouse is moved.

For very slow and small movements the cursor is scaled with a very low value to give fine control over its position. Conversely if the mouse is moved rapidly, the cursor is scaled with a high value and moves very quickly and coarsely across the screen. This type of control is very attractive for CAD applications or for manipulating large spreadsheets.

There are basically two mouse protocols: the Mouse Systems three-button and the Microsoft two-button. The majority of application software which uses a mouse normally requires emulation software for either of these protocols. The choice of mouse protocol (and mouse design) is dependent upon the nature of the principal application for the 386 PC. With a three-button mouse the number of possible press options is seven. The Logitech C7 Mouse Systems three-button design allows the user to program the seven possible button combination presses. In some CAD applications the additional button presses can be programmed to specific functions which can be time saving.

For most menu-driven application software, in or out of a Windows environment, a two-button mouse is quite adequate. Sometimes it's impracticable to have a mouse with a cable attached to the 386 PC. Should this arise a cordless mouse may be considered. The Mouse Manager, from TDS-Numonics, is one possible solution. Based on infrared technology, it transmits to a small receiver which is attached to any surface on the 386 PC. The receiver is interfaced to the 386 PC via one of the serial RS-232 ports. It is a rechargeable device and can operate for 10 hours with a maximum separation of 2.5 metres from the PC.

3.5.1 Mouse Drivers

To initialise the mouse operation, a software driver supplied with the mouse must be installed. There are two methods of doing this: either through the AUTOEXEC.BAT file as a MOUSE.COM file or through the CONFIG.SYS as a device driver (DEVICE = MOUSE.SYS). The mouse driver software is usually loaded into the 640K base memory (Section 2.3.1) and is a typical example of a terminate and stay resident (TSR) routine. It is possible that some mouse drivers may be installed in the extended memory (Section 2.3.4) of the 386 PC and this is a preferable location to the base memory.

If during installation, there is an option for a dynamic acceleration on the mouse then this should be considered in the light of this discussion, bearing in mind that dynamic acceleration software will require more memory.

Some development software packages have their own mouse drivers, MicroSoft's QuickBASIC 4.5 for example, and this is an alternative to installing the mouse driver during the power up BOOT phase. However this driver cannot be installed directly into extended memory.

3.6 The Power Supply Unit

The function of the power supply in the 386 PC is to provide the proper voltages and power for the motherboard and the I/O expansion card connectors. The voltages produces will be derived from the mains power and should clean with less than 5 mV RMS AC ripple. Many ICs are very critical on voltage levels and their tolerance is very tight. On a number of power supplies there will also be a filter network to ensure that the majority of voltage spikes on the mains power line are filtered out before they reach the power rails on the motherboard. The voltages which are normally required are +/- 15V, +/- 12V and + 5V with sometimes two ground levels (analogue and digital). On the motherboard of the 386 PC there will be rails carrying these voltages to the various components and devices.

Most of the digital circuitry will be of CMOS technology are this will require power from the 5V power rail. However the disk drives will require power from the other voltage rails. Also important is the power rating of the power supply and this refers to the amount of current which can be drawn from each rail. The power supply will rate in power (VAs), the product of the voltage and the available current at that voltage level. A typical DC power rating would be 180 VA which indicates that the sum of the power loads must not exceed 180 VA. For example the power supply could have the following specification:

+12V @ 3 amps giving 36 Watts
-12V @ 3 amps giving 36 Watts
+5V @ 21 amps giving 105 Watts

Whatever the loading may be on the power supply it will be expected to maintain the defined voltage levels without any voltage drop. The power supply rating need only be considered if a number of heavy-duty input/output (I/O) expansion plug-in cards are to be installed in the 386 PC. If the 386 PC is likely to have a number of hard disk drives, two floppy drives, a CD-ROM, a tape drive back-up or other power hungry devices feeding off the I/O expansion connectors, then a suitable power supply will be required.

If there a strong likelihood that several devices will be installed in the 386 PC on the I/O expansion bus, then the option of a tower system should be considered as these normally have higher rated power supply units (Section 10.1.1). One of the features of the extended industry standard architecture (EISA – Section 7.3.4) is its ability to sense power surges from several peripherals coming on together. EISA will stack the peripherals thereby minimising the power surge.

Paramount in the internal design of the 386 PC is the cooling fan which is needed to remove most of the heat generated by the ICs on the motherboard and the additional expansion boards in the card cage. If the fan should fail do not continue operating the 386 PC without it, as overheating the electrical components will lead to partial or complete failure. Partial failure is the most sinister; the computer continues functioning but does the wrong things and produces the wrong answers.

3.7 Tape Back-ups or Streamers

The information on the 386 PC, whether application programs or data, will increase in value as the machine is used more and more. It is therefore prudent to consider methods of backing up or making copies of the data. Although the hard disk units can give months and months of excellent, trouble-free service, they are not 100% reliable and can go wrong. The consequence of this can vary from a small loss of data or total loss of all data if a head crash occurs. If the 386 PC is moved while data is being read to the hard disk unit, this can result in a head crash; even power cuts can upset the unit. If the information is therefore of value, it is worthwhile installing a tape streamer to enable back-ups to be made. Back-ups on floppy disks can be very time consuming and in many instances are only a viable option for small amounts of data (10 Mbytes).

Figure 3.6 The Irwin 2000 series 5.25 inch tape drive streamer

There is a variety of back-up systems for PCs but the majority use the industry standard **Quarter Inch Cartridge** (QIC) data cartridge with 1/4 inch tape as the storage medium, for example the Irwin 2000 Series shown in Figure 3.6. Tape streamer units are available in two designs, as an internal unit or an external unit. The integral designed unit is fitted into the 386 PC and occupies a half-height disk space and draws its power from the 386 PC, for example the Wangtek 5125PK and Alloy Retriever 40. In the other design, the unit remains external to the 386 PC and an example of this design is the Irwin 455A. The tape cartridges for the streamers are available from 3M – type DC600 and DC300. The DC600 series cartridges can hold up to 150 Mbytes and the smaller DC300 can hold up to 40 Mbytes. The QIC cartridges carry a high cost because of the precision manufacturing techniques involved, tape guides, rollers and precision mechanics.

A tape streamer, like the disk drive, requires a control card which is accommodated in the card cage and installation is straightforward and should not give rise to any problems for a well designed 386 PC. However some devices require prior knowledge of the DMA port (Section 2.3.5) and its address.

Accompanying the tape streamer will be a floppy disk with back-up and restore utilities. These utilities may include routines for selective file back-ups and for copy verification. There may even by a selection of macros which can be used for automatically issuing back-up commands related to the system clock and these lend themselves very favourably to regular back-up procedures. A number of tape streamers, for example the Wangtek 5125PK, are accompanied by software from Sytron called **Sytos Tape Operating System** which can be either menu driven or act as an extension to DOS.

Data transfer rate with tape streamers can vary from model to model but this is not an important feature since provision should be made to perform the back-up task at the end of each session. A problem may arise from the DOS imposed limit of 32 Mbytes which may require each volume to be backed up separately. A tape streamer may only support one volume per tape which results in an inefficient use of the cartridge. In the true spirit of the device (streaming) one would expect a sector-by-sector image of the hard disk to be stored on the tape cartridge. However this not a wholly desirable feature as any new files on the hard disk would be deleted during the restoration process, but this facility is available on a number of models.

The majority of tape streamers provide software which allows the user to store data by using the information attached to each file by DOS, time of creation, alphabetical order or by using wild cards. After the tape streamer has been installed, it would be normal to create a directory for the streamer software, although some devices do this during the software installing procedure. It is sometimes desirable to have menu-driven software, as with the Cristie TS1500 Turbo, or a direct access to its operation, which is found on the Achieve Xle. Before a back-up can be performed the tape cartridge must be formatted. This procedure will be model dependent and can be a lengthy operation.

During formatting of the cartridge the tape is partitioned into sectors or streams and segments of a stream can mimic a track of a disk. Both sides of the tape are used. It may be desirable to restrict entry to the back-up facilities and an attractive feature of the Cristie TS1500 Turbo is a request for a password before the backed up files can be accessed. Incidentally, the Cristie device highlights the bad sectors on the hard disk during back-up.

3.7.1 WORM Back-up

A Write Once Read Many (WORM – Section 6.10) can also be used as a method for backing up hard disk information. Although at the outset it may appear expensive, it is a very effective method of obtaining a permanent copy of the current contents of the HDD. If this is a critical factor then the additional investment in WORM technology may well be worthwhile, as it is probably the most reliable back-up available. If a copy of a file is made onto a WORM where a file of the same name already exists then the new file takes on the file name. The original version is not actually lost but the new file will be accessed when that file is recovered. Since the original file is still on the WORM it is possible to recover it if need be. As new files are stored on the WORM they occupy unused areas of the disk, repeated writing and 'erasure' will eventually use up all the WORM.

3.7.2 Digital Audio Tape (DAT)

There are alternative back-up storage devices which use Digital Audio Tapes (DAT) as tape streamers. These are capable of providing very large amounts of storage, typically 1,300 Mbytes per DAT. The Model 1300 4mm DAT Cassette Tape Drive from WangDAT (Figure 3.7 opposite), supplied by Summit Board Computing, uses this technology. The tape in the DATA cartridge is very thin and the writing is diagonal across the tape using a **helical scan** technique. This provides very high-density data storage of 50 Mbytes per cc of tape compared to 570K for QIC. A clever feature of the Model 1300 is that during a fast·wind, the tape is still in contact with the reading head and this enables fast searches for random access.

Although DAT technology is well matched for the purposes of archiving, the search periods tend to lengthen as more information is stored on the DAT. The data transfer rate for the Model 1300 can be as high as 4 Mbytes/sec in its burst mode or 183K for sustained, continual operation. The expansion bus interface protocol for the Model 1300 is based on SCSI (Section 6.5.3) and the unit can be accommodated in a single half-height space in the disk compartment of a 386 PC.

3.8 Personal System/2 (PS/2)

IBM firmly established the personal computer market in the 80s with its models PC, XT and AT. However most of the market was creamed off by other manufacturers who cloned IBM machines and yet effectively evaded copyright violations. IBM, not wishing to see the same scenario occur with its new range of personal computers, introduced copyright protected chip sets for the new range called Personal System/2 or PS/2 as it has become known.

The two special features of the PS/2 range of computers are IBM's OS/2 operating system (Section 5.4.2) and the bus design for expansion cards known as Micro Channel Architecture (MCA).

Figure 3.7 WangDAT's Model 1300. (Photo: Courtesy of Summit Board Computing)

Although OS/2 has been designed to run on a 80286-hosted PC, it will also run on the PS/2 machines which hosts the 80386. The range of PS/2 machines has many commendable features, not least the establishment of the VGA (Section 4.3.3) as a graphics standard. The 3.5 inch floppy disk drive has also become a standard feature on the range of PS/2 machines and this has lead to its general widespread acceptance.

The IBM range includes a number of PS/2 computers based on the 80386 CPU and these are at the top of the range. There are currently three versions of the Model 70:

❑ Model 70-F61 – 60 Mbytes HDD

❑ Model 70-121 – 120 Mbytes HDD, 20 MHz

❑ Model 70-A21 – 120 Mbytes HDD, 64K memory cache, 25 MHz.

All three models are supplied in the normal PS/2 footprint package. There is a portable version of the Model 70 supplied with either a 60Mbyte HDD (P70-K61) or 120Mbyte HDD (P70-121) and comes with 4 Mbytes of RAM as standard. The Model 80 is of tower design and is available with a variety of HDDs and clock speeds:

❑ Model 80-041 – 44 Mbytes

❑ Model 80-071 – 70 Mbytes, with CPU operating at 16 MHz

❑ Model 80-111 – 115 Mbytes, with CPU operating at 20 MHz

❑ Model 80-311 – 314 Mbytes.

IBM also manufactures the Models 55SX and 65SX which are based on the reduced 80386SX (Section 2.2.5). The 55SX is available with either 30Mbyte (55SX-X31) or 60Mbyte HDD (55SX-X61) whereas the 65SX, which has a SCSI disk controller, is available with a 60Mbyte (65SX-61) or a 120Mbyte (65SX-121) hard disk. The Model 55SX represents the lowest cost entry point into the range of 80386-based IBM computers.

The Model 55SX can accommodate 4 Mbytes of RAM on the motherboard and like the other PS/2 machines has the MCA. All these machines can be supplied with the optional IBM OS/2 operating system, but OS/2-1.2 does not fully exploit the software protection features of the 80386. However the release of OS/2-2 (Section 5.6) is better matched to the architecture of the 80386 CPU.

IBM also has a UNIX derivative operating system, **Advanced Interactive eXecutive** (AIX) which only runs on PS/2 386 PCs. Although some UNIX application programs can run under AIX, to run DOS programs under AIX, the user will require the DOS Merge utility which performs as a concurrent task in the UNIX environment. There are limitations however; in a system with a AIX PS/2 linked to several dumb terminals, DOS graphics application programs cannot be executed from the terminals, and can only run on the PS/2 machine.

3.8.1 Micro Channel Architecture

IBM in the design of its PS/2 computers introduced a new input/output (I/O) standard which is referred to as the Micro Channel Architecture (MCA). The diversity and number of I/O expansion cards was proving to be exacting upon the PC I/O bus and IBM sought a solution to this ever increasing problem. For a single user PC the I/O tasks can be executed in a sequential manner, but this does present difficulties when the PC forms part of a multi-user network where resources are expected to be shared. The MCA was therefore designed with the aim of satisfying the enhanced I/O demands of a multi-tasking and multi-user personal computer system.

When the PC is operating in either multi-tasking or multi-user modes, with a number of I/O expansion cards in the system, it is quite possible that the tasks or users may simultaneously request the use of one of the PC's resources and cause a conflict on the I/O bus. By assigning priorities to resources, conflicts of this nature can be avoided.

One of the features which makes the MCA an attractive vehicle is the **Program Option Selection** (POS) function. It is responsible for resolving potential I/O bus and resource conflicts and is wholly software controlled. I/O expansion cards built to the MCA standard do not have configuration switch settings, which are a common feature on conventional expansion cards. The configuration is performed in software by the programmer and this improves the flexibility of the I/O card usage as the POS can identify the type of card in each expansion slot.

Another interesting characteristic of the MCA is the Multi Master capability which allow certain adaptor and I/O expansion cards to take complete control of the I/O bus and basically act as bus controllers or masters. The interchange of data between the adaptor card and the system or other cards is therefore greatly heightened through direct communication.

Two examples where this design feature is appealing are: in local area network adaptor cards to allow other users to access the resources on the 386 PC, and adaptor cards which have enhanced computational facilities like coprocessors. Up to 15 additional bus masters can be supported on the MCA and these have free access to the PC's memory and other I/O devices. The concept of the Multi Master design relies on distributing the system's resources to localised management and thereby minimising the involvement of the CPU.

To accommodate the potentially high degree of bus activity, MCA has a complex bus arbitration. The arbitration comes into effect when the activity on the buses ceases after a task completion. Part of the MCA electronics, referred to as the **Central Arbitration Point** (CAP), asks all the devices on the system to signify if they wish to request access to and take control of the system bus. Each waiting device applies to become the bus master by sending its assigned priority level to the CAP. In the event of a device discovering that a higher priority device is also applying for bus access it withdraws its request. All the requesting devices will withdraw bar one. The result will be a single device gaining access to the system bus and becoming the bus master.

One of the attributes of the MCA is the interrupt mechanism from I/O devices, referred to as level triggering as opposed to edge triggering (Figure 3.8). This improves the reliability of the system as the falling edge of a spurious noise pulse propagating through the system may be mistaken for a legitimate interrupt. With level sensing circuits the actual voltage must be maintained for several microseconds before it registers as an interrupt. The loss of an interrupt in a multi-user, multi-tasking system can degrade synchronism between the PC and the I/O devices.

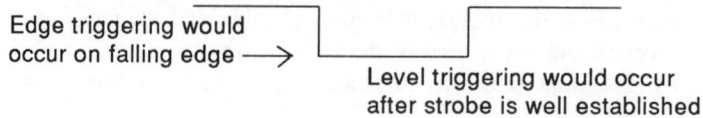

Edge triggering would
occur on falling edge ——>

Level triggering would occur
after strobe is well established

Figure 3.8 Digital Strobe showing the difference between Edge and Level triggering

The MCA bus configuration can support eight I/O cards (or channels) which can be placed in a priority order. Although the MCA is standard on the IBM PS/2, the manufacture of MCA-based 386 PCs is only granted under licence from IBM and this has lead to alternative bus standards such as EISA (Extended Industry Standard Architecture – Section 6.6.4) being adopted by other 386 PC manufacturers.

It must be stressed that I/O expansion cards, designed for the IBM XT or AT, with the Industry Standard Architecture (ISA), are not compatible with 386 PCs hosting the MCA bus structure.

Appendix 3A: Floating Point Numbers

The majority of microprocessors deal with numbers in a fixed point format of binary numbers. In order for binary numbers to represent negative numbers, the majority of microprocessors use what is known as the 2's complement scheme. As an illustration, an 8-bit byte can represent all integers between -127 and +127:

7	6	5	4	3	2	1	0		Bit number
0	1	1	1	1	1	1	1	=	+ 127
0	0	0	0	0	0	0	0	=	0
1	0	0	0	0	0	0	0	=	- 127

where the most significant bit on the left-hand side represents the sign of the number – 0 for positive and 1 for negative. The dynamic range for an 8-bit number is therefore 255. The Intel 80386 microprocessor deals with 32-bit fixed-point numbers and the maximum positive number in this format is $2^{31} - 1 = 2,147,483,647$. Although this appears large, for many calculations it is far too limited.

The question now arises: How can the range of a 32-bit number be extended by using the same number of bits?

The normal method is to assign part of the number to a power index and part to a fraction. This is the essence of the floating point number. For example, the number 152.7 can be written as $0.1527 \ 10^3$, where 3 is the power index and 0.1527 represents the fraction. In a similar manner, in our 32-bit number we could assign bit numbers 0 to 22 to the fraction and 24 to 30 to the power index. The fractional part is normally called the mantissa and the power index is called the exponent:

31	.	.	.	24	23	22	.	.	.	0
Es	E6	Exponent		E0	Ms	M22	...	Mantissa ...		M0

Sign ← ——— 8 bits ——— → Sign ← ——— 23 bits ——— →

Ms is the sign of the number; *M22, M21, ... M0* are the mantissa bits; *Es* is the sign of the exponent; *E6, E5 ... E0* are the exponent bits.

The exponent must cope with positive numbers greater and less than 1 and it is therefore given a sign bit (*Es*). With this notation, the floating point number can be expressed as:

$$(-1)^{Ms} * 2^{(\pm E)} * (1.f)$$

where f is the fractional part which always has a 1 on the right of the decimal point and in this format is referred to as normalised. In 2's complement the range of the exponent is:

$E = \pm 1\ 1\ 1\ 1\ 1\ 1\ 1$ (binary) or -128 to 127.

The mantissa on the other hand, can have values between:

$M \geq \pm 0.1\ 0\ 0 \ ...$ (binary) = 0.5 (decimal) to:

$M \leq 0.1\ 1\ 1\ 1 \ ... = \pm (1 - 2^{-23})$ binary = .999 999 88..(decimal).

The maximum values for this 32-bit example will therefore be:

$\pm 1.0 \ 2^{(127)} = +1.7014118 \ 10^{38}$

and the minimum values are:

$\pm 0.100 \ 2^{(-127)} = +2.9387358 \ 10^{-39}$

The circuitry within the Intel 80387 coprocessor manipulates floating point numbers by separating the mantissa from the exponent and treats them individually. Before recombining the mantissa and the exponent, the mantissa is normalised by left shifting until a 1 is on the immediate right-hand side of the decimal point.

The 80387 can cope with a range of floating point numbers up to a 96-bit format and this is achieved by evoking the instructions from the coprocessor instruction set when the source code of an application program is compiled. There is a floating point standard which was defined by the American Institute of Electrical and Electronics Engineers (IEEE) and is known as the ANSI/IEEE 754-1986 and the Intel 80387 performs its floating point calculations in compliance with this standard. There are three formats for REAL floating point numbers within the IEEE-754 standard.

The **Single Precision** binary REAL 32-bit format has the form:
        1-bit sign field
        8-bit exponential field
        23-bit mantissa field.

The **Double Precision** binary REAL 64-bit format has the form:
        1-bit sign field
        11-bit exponent field
        52-bit mantissa field.

The **Double Extended Precision** binary 96-bit REAL has the form:
        1-bit sign field
        15-bit exponent field
        64-bit mantissa field
        16-bits reserved.

Further Reading:

Coprocessors:

1. 8087/80287/80387 for the IBM PC and Compatibles, R Startz, (3rd edition) Brady.

2. 80386/387 Architecture, P S Morse, Wiley (1987).

3. 80387 Programmer's Reference Manual, Intel Corp (1987).

4. FasMath 83D87 User's Manual, Cyrix Corp (1989).

RS-232:

1. The RS-232 Solution, J Campbell, Sybex.

4

Display Units

One of the standard features of the 386 PC is the monitor or display unit and in the majority of applications this is an important element in the 386 PC design. It has often been said that the highly visual characteristics of the personal computer have lead to its widespread adoption in industry, commerce and education. There are various designs for display units based on quite different technologies and their adoption for a particular system is often closely related to the constraints of their applications and working environments. These constraints may include power available, light levels, financial budgets, portability and working space. The flexibility of the 386 PC allows a large variety of monitor designs, and the mix and match principle can be exercised with great effect to produce an optimum system.

4.1 Screen Resolution

In the graphics mode, the resolution is the number of dots on the screen. It is measured as the number of horizontal dots by the number of vertical dots, for example 600 x 480. A monitor used on a computer consists of a large array of dots, in the case of a cathode ray tube, these are minute fluorescent nodules. A screen pattern appears when a combination of these dots is illuminated. In the case of a colour monitor, each dot will consist of three secondary dots which when illuminated in different portions, provide the full colour range.

For a display monitor on a PC there are two modes of operation, the text mode and the graphics mode. In the normal text mode, the screen is partitioned into character positions of 25 rows and 80 columns. Each position can be occupied by a single ASCII character. A full screen can therefore display 2,000 characters which means that there are 2,000 uniquely addressable positions on the screen. If each character requires one byte of data then a single screen would require 2K of memory and this is referred to as the **text screen buffer.** Each ASCII character is constructed from a matrix of 14 x 8 dots. In special cases, the column width can be increase to 140 and the number of rows to 50 giving a screen capacity of 7,000 characters. However each ASCII character is defined in a smaller dot matrix.

In the second mode of operation, **the graphics mode,** the screen memory is considered as one large array of dots which are uniquely addressable. A graphics image in the memory of the 386 PC consists of an array of picture elements or **pixels** and the graphics circuitry maps this aaray on to the monitor screen. When there is a one-to-one mapping between the number of pixels and dots on the monitor the screen dots are also referred to as pixels. However, there is not always a match between the number of screen dots and number of pixels in the screen memory. When this occurs not all the image is accommodated on the screen or conversely the image only occupies part of the screen. Part of the graphics standard is defined by the number of pixels in its array area and a graphics board designed to that standard must have adequate memory to support the pixel array. In general the greater the number of pixels the greater the screen resolution and the more memory needed to support it. For well designed systems, it is assumed that there is a match between the number of pixels and the number of dots on the screen. When this occurs the screen dots are also referred to as pixels (picture elements). The separation between them is known as the pixel pitch and is an important parameter in the screen specification.

4.2 Cathode Ray Tubes (CRTs)

Monitors based on the cathode ray tube design are the most widely used with 386 PCs and they have many features to commend them. High resolution, low image distortion, in a myriad of colour variations, has been achieved through high-quality manufacturing methods. This ensures that eye strain is kept to a minimum while the screen is virtually flicker free to present relaxed viewing. The screen of the monitor is made up of very closely spaced dots which, when struck by the electron beam of the CRT, fluoresce, emitting their respective colour. The distance between the pixels, the **pixel pitch,** is one of the parameters which reflects the quality of the monitor and this should be not exceed 0.28 mm.

Monitors are available in either colour or monochrome and although the monochrome, with variations of grey, will represent a lower capital outlay, it will not be as aesthetically pleasing as the colour monitor. Each pixel on a colour monitor is made up from three phosphor dots: green, red and blue. The electron gun in the CRT issues three separate and independently controllable beams, one for each colour. The variation of colours is therefore controlled by adjusting the intensity of the electron beams.

Another factor which determines the quality of the monitor is the **beam convergence,** which is a measure of how well each beam strikes its respective colour dots. Any misalignment in the control in any one of the electron beams causes partial fluorescence of the other colours. The effect is for an image to lose its sharpness with spurious colours on edges and borders. Poor beam convergence usually shows up in the corners of the tube where it is more difficult to control. On a good quality monitor the beam convergence misalignment should not exceed half the pixel pitch. The **persistence** or the time the dot remains fluorescent after being excited by the electron beam, is also important. For a screen which does not have a high refresh rate the persistence should be high, whereas in high-performance monitors the persistence should be short. It is customary to match this requirement with the graphics card.

4.2.1 Multisync Monitors

Some good quality monitors will cater for a variety of graphics cards and these are of the multisync design. Such a monitor will operate in either **digital** (TTL) or **analogue mode** for the high-resolution graphics requirements. They are normally switchable from one mode to the other by a set of DIP switches situated on the back of the monitor. The term multisync derives from the fact that this type of monitor can operate with several output frequencies to accommodate differing graphic standards. The analogue option was adopted by IBM to avoid signal distortion which can occur in the connecting cable from the monitor to the main PC unit.

The multi-scan monitor design, which would be used for CAD and desktop publishing applications, will have a pixel density ranging from 800 x 600 to 1024 x 768, or even 1024 x 1024 for full A4 size screens. The cables from multisync monitors have D-type connectors which are normally distinguishable by their three rows of holes. D-type connectors on TTL monitors have two rows. Many graphics cards have connectors for both TTL and analogue outputs and they are easily distinguished by the three rows of pins in the analogue connector and the two rows of pins in the TTL.

There are two parameters which portray the performance of a CRT monitor: the **Horizontal Scan Frequency** (HSF), and the **Vertical Scan Frequency** (VSF). They provide measurements of how fast lines can be drawn horizontally and vertically on the screen. The **bandwidth** is also an important parameter when specifying a monitor, and is related to the number of pixels that can be illuminated per horizontal sweep and will range from 14 MHz to 34 MHz. Therefore for a screen with 600 horizontal pixels the horizontal frequency range would be from 23 kHz to 57 kHz. The vertical scan frequency is a measure of the screen refresh rate and this can range from 50 Hz to 80 Hz.

Differing graphics standards will require different combinations of VSF and HSF. If the horizontal frequency is too low a technique known as **interlacing** is used, allowing say, one in every two rows of pixels in the video image to be refreshed during a single vertical scan. In one vertical scan, all the odd numbered rows would be refreshed and in the next scan all the even rows. The effect of interlacing is to reduce the screen refresh rate, but there would be an increase in screen flicker. Non-interlacing schemes scan every horizontal row during each vertical scan and when selecting a CRT monitor a non-interlaced model with vertical scan frequency of at least 60 Hz should be sought. The specifications of a multisync monitor, VSF and HSF, can normally be exceeded, but at a cost. A monitor working beyond its prescribed limits will experience additional heating in the tube inductive circuitry which has the effect of shortening its lifetime.

A convenient option with a multisync monitor is the **auto-sizing** facility. If one application program uses a 640 x 480 resolution and another requires 800 x 600 then to ensure that all the image remains on the screen, the monitor should auto-size the display for the program. If this does not happen then manual adjustments will have to be made to the monitor to resize the picture. However this auto-size option is only available with some Video Graphics Array (VGA) cards which are able to send information on the number of scan lines to the monitor.

An example of a multi-sync colour monitor is the 14 inch Samsung CS4551 which has a resolution of 720 pixels by 480 lines. It can support a variety of graphics standards with a horizontal scan frequency range of 15 to 35 kHz and a vertical scan rate (refresh rate) range of 57 to 73 Hz. The dot pitch of the CS4551 is 0.31 mm and its display area 250 x 180 mm.

4.3 Graphics Standards

There are several graphics standards and the choice of a particular design is conditioned by the application of the 386 PC. However, the number of general purpose options has narrowed down to just a few and these are offered as options when buying the 386 PC.

The graphics options usually come in the form of a plugin expansion board(s) which slots into the card cage of the 386 PC. Sometimes the graphics circuitry is resident on the motherboard of the 386 PC. A compatible monitor will also be required and care will have to be taken to ensure that the graphics card and the monitor are perfectly compatible, otherwise damage can occur if there is a mismatch between them.

An attractive feature of the graphics aspect of the 386 PC is the option of upgrading the standard at a later date. However, as a cautionary note, the IBM **Colour Graphics Adaptor** (CGA) should never be considered as the graphics option for a 386 PC due to its very poor resolution. Several high-resolution graphics cards have an auto-select facility. If the monitor is operating in a high-resolution mode and an application program does require a CGA then this should not create any problem because the graphics boards will auto-select the lower resolution graphics standard.

What distinguishes various graphics standards is the resolution, given in terms of the number of pixels which can be uniquely addressed and range of colours. The higher the quality of the graphics the greater the number of pixels and the sharper the definition on the screen. On the other hand, the choice of colours is usually defined in terms of the **palette**. The palette may have a massive range of colours but only a limited number of colours from it can be on the screen at any one time. If for example, a graphics standard offers 16 colours out of a palette of 256 then this indicates that there are 16 different sets of 16 colours available.

Although there are numerous graphics standards in existence, this chapter will cover the Hercules, EGA, VGA and very high-resolution graphics standards. The first three from this category are generally recognised by the majority of application programs and they are likely to be used on the 386 PC for most of them.

4.3.1 Hercules Monochrome

When IBM released its first personal computer in the early 80s it had a text-based screen displaying 25 lines of 80 characters. There was no allowance for pixel addressing on the screen which meant that there was no graphics capability. This deficiency was seized upon by Hercules who produced a monochrome graphics card which allowed a screen addressing area of 720 x 348 pixels in the graphics mode and 80 columns by 25 characters in the text mode. Hercules therefore became the monochrome standard which is still with us today and represents the low-cost graphics format. Many software packages with high graphics content offer the Hercules as an option and it is now widely accepted among software houses.

It is customary these days not to have to include the once obligatory terminate and stay resident (TSR) drivers, HGC.COM and INT10.COM, before the application program can run. More than likely the program will carry its own Hercules driver. Hercules has two graphics pages, PAGE 0 and PAGE 1, and during the installation of some application programs, the user might be asked to specify which page is used. As a general rule PAGE 0 seems to be the most common option. However once in the graphics mode, Hercules in the graphics mode will emulate the text mode screen display, but the screen writing will be slightly slower due to the extra processing required.

Microsoft, with its version of QuickBASIC 4.5, has embraced the Hercules option and this is a very attractive route for graphics programming in monochrome. The Hercules graphics option is normally supplied with the majority of 386 PCs as a standard feature with the opportunity of upgrading to higher resolution colour standard. However if monochrome is desirable on the 386 PC it is advisable to choose the alternative VGA mono which has a greater resolution and provides 16 levels of grey shading.

In June 1986 Hercules released an update graphics board HGC+ which has RAM based alphanumeric characters to accommodate a variation on fonts. It also has a faster writing speed than its predecessor. To meet the challenge of colour requirements Hercules issued the InColor card which is a 16-colour version of HGC+ with a pixel area of 720 x 348. It is compatible with the EGA standard and will work with an 350 vertical line EGA colour monitor.

4.3.2 Enhanced Graphics Adaptor (EGA)

This standard was IBM's response to the need to have good quality colour graphics on personal computers. Introduced in 1984, the original board only had 64K of RAM but this was later updated to 256K. In the EGA standard the total number of different colours is 64, referred to as the palette, but only 16 of these can be in use at any one time. EGA has 17 modes of operation, four for text display (Mode 0 to Mode 3) and 13 for graphics (Mode 4 to Mode 16). This large number was considered necessary to ensure that the EGA standard is compatible with the earlier standards and monitors. These display standards include the **Monochrome Display Adaptor** (MDA), the **Colour Graphics Adaptor** (CGA) and for monitors, **Enhanced Colour Display** (ECD) and **Monochrome Display** (MD). The resolution of each of these standards with their respective colour range is shown in Table 4.1.

Graphics standard	Resolution	Colour Range
Colour Graphics Adaptor (CGA)	640 x 200	1
	320 x 200	4 / 16
Hercules Graphics Controller (HGC)	720 x 348	Monochrome
Monochrome Display Adaptor (MDA)	80 x 25	Chars
Enhanced Graphics Display (EGA)	640 x 350	16 / 64
Enhanced Colour Display (ECD)	640 x 350	16 / 24
Multi-Colour Graphics Array (MCGA)	640 x 480	2
Video Graphics Array (VGA)	640 x 480	16
	320 x 480	256 / 262, 144
Super-VGA	800 x 600	256

Table 4.1 Comparison of several display standards

In mode 16, the pixel resolution reaches 640 x 350 and produces medium quality colour graphics. Each character in the text can be displayed in a box size of 8 x 14 pixels which gives a clear definition and allows foreign characters to be generated with high clarity.

Many 386 PCs are sold with an EGA graphics card and compatible monitor as this combination is quite acceptable for applications which do not require high-resolution graphic intensive facilities. IBM also issued a new medium graphics standard for its PS/2 models 25 and 30, named the **Multi-Colour Graphics Array** (MCGA). It requires a multisync monitor and gives a pixel area of 640 x 480 which is slightly better than the EGA. To support the EGA standard, an EGA monitor must have a minimum scan frequency of 22.1 kHz.

4.3.3 Video Graphics Array (VGA)

The VGA represents the latest high resolution graphics standard sanctioned by IBM and has been adopted in its PS/2 series of personal computers. This standard covers both monochrome and colour and requires an analogue monitor with a bandwidth of 32 MHz. The maximum resolution for the standard VGA is 640 x 480 pixels and the number of colours on the screen at any one time can be 256. There are provisions within the VGA standard for coping with monochrome requirements which rely on extensive grey shading. This allows the output from a VGA card be fed directly to a monochrome VGA monitor and the colours will be translated to shades of grey. This has been achieved by making the video modes independent of the display type (the monitor) and this relieves the application program of having to cater for various graphics attributes.

There is an enhancement on VGA generally called super-VGA, distinguishable by the higher resolution which starts from 800 x 600 with a minimum display of 256 colours. High-quality multisync monitors can normally accommodate this degree of resolution, however the monitor specification should be checked to confirm this requirement.

In the VGA standard there are several video modes of operation, with each video mode representing a particular format of screen operation. For the VGA to retain its compatibility with previous standards the old video modes have been incorporated in the new set of VGA modes, which allows application programs requiring CGA or EGA to run with VGA. VGA has five more alphanumeric text modes than the EGA standard. Each ASCII screen character is represented on the screen as a matrix of 9 x 16 pixels which provides good quality screen writing. In the VGA there is a character generator RAM which enables two out of eight different fonts to be on the screen at any one time. This gives rise to the opportunity of using italics, bold or other types of characters.

The number of graphics modes has been increased by two: Mode 17 with 640 x 480 pixels has a choice of two colours and Mode 18 with 640 x 480 pixels has a choice of 16 colours. Mode 17 with its two colours matches the **Multi-Colour Graphics Array** (MCGA) which is used in the IBM PS/2 Model 30. The colour range for VGA could be drawn from a palette of 262,144 and the lower resolution (Mode 19) of 320 x 200 pixels could access 256 different colours. Mode 19, with its good colour range, is particularly attractive for video digitising. Its screen size of 320 x 200 pixels is equivalent to television quality displays. However, TV images from video cassette recorders can be captured and accurately represented in Mode 13 (Section 9.5).

To enable the VGA to support a monochrome display by translating its normal colour output signals into varying shades of grey a technique known as **Colour Summing** (CS) has been used. In the Basic Input/Output System (BIOS – Section 2.8) there are three colour 6-bit registers, one for each primary colour, which feed three digital to analogue converters (6-bit ADCs for video generation) for the monitor.

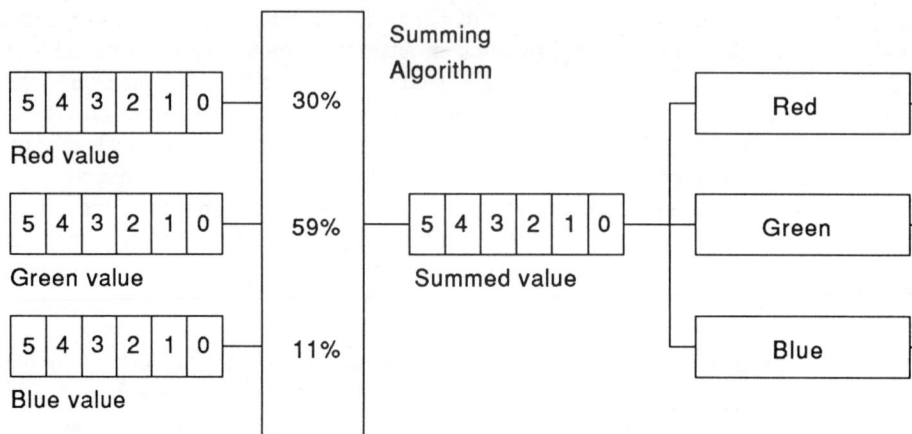

Figure 4.1 Colour Summing Mechanism

The purpose of the CS algorithm is to generate 16 shades of grey, from the 16 possible colours, by mapping 18-bits into 6-bits. The 6-bit grey shade is then loaded into each of the three BIOS registers. As seen in Figure 4.1 the three 6-bit colour inputs pass into the summing CS algorithm and the red is weighted by 30%, the green by 59% and the blue by 11%. These values are chosen, on account of the sensitivity of the human eye, to give 16 distinct shades of grey. Any one of the outputs can be used to drive the monochrome monitor since they all contain the same value. With the arrangement shown in Figure 4.1 if there were 64 colours, then these could be mapped to form 64 (2^6) different shades of grey.

For producing the 256 colours in the low resolution Mode 19 a **Colour Lookup Table** (CLUT) is used. An 8-bit word, representing a colour, can address one of 256 registers ($2^8 = 256$) in the CLUT and each entry in the CLUT is 18 bits wide, six bits for each of the primary colours (see Figure 4.2 opposite). Once a register has been addressed by the colour word, the contents of each address are fed into the three colour analogue to digital converters. The size of the CLUT determines the number of different colours which can be on the screen at any one time. The CLUT can be changed by drawing a new set of colours from the palette via a call to the BIOS.

After the original VGA standard was issued for the IBM PS/2 range of personal computer, a number of manufacturers held the opinion that the maximum resolution was too low and this spurred the emergence of the super-VGA. A VGA card which can support a resolution of 800 x 600 pixels or greater with an 8-bit or 16-bit data bus is frequently referred to as super-VGA, or Extended VGA, or Enhanced VGA or VGA+. The standards for the super-VGA were established by the **Video Electronics Standards Association** (VESA) which is made up of nine companies. They actively encourage software manufacturers to support the super-VGA standard by providing high-resolution drivers with their products. Many multisync monitors are built to accommodate the VESA standard and they can operate with a resolution of 800 x 600 pixels without any long term damage.

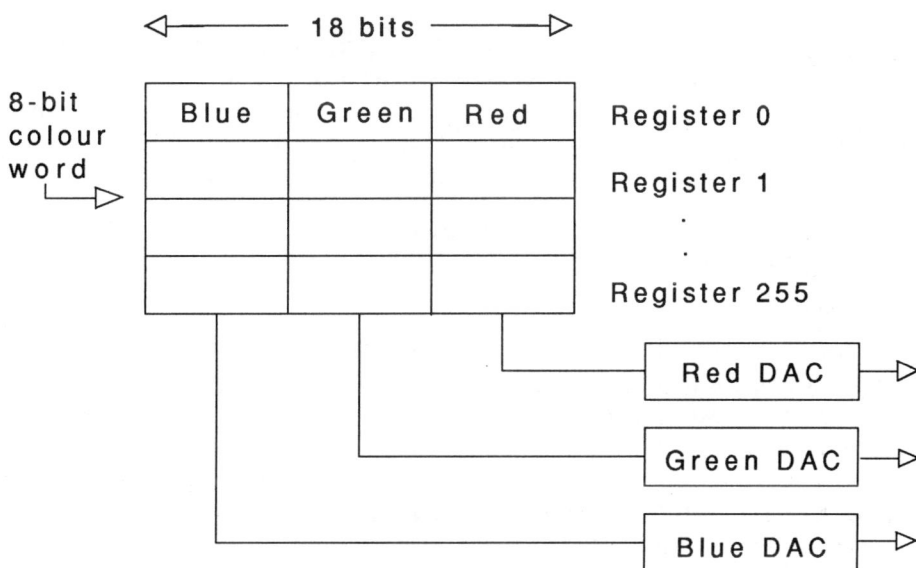

Figure 4.2 Block diagram of Video DACs with colour look-up table

To speed up the performance of the super-VGA card in a 386 PC it is common practice to relocate the BIOS (or shadowing – Section 2.8.1) to extended memory. But this only offers an advantage if the BIOS-ROM on the mother-board has a slower access time than the dynamic RAM of extended memory. However a number of application programs by-pass the BIOS (Windows/386, Lotus 1-2-3 for example), therefore relocating the BIOS will have no effect upon the speed of the super-VGA. The majority of super-VGA cards have their own memory and the fastest display is achieved by using dedicated **Video-RAM** (VRAM). VRAM chips are dual ported, one parallel bus and one serial bus, which means they have two sets of buses. This design allows parallel addressing of the VRAM by the 80386 CPU at the same time that serial data is output to the display monitor.

The range of colours available on a super-VGA card is dependent upon the amount of memory, but in general the greater the resolution the fewer the number of colours. A super-VGA card, with 512K of memory, will give 256 colours with a resolution of 800 x 600 or 16 colours with a resolution of 1024 x 768.

When selecting a super-VGA card it is important to ensure that the application program, for which the super-VGA is intended, has the appropriate software driver, otherwise the default VGA will occur. The advantage of the super-VGA can only be gained if the proper software driver is used. Several manufacturers of super-VGA cards provide drivers for AutoCAD (Section 8.3.2), Ventura (Section 9.21.), GEM, Windows/386 and other well known application programs which are highly graphics intensive.

An example of a VGA board is the Video Seven V-RAM VGA which hosts its own 256K of video RAM which can be increased to 512K. The V-RAM VGA has a 14-pin connector for a multisync monitor and the software supplied allows the BIOS ROM to be relocated or shadowed into RAM to improve the writing speed. Various colour and resolution combinations are possible with the V-RAM VGA:

800 x 600 (512K) or 640 x 480 (256K) in 16 colours
640 x 480 pixels in 256 colours
1,024 x 768 pixels in two or four colours.

Other software supplied with this card includes drivers for AutoCAD, AutoShade (Section 9.2.1), Ventura, GEM, Windows/386 (Section 5.5.1) and there is also an enhanced text driver suitable for Symphony and Lotus 1-2-3 which gives a 132-column screen.

4.3.4 Very High-Resolution Graphics

Certain applications for 386 PCs require very high-resolution colour graphics – computer-aided design (CAD – Section 9.3) and high-quality desktop publishing (Section 9.2) are examples, and special graphics cards and monitors should be considered. Resolution requirements for pixel densities in excess of 1,024 x 760 demand high-performance graphics, but the more common requirement is pixel density of 1,600 x 1,200. Not only does the resolution enter in the equation, but also the image manipulation speed.

To achieve high-performance image manipulation, graphics controller cards must host dedicated graphics processors and provide sufficient memory for supporting the screen image. It is also essential that during screen refreshing and screen updates every pixel is addressed. However in order not to confine the 386 PC to a specific application, the high-resolution graphics option must be able to support application programs which call for EGA or VGA graphics.

To ensure that every pixel is updated during every screen refresh, a number of high-resolution graphics cards use a **raster scan** design method which operates in a non-interlacing mode. A commercially available package which provides high-performance graphics is the Xcellerator 1600 from Cambridge Computer Graphics. It consists of a colour monitor and a graphics controller card which is accommodated as an I/O expansion card in the 386 PC card cage. The controller card hosts a Texas Instruments TMS34010 graphics processor with one Mbyte of RAM which can be augmented if necessary.

The Xcellerator has three modes of operation: in Mode 1 the display resolution is 1,600 by 1,200 with 16 colours from a palette of 4,096 and the horizontal scan frequency is 75 kHz. Mode 2 has a display resolution of 1,024 by 768 with 256 colours out of a palette of 16 million with a horizontal scan frequency of 48 kHz. Mode 3 is equivalent to the VGA standard and is also able to emulate the EGA and CGA standards.

For alternative high resolution graphics cards there is the Cobra from Vermont Microsystems and Compaq's very own AG 1024 graphics adaptor. The Cobra derives its power from a combination of processors, an Intel 80186 and a Quad 2901 which are supported with one Mbyte of RAM. The resolution can either be 1,024 x 768 or 1,024 x 800. The colour choice is very similar to the Xcellerator 1600, however being a three card (AT) set, much of the card cage of the 386 PC will have to be given over to accommodating them. Compaq's Advanced Graphics system AG 1024, which can be hosted by Compaq's 386 PCs, has a maximum resolution of 1,024 x 768 and is generally well suited to CAD applications where a medium graphics resolution is required.

The AG 1024, powered with a Texas Instruments TMS34010 graphics processor, comes with software drivers for AutoCAD and Windows/386. In the specification of the AG 1024 two graphics standards have been supported, the **Texas Instruments Graphics Architecture** (TIGA) and the **Direct Graphics Interface Standard** (DGIS) from Graphics Software Systems. This may be attractive for programmers involved with the preparation of code for high-performance graphics applications and should render the AG 1024 compatible with many application programs which recognise these standards.

4.4 Liquid Crystal Displays

Although the CRT has dominated the display unit market there are other methods for displaying the visual information. There are disadvantages with CRTs, namely they are bulky, consume a lot of power and are unsuitable for portable systems. It has been argued that there is a health risk associated with the electromagnetic emission from CRTs, however there is not a great deal of convincing evidence to confirm this belief.

The long term effects of viewing CRTs close up affects some individuals but generally this has yet to be fully investigated.

My personal conviction is that monochrome, paper white monitors, with grey shading is preferable to colour for long-term viewing. An interesting alternative to the CRT is a liquid crystal display (LCD) screen which has attracted the attention of lap top PC manufacturers. Developments in LCDs have progressed over the past 10 years to achieve devices which give quite a respectable performance. With their slim format, LCDs lend themselves to PC designs where volume is at a premium. Their high contrast and the wide viewing angle are essential features of their design. Although high-resolution LCDs have been realised they suffer from one major drawback – their response time is slow and this leads to long screen refresh times.

LCDs consist of organic molecules which have a helix-like structure and one of their properties is their effect on the polarisation of light – they are optically active. As polarised light passes through the liquid crystal, the polarisation of the light is rotated. When liquid crystals are subjected to an electric field they untwist, align themselves with the field and no longer have a polarising effect upon the light (Figure 4.3).

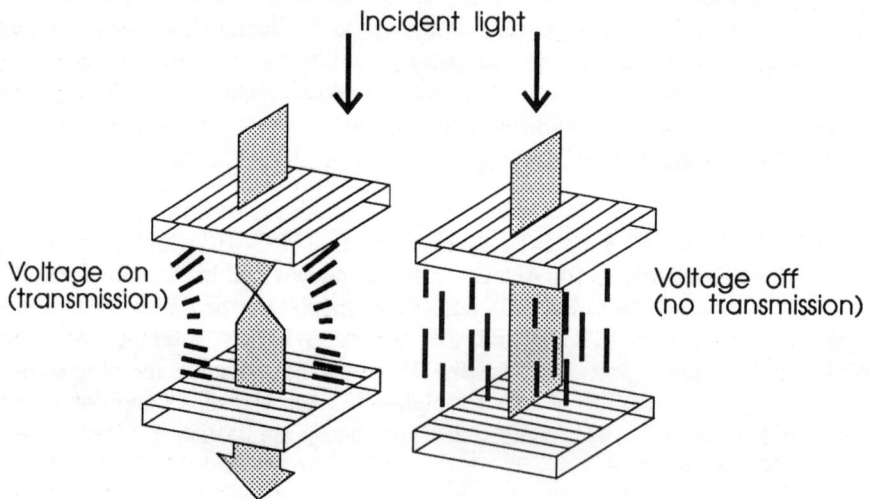

Incident light

Voltage on
(transmission)

Voltage off
(no transmission)

Figure 4.3 An LCD display

In a working system, the liquid crystal material is sandwiched between two crossed polaroids and forms a flat structure. As a localised electric field is applied the transmission properties of the sandwich change. For conventional **twisted nematic Liquid Crystal Displays** (tn-LCDs) the viewing angle is limited due to the poor contrast and this has limited their application in personal computers. However this problem was overcome with the invention of super twist LCDs which have a critical twist angle of 270 degrees. These allows a larger viewing angle with high contrast and this technology has been applied to the manufacture of dot matrix arrays of 640 x 200 and 640 x 400 which are suitable for PCs.

LCDs can be designed in the reflective or transmission mode, however when operating in the latter mode a blue colouration is visible. To improve the 'blackness' a **Neutralised Twisted Nematic** (NTN) display has been developed which is basically two layers of super twist LCDs. This structure has four thin-film polarising layers and four layers of glass which leads to 16 levels of grey to be realised. A good quality contrast ratio of 12:1 is achievable with this design.

LCDs are not only light weight, but take very little power and this is an attractive feature for portable PCs. An example of a double supertwist LCD with very high contrast (black on white) is the Sharp LM64048Z which has a dot format of 640 x 480 and a viewing area of 237 mm x 180 mm. The actual dot size is 0.33 x by 0.3 mm and this able to provide the resolution required for the VGA standard. The LM64048Z is back-light illuminated to provide a very agreeable display with impressive contrast. Coloured LCDs are edging onto the market with a ferroelectric liquid crystal design. These are characterised by their fast response times and wide viewing angle. The Sharp 14-inch colour LCD has 308,160 pixels and each pixel consists of four dots to give over 1.2 million active elements. To illustrate the difficulty in fabricating this type of display, each dot is controlled by its own amorphous silicon thin-film transistor – 308,160 pixels require a lot of transistors.

4.5 Gas Plasma Displays

An alternative display technology is based on the gas plasma design and these displays fall into two groups, AC and DC displays. In the construction of a gas plasma display (Figure 4.4 overleaf), an array of parallel ribs is affixed to a sheet of glass which acts as the front of the display. Between the ribs lie strips of a transparent dielectric material which act as the anodes. This parallel array is fastened to a perpendicular comb of cathodes, which is attached to the rear glass sheet of the display to form a crisscross structure. The gap between the cathodes and the anodes is filled with low pressure neon gas with each space within the crisscross acting as a pixel element.

Once the localised neon glow discharge has been excited, it remains active until switched off and the AC design is characterised by this high brightness orange display. As a result of the sustained plasma discharge, there is no requirement for pixel refresh. Screen areas of 1024 x 1024 and larger can be fabricated with this technology and this is particularly attractive for pictorial, touch screen devices. There are methods for reducing the power consumption of AC gas plasma displays and one such technique is based on the **Independent Sustain and Address** (ISA) design which has an integral energy recovery circuit and a reduced number of pixel drivers. Display resolutions of 640 x 400 pixels have been fabricated with the ISA design.

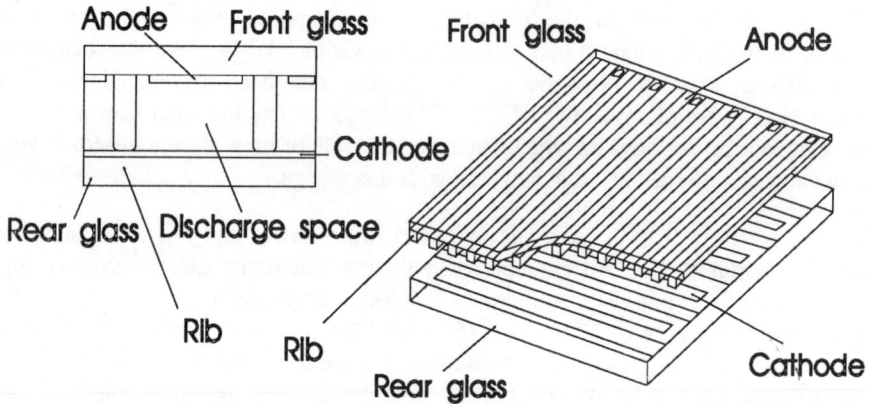

Figure 4.4 The structure of a gas plasma display

The second design, DC, has the disadvantage of requiring pixel refresh to sustain the plasma discharge. However the power consumption is much lower than early AC plasma displays and although they do not possess the brightness of the AC design, they do have a wide viewing angle. Pixel arrays of 640 x 480 are available and they are finding applications in portable 386 PCs as an alternative to the liquid crystal display.

A 386 PC which uses the a gas plasma display is the CD-Portable 386-100 from Comcen Technology. The standard for the monochrome graphics this 386 PC is VGA and it comes with integral CD-ROM.

Further Reading:

1. Programmer's Guide to the EGA/VGA,G Sutty & S Blair, Brady.

2. EGA/VGA: A Programmer's Reference Guide, B D Kliewer, McGraw-Hill.

5

Environment Software

When a 386 PC is first powered up, the boot software (derived from the boot-strap principle) is loaded into the PC's memory and creates a working environment for using the machine. It does in fact form a software interface between the user and the system of the 386 PC and all operations and requests, made by the user, are handled by this interface. This environment software is referred to as an operating system and constitutes the interface between the 80386 CPU, the user and the other resources within the PC.

By this we mean that the operating system is responsible for the basic operations of the 386 PC which include servicing peripherals – such as disk control, writing to the screen, reading the keyboard and controlling the flow of information through the communications ports. These peripherals gain the attention of the CPU by generating an **interrupt.** The CPU responds accordingly by executing a service routine specifically for the interrupting peripheral. The operating system is also responsible for detecting conditions which may be generated from software and hardware errors. This prevents the 386 PC from hanging up and the operating system will normally highlight the source of the error condition with an appropriate banner on the screen.

5.1 Function of an Operating System

The current generation of microprocessors, 16-bit and 32-bit devices, have been designed with the aim of providing the user with considerable protection during the execution of an application program or during the development phase of a program. The latter will involve correcting software errors and this is usually a lengthy process where every ounce of assistance from the hardware is appreciated. When the programmer is testing a piece of bug-ridden code, instead of the whole system crashing when a bug is encountered, the system will relax into a known recoverable state. This has been achieved by designing the microprocessor to detect errors generated by software or hardware bugs and thereby preventing further damage from occurring. To achieve this, modern microprocessors can operate in a dual mode configuration, a **user mode** and a **supervisor mode** (Figure 5.1). In the supervisor mode, the microprocessor runs the operating system software. Programmers develop and run their programs in the user mode. When certain conditions are encountered an **exception** is generated and the 80386 changes over to the supervisor mode where the operating system takes over.

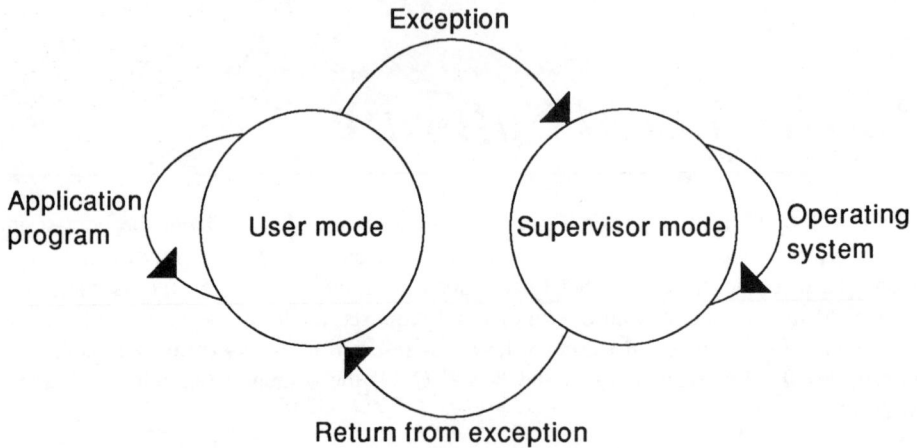

Exception

Application
program   User mode   Supervisor mode   Operating
system

Return from exception

Figure 5.1 Transitions from the two modes of operation

Each exception generated in the user mode will have a **service handling routine** in the operating system software. Once the service routine has been executed, the 80386 will either return to the user mode, providing the condition was not fatal, or otherwise relax into a recoverable state by exiting completely from the user's program. The facility of the supervisor mode, with its operating system, is referred to as the environment and the user works under the protected environment of the supervisor mode.

Figure 5.2a opposite shows schematically the environment of the Intel 80386 featuring the operating system in the supervisor mode at the core (level 0) and the user mode at the periphery. All inputs, outputs and interrupts are conditions which generate exceptions and are handled by the microprocessor in its supervisor mode through the operating system. The user/supervisor mode represents a single level of protection. However the 80386 has up to four levels of protection (Figure 5.2b) and this offers substantial scope for 80386 to support more than one operating system simultaneously if required. The operation of the 386 PC in its Virtual 8086 Mode (Section 2.2.2) can be represented by Figure 5.2c where several DOS programs are running on the periphery in level three of the protection scheme. Although much of what goes on at the system level is transparent to the user, it is instructive to understand the overall concepts of its operation.

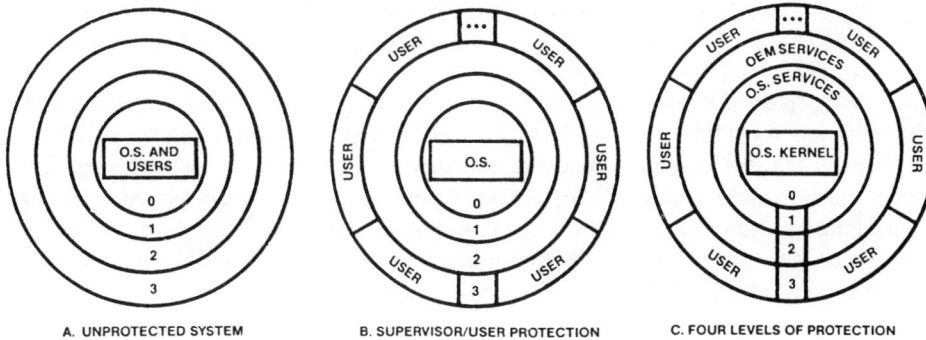

A. UNPROTECTED SYSTEM   B. SUPERVISOR/USER PROTECTION   C. FOUR LEVELS OF PROTECTION

Figure 5.2 Protection levels of the Intel 80386

5.2 Multi-tasking and the 80386

A 386 PC system will be expected to perform many tasks or processes: running several user programs, overseeing the inputs and outputs and responding to interrupts from peripherals. In order to realise multi-tasking, the 80386 must be able to switch between tasks and thereby it will only execute 'thin slices' of each task at any one time. To cope with these needs, two system aspects are required: firstly a scheduling technique which allocates the tasks and secondly a method of switching between them. The former is called an operating system whereas the latter is the interrupt mechanism.

A challenging question therefore arises: How best can the resources of the computer be used? An operation of the 80386 CPU should have optimum response while still allowing efficient use of the system's resources, whereas multi-tasking requires optimum use of resources within a reasonable response time.

The 80386, in addition to its general purpose registers, has a set of system registers which can be used by the operating system (Figure 5.3 overleaf). The operating system initialises these registers during power up and may use them if a paging error should occur, with the address of the error service routine found in CR2. The system register also contains descriptor information which is sometimes required for memory addressing purposes. At the core of every operating system there is a supervisory program called the **kernel** which is responsible for three functions: to deal with interrupts from the system and the peripherals, to determine the sequence (the priority) of the tasks to be executed and finally to allow tasks to exchange data.

To add to the versatility of the system, more than one task could be running the same program. This would occur in a multi-user system where several users are running the same compiler for example. In the kernel there is a facility for allocating a Task State Segment (TSS) for each task and the TSS contains a number of registers relating to each task (Figure 5.4 opposite). Each task will therefore have a TSS which contains the information required to set-up the CPU to execute it. The lower part of the TSS is defined by the 80386 architecture and contains the processor's register values. The upper half is defined by the operating system and holds task-related data for scheduling the priority and the time allocated to the task. When a new task is introduced into the system, a TSS is allocated to it and is loaded with necessary information needed by the operating system to execute it.

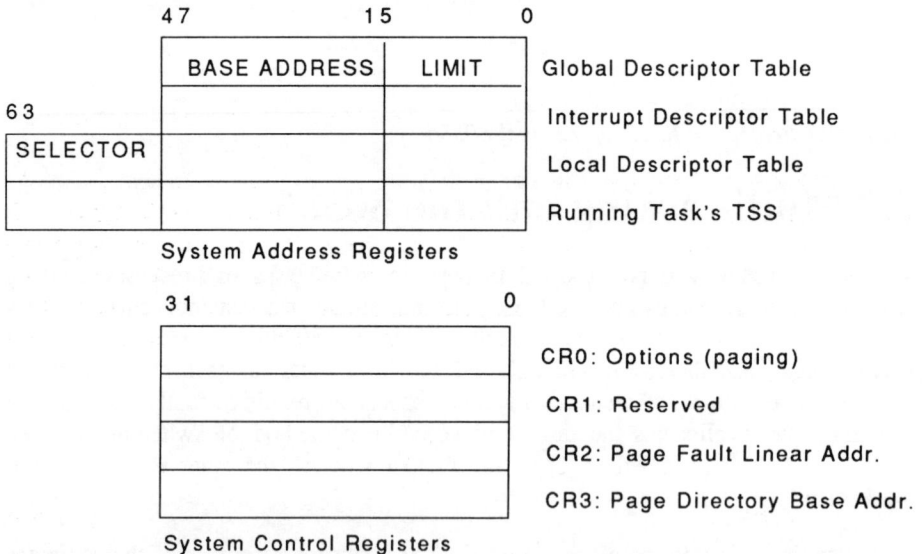

4 7		1 5		0	
BASE ADDRESS		LIMIT			Global Descriptor Table
					Interrupt Descriptor Table

6 3

SELECTOR					Local Descriptor Table
					Running Task's TSS

System Address Registers

3 1	0	
		CR0: Options (paging)
		CR1: Reserved
		CR2: Page Fault Linear Addr.
		CR3: Page Directory Base Addr.

System Control Registers

Figure 5.3 80386 System Registers

When multi-tasking, the CPU executes several instructions of one task and then switches to the next, executes a few instruction of this task and then switches to another and so on. It will return to the first task and pick up from where it left off and possibly repeat the process. The kernel of the operating system is responsible for interleaving these tasks on the 80386 CPU and this is done according to a scheduling scheme which defines the order of task execution. As the CPU switches from a task, the current CPU state is loaded into a dedicated TSS for the task, since this state is required when the CPU returns to it.

The CPU state for the next task is then loaded into the CPU from the appropriate TSS. This task switching is referred to as **context switching** and the time to perform a switch is referred to as the **context latency**.

(Defined by the operating system)
Local Descriptor Table Address
Page Table Directory Address
General CPU registers
Flag Register
Instruction Pointer
Segment Registers
Supervisor Stack Pointers

Figure 5.4 Task State Segment

To switch tasks, the operating system issues a jump or call command whose operand is a selector for the TSS of the next task. Once the address of the new TSS is in the CPU's Running Task Register, the CPU can commence executing the task. The tasks can be in one of either three states: running, ready to run or blocked and their condition is indicated by the task status. The running task is the one currently being executed, a ready-to-run task will be waiting its turn and a blocked task is one which is suspended while waiting for the outcome of another task or is just inactive. In a multi-tasking environment the tasks can have different priorities and the level of each is defined from within the operating system.

5.3 Disk Operating System (DOS)

The first operating system to be provided with the IBM PC was PC-DOS commissioned by IBM from Microsoft. Microsoft later issued its own version, MS-DOS, which has very similar functionality to PC-DOS. The early versions of DOS catered for the facilities which were standard on the early design of the IBM PC. Over the past few years with the proliferation of additional hardware features, DOS has been upgraded to accommodate the expanding requirements of the operating system.

The inclusion of the hard disk drive, the 3.5 inch floppy drive and the option for networking are examples of the extra workload placed on the operating system. One of the attractive features of DOS is the vast array of application programs that run under it and this has lead to its continuing popularity. It still has a promising future in spite of the competing operating systems such as UNIX and OS/2. The cost of running DOS application programs is low and this will remain within its favour for the time being.

There are variations of DOS and among the most well known is DR DOS from Digital Research. There are a number of differences between MS-DOS and DR DOS and some will be apparent to the user. DR DOS can reside in ROM chips in a PC and this has an obvious attraction for portable and lap-top PCs or even industrial imbedded systems. The advantage of a ROM-based DOS is the speed of rebooting the system in the event of a crash. To tailor DR DOS to the user's own system needs, Digital Research supplys a DR DOS System Builder's Kit. One major difference with MS-DOS 3.3 is the provision for a three-level protection requiring passwords for access. DR DOS has also breached the 32-Mbyte hard disk partition boundary (Section 2.5.1) of MS-DOS and has extended it to 512 Mbytes.

5.3.1 DOS Version 3.3

This version of DOS offers a few additional commands over DOS Version 3.2 and some of these greatly enhance the functionality of the 386 PC. From a hardware perspective, DOS 3.3 offers support for four serial ports (COM1 to COM4) and a 3.5 inch 1.44-Mbyte floppy disk drive. There is a device driver in DOS 3.3 for supporting extra memory which conforms to the LIM 4.0 specification (Section 2.3.4). DOS 3.3 also has a file cacheing utility FASTOPEN which can be located in Expanded Memory by using /E in the AUTOEXEC.BAT file.

Under normal operation, every file on a hard disk is allocated to a directory of 32 bits and when a file is accessed, its directory is loaded into the system buffer. Subsequent references to the file use the copy of the directory in the buffer. Due to limited buffer sizes this mechanism does not lend itself too well to several concurrent open files. FASTOPEN overcomes this limitation by making a copy of the disk directories in expanded memory which are references for file information. This has the effect of improving the performance by hastening data transfer between disk memory and on-board memory.

There have been several excellent texts written on DOS and it is not the purpose of this chapter to cover this subject in any great depth. See *Further Reading* at the end of this chapter for more information. Many 386 PCs are sold with DOS Version 3.3 and it is normal to find the manufacturer's DOS manual bundled with the machine. The DOS manual should give enough information to obtain a good working knowledge of the many DOS Version 3.3 utilities.

5.3.2 DOS Version 4

There are several new features with DOS Version 4 which include larger HDD partitions, a user Shell, Expanded Memory support, VGA graphics screen dump, upgraded national language support and several new commands. One of the most obvious differences between DOS Version 4 and its predecessors is the full screen interface shell or **Systems Application Architecture** (SAA) which is similar to the Windows environment. It is of the **Window Icon Mouse Pull-down menu** (WIMP) design, where the user interface is strongly mouse and screen icon dependent. It can however still be used in the text mode via the keyboard. The Shell conforms to the design laid out in the **Common User Access** (CUA) documentation of the SAA and requires very little learning for the user who is familiar with other IBM systems.

DOS Version 4 offers greatly enhanced resources for memory management and it is this aspect which is of singular significance over DOS 3.3. For example, the hard disk drives (HDDs) have been extended by using 32-bit logical sector numbers for the file allocation table (FAT – Section 2.5) values as opposed to the 16-bit for the previous version. Three differences arise from this: firstly the maximum number of sectors now becomes 4,295 Mbytes which should be adequate to address even the largest HDDs. Secondly the maximum number of clusters per sector becomes 128 and thirdly the maximum number of entries or clusters is 65,536.

Another important area where DOS Version 4 has been improved is in the use of LIM-EMS or EMS (Lotus/Intel/Microsoft – Expanded Memory Specification Section 2.3.3). DOS Version 4 recognises the LIM-EMS interface and it is therefore unnecessary to install a device driver to enable the extra memory. It is also possible to place the 386 PCs BUFFERS in Expanded Memory by adding the /x switch to the BUFFER entry in the CONFIG.SYS file.

In a similar vein DOS Version 4 occupies a greater area within the 640K conventional memory and this places a greater need to have Expanded Memory to accommodate additional drives.

5.4 UNIX and XENIX

An alternative operating system to DOS is UNIX, a product of the 1960s from the AT&T labs. Designed mainly for minicomputers it has stood the test of time primarily due to its provisions for multi-tasking and multi-user needs. These are now strong requirements of current personal computer systems and UNIX lends itself admirably well to these needs. Until the advent of the 386 PC, UNIX was not a viable operating system for personal computers, due in part to UNIX being a memory hungry operating system which requires several Mbytes to run effectively. The introduction of the 80386 microprocessor with its vast physical address space (PAS) heralded a supreme opportunity for UNIX to make an entry into the personal computer market.

UNIX provides a file system which holds three different types of files. The first type consists of document and binary executable program files which has no specific record structure. The second type are directory files which maintain a list of all other types of files and the third type consists of input and output device mechanisms. These files are configured with a high degree of security which is afforded by UNIX to prevent unauthorised entry to the files. UNIX is furnished with an array of facilities which are detailed in the following sections and these tools are accessed through a command language interface referred to as the **shell**. The shell therefore serves as the user interface to the UNIX operating system where the user commands are executed.

Application programs written in the command language are often called **Shell Scripts**. The execution of a command is called a **process** which involves a program file(s) being accessed and a list of commands may be concatenated into a file, itself being ascribed to a command status and executed as a command. Within UNIX there are standard input/output mechanisms and the commands which process data in this manner are referred to as **filters**. Filters often require the exchange of data and this is achieved by means of **pipes** which link processes together. This enables the output of one command to feed into the input of another. One of the attractive features of the shell is the ease by which these pipes are implemented.

The source code for UNIX is C and this feature makes it very transportable and a 386 UNIX operating system can easily be created once the source code is in place with a 80386 C compiler. C as a source code for a 80386 operating system is by no means ideal. The 80386 architecture supports a four-level hierarchical memory protection scheme and segmented and paged memory. In general C does not contain any constructs for using segmented and pages memory since it presupposes that memory space is linear. This means that a C compiler would not produce code which employs the segmented and paged handling mechanism. Consequently none of the protection features of the 80386 architecture would be used by an operating system written in standard C. The input/output drivers of UNIX rely on general purpose memory-mapped I/O for the 80386. However the 80386 has special features for restricting I/O depending on its priority and these cannot be recognised with a general C compiler. To address some of these deficiencies a version of the UNIX operating system has emerged for the 386 PC, known as SYSTEM V/386 Release 3.2, from AT&T.

5.4.1 UNIX System V/386

UNIX has become an accepted operating system for the 386 PC, especially when the machines are part of a local area network (LAN) where resources can be shared. UNIX as an operating system is memory demanding and this aspect lead to the initial reluctance of it being widely accepted. However, now that memory is competitively priced, UNIX 386 PCs are becoming more commonplace.

A UNIX 386 PC should be furnished with a hard disk drive of at least 80 Mbytes and a minimum internal RAM of 4 Mbytes. It is quite probable that the internal memory will have to be augmented if the UNIX 386 PC is to be used for multi-tasking. As a safeguard, ensure that there is sufficient space within the 386 PC to accommodate at least 16 Mbytes of RAM. Application programs running under UNIX, will in general be more expensive than the equivalent DOS version and this factor should be included in the costing of a UNIX 386 PC system.

UNIX System V/386 is a multi-user, multi-tasking operating system which uses the paging mechanism of the 80386 thereby exploiting to a greater extent its architecture features. It is matched to the 80386 since the processor itself supports several modes of operation which accommodate multi-tasking and multi-user within a protected environment which is underpined by virtual memory addressing (Section 2.2.4) via its on-board Memory Management facility.

When running in a multi-tasking mode, the V/386 operating system increases reliability by employing some of the protection features of the 80386. It does this by isolating each task by ensuring that it does not intrude into the memory space of other tasks. This results from a special feature of the 80386; when a memory address is generating it also has a hidden attribute field which contains information regarding the memory. This information pertains to whether the memory is read only, read-write or protected and restricts the manner in which the memory is used.

Efficient and effective context switching from task to task, which is a fundamental operation in multi-tasking, is accomplished in the 80386 by using a few special assembly language instructions. A context switch from one task to another can be performed in only a few clock cycles, (16 micro seconds for a 16 MHz CPU) and this leads to a very low **context latency** which permits rapid process changes. This in turn contributes greatly to the multi-tasking performance of the 80386 processor.

V/386 will allow each user to address up to two Gbytes of physical memory which is controlled through the 80386's resident Memory Management Unit (MMU – Section 2.2.4). This supports page demand and virtual memory addressing which is almost transparent to the user(s). The multi-user aspects of V/386 also support other concurrent operating systems. When running under V/386, a MS-DOS software monitor can be added to the system to allow DOS programs to run.

There are a number of UNIX operating systems for the 386 PC and for illustrative purposes, consideration will be given to two of them: INTERACTIVE UNIX from INTERACTIVE Systems Corp. of Santa Monica, California and SCO System V from the Santa Cruz Operations Inc. The SCO System V includes two products: SCO XENIX 386 and UNIX System V/386. Both companies supply a family of UNIX products for the 386 PC which support a multi-user and multi-tasking UNIX platform and these products are derived from the AT&T UNIX System V/386. Many features are common to both INTERACTIVE UNIX and SCO System V and a brief discussion of their characteristics will illustrate their differences and similarities.

5.4.2 INTERACTIVE UNIX

The operating environment for the INTERACTIVE System hosts a front end menu-driven display which permits the user easy access to the UNIX 386 PC resources. As new options are added to the system the appropriate administration menu is amended. To implement INTERACTIVE UNIX the 386 PC must have a minimum of four Mbytes of 32-bit RAM and a 44-Mbyte hard disk drive. It supports either the Micro Channel Architecture (MCA) or Industry Standard Architecture (ISA) 16-bit format expansion buses.

One aspect which is featured is STREAMS which defines a standard interface for input/output functions between the UNIX kernel and the 386 PC system. To add to the functionality of the product, INTERACTIVE UNIX supports shared libraries which allow UNIX application programs to share a single copy of the runtime library. When an application program is running and makes a call for a library routine, the routine is dynamically linked into the program. This reduces the amount of memory required by each application since the program does not have to include the library routines. INTERACTIVE UNIX also provides a range of peripheral device drivers for the standard array of 386 PC devices.

The concept of the INTERACTIVE product range is of a modular design with a series of additional options depending on the intended configuration of the UNIX system. The configuration can be tailored for a single user only running application programs, a single user developing application programs or networked versions of these. Under the operational environment of INTERACTIVE UNIX, the 386 PC therefore has access to a comprehensive range of facilities which can be broadly grouped into:

❏ DOS and User Utilities

❏ Software Development

❏ Networking

❏ Window Functions.

It will be instructive to outline the options offered in each of these groups so that general appreciation of the INTERACTIVE product can be gained.

DOS and User Utilities

To enable MS-DOS programs to run under INTERACTIVE UNIX there are a number of features provided. There are four levels of support offered to DOS requirements. The first, DOSSETTE is a set of utilities which permits the copying of DOS data files from a DOS medium into a UNIX file. Secondly, the **File System Support** (FSS) will allow DOS or UNIX files systems, on a disk partition, to be treated as a mutual resource by either UNIX or DOS. FSS will also ensure against DOS partition integrity for simultaneous access during multi-user activity. Thirdly the operating system can be extended with VP/ix. With this extension UNIX and DOS application programs can run concurrently on the same UNIX 386 PC and this is particularly attractive for a user who already has a sizable investment in DOS software and is making exploratory investigations into UNIX.

VP/ix also facilitates the creation of DOS terminal workstations by exploiting the Virtual 86 Mode of the 80386 CPU (Section 2.2.2). Each terminal takes on the role of a virtual machine (VM) and gains access to the resources of the UNIX 386 PC via a RS-232 serial link. There is provision within VP/ix to permit DOS or UNIX users to access files which reside on either UNIX or DOS disk space partitions.

There is also file and record locking protection to ensure proper access procedures to stored data. In the event of a resource only having a DOS device driver, VP/ix can access the resource by means of the **Direct Device Attachment** (DDA). There are limitations on the use of DDA: the resource must not use direct memory access (Section 2.3.5) and only one user can access the resource at a time. However the DDA facility contributes to the integration of a previously acquired DOS-based PC system with a UNIX 386 PC facility.

The fourth level of support for DOS users is covered by INTERACTIVE PC-Interface which provides a distributed UNIX file system over a LAN for DOS users. One possible configuration which can be realised is to have one 386 PC, on a LAN, dedicated to DOS services and a DOS working environment. By using PC-Interface, another user can remotely load up a DOS application program as a concurrent task on the dedicated 386 PC and control it from their own 386 PC. PC-Interface will also allow users on a DOS 386 PC to access and run UNIX application programs on other PCs and there is provision for extensive data transfer between the two working environments.

PC-Interface consists of two sections: the **UNIX Server Module,** which is supplied as part of the INTERACTIVE UNIX operating system and the **DOS Bridge Module,** which is acquired separately. To establish PC-Interface the two modules are used in conjunction with suitable hardware interfaces – multiple RS-232 links (Section 3.3.2) or an Ethernet expansion card. If connected to a LAN the INTERACTIVE TCP/IP will be needed on the UNIX server.

The user utilities have a sub-family of products covered by the TEN/PLUS Environment. TEN/PLUS has a facility for creating custom menus to the user's specifications by means of the **Profile Helper**. There is also a **File Manager** and **Print Helper** for performing the tasks associated with these activities; file manipulation and print spooling. The functions of the UNIX shell can be accessed through the TEN/PLUS software interface. TEN/PLUS has a number of other features; **Mail System** for transmitting and receiving messages, mail can be targeted to single users or a prescribed list of LAN users. For the more regimented user the **Time Management System** (TMS) may have some appeal – the user can plan meetings by accessing other LAN user's calendars. The time spent on specific tasks by a user can be monitored with TMS for management and costing purposes. Lastly the **User's Tool Kit** and **Programmer's Tool Kit** are for customising documents and the TEN/PLUS environment respectively.

Another utility is INTERACTIVE **Text Processing Workbench** which contains the normal features of an advanced text editor and is a derivative of AT&T's Workbench Release 2.0. Workbench enables users to format documents to their own design with options for writing equations and creating tables. A number of printer drivers are contained within Workbench for a popular array of printers.

INTERACTIVE **MultiView** is an interesting utility which provides a window environment as part of a user interface to the UNIX 386 PC. It permits multiple, concurrent windows, each representing an active application program or a current resource. MultiView has pull-down menus to enable easy access to the system services and each window can be panned, scrolled and resized to occupy the full screen. For moving ASCII data from one application program to another, the cut and paste facility may be evoked and the menus may be redesigned to suit the user's wishes. MultiView also offers support for multiple terminals linked to a host UNIX 386 PC via an Ethernet LAN or the RS-232 serial interface (Section 3.3.2).

To compliment MultiView, INTERACTIVE also supplys **MultiView DeskTop** which runs under Windows/386 (Section 5.5.1). It provides the user with a Graphics User Interface (GUI) where multiple resources of the UNIX 386 PC can be accessed whether they are UNIX or DOS based. Like Windows/386, data can be transferred from application to application by using the clip board facility. DeskTop is an effective means of integrating the DOS and UNIX environments without losing the functionality of either operating system.

INTERACTIVE Software Development

The UNIX environment based on 386 PCs is admirably suitable for developing software due to its multi-tasking, multi-user features and the ability to manage software development. Typically each member of a team of software engineers will need to access the development tools and share common software libraries. Often an engineer will need to test the operation of their code with an input from their colleagues' code and the facilities afforded by a multi-tasking, networked system make this task much easier. Managing the progress of a software project is a difficult task which can be made easier if the software manager is provided with the ability to monitor the progress of each engineer and their code. The software development tools of INTERACTIVE UNIX include:

❑ AT&T's C compiler

❑ 80386 macro assembler

❑ A syntax checker

❑ A symbolic debugger

❑ A linker

❑ New C

❑ POSIX and FIPS 151-1 compliance development libraries

When there is a need to use high-level languages INTERACTIVE can supply compilers provided by Language Processor Inc. (LPI) and a list of them is given in the section on SCO XENIX 386 (Section 5.4.3) which uses the same products. Each compiler produces 32-bit code specifically for the 80386 CPU.

Two additional utilities which INTERACTIVE supplys as part of the package are CodeWatch and CoEdit. CodeWatch can be used to correct software errors at source code level. The code can be executed line by line and the progress monitored. CoEdit on the other hand is a language-sensitive editor for writing the source code which performs syntax checking as the code is written. The compiler can be called from CoEdit and any compilation errors are highlighted in the source code.

INTERACTIVE Networking

Network facilities are strongly featured in the INTERACTIVE product family. For internetworking applications, INTERACTIVE supplys TCP/IP (Section 8.1.4) which conforms to the IEEE 802.3 standard (Section 8.6.3). It is appropriate software for permitting communication between a UNIX 386 PC and remote, dissimilar computer systems via a LAN. The full range of TCP/IP facilities are supported by this product including File Transfer Protocol (FTP), Simple Mail Transfer Protocol (SMTP), SLIP To System V STREAMS and Telnet (Section 8.1.4). A number of Ethernet adaptor cards are supported by INTERACTIVE TCP/IP and these include the INTERLAN NI15210, the Western digital WD8003E, the 3Com 3C501 and the Ungermann-Bass PC-NIC.

A version of the Sun Microsystem Network File System (NFS), called INTER-ACTIVE NFS, is also available and provides a method for sharing files between UNIX and non-UNIX based computers. It also provides the user of a UNIX 386 PC access to the resources of other computers, which host NFS, across a variety of networks, and provides support for BIOS. NFS has three management utilities: **Network Lock Manager** is able to issue record locking commands across a LAN, **Status Monitor** provides the user with the NFS locking status of an accessed file and **Yellow Pages** gives a list of the network resources.

INTERACTIVE Windows

INTERACTIVE's concession to the growing need for graphics-based window environments is INTERACTIVE X11. This is derived from Release 3 of the Massachusetts Institute of Technology (MIT) X Windows X11 which has become the network-based standard Graphics User Interface (GUI) windowing system for UNIX 386 PCs. With it, every networked UNIX 386 PC can operate with a graphics window front end even if the source application program is running on another machine. This is sometimes referred to as **Client Server Architecture** (CSA).

The system can support a range of high and low-resolution graphics standards, however its attractive feature is its ability to download the X11 processing to intelligent graphics cards which host their own microprocessor (Section 4.3.4). This is achieved by means of the **Smart Board Interface** (SBI) which supplies an operating environment for graphics-intensive application programs. Offloading the processing onto the graphics card has the effect of reducing the workload on the 80386 CPU. Each manufacturer of an intelligent graphics board can therefore write their own device driver which acknowledges SBI and performs offload processing.

Network-based graphics application programs and their data files can be processed with a minimum degree of intervention from the 80386 CPU since much of the processing will be exercised by the intelligent graphics cards. For a standalone UNIX 386 PC using INTERACTIVE X11, the data exchange is accomplished by means of a high-speed interprocess communication (IPC) protocol.

However for network data transfer, INTERACTIVE TCP/IP will have to be used to achieve window displays of processes on remote 386 PCs. INTERACTIVE X11 (Runtime) is also available and contains all the software call routines to implement the full facilities of X-Windows. One of its features, the Xlib library, has a set of routines of a variety of display standards and other resources. This library is shared by all users of and the routines are called as required.

INTERACTIVE has also issued two other X-Window products: INTERACTIVE X11 Development System, for designing X Window user interfaces, and INTER-ACTIVE X11 Server Kit (under special agreement) for creating display support routines for new devices.

5.4.3 SCO System V

A product from the SCO System V range is SCO XENIX 386 and is supplied in the UK by Level V. XENIX 386 conforms to the AT&T **System V Interface Definitions** (SVID) and offers a full 32-bit performance UNIX operating system for 386 PCs hosting either the Industry Standard Architecture (ISA) or the Micro Channel Architecture (MCA) buses. There are three modules within SCO XENIX 386: the Operating System, the Development System and the Text Processing System.

The Operating System provides a UNIX System V shell for file editing, communication with other users and running UNIX application programs. XENIX 386 can work side by side with DOS, since the system hard disk drive can be shared by both operating systems. A user can easily change from a XENIX environment to a DOS environment and there are utilities for transferring data between the two. Generous support is afforded by XENIX 386 for an extensive range of peripherals including graphics standards, disk controller and back-up tape drives.

The Development System provides a graphics interface and a range of XENIX cross development software tools for writing C language and assembly language programs for the 80386. This also includes an extensive array of library utilities for accessing UNIX resources within the 386 PC. For high-level language program development, there is available a range of compilers specifically for producing 80386 object code modules, and modules from different compilers can be linked to form executable application programs.

The compilers, from Language Processors Inc. (LPI), include:

❑ LPI-FORTRAN (ANSI X3.9-1978, FORTRAN 77)

❑ LPI-COBAL (ANSI X3.23-1985)

❑ LPI-BASIC (ANSI Minimal BASIC X3.6-1978)

❑ LPI-PASCAL (ANSI and IEEE standard)

❑ LPI-PL/I (ANSI and General Purpose Subset)

❑ LPI-RPG II (compatible with IBM System/3 and System/34).

To test generated code and correct the software errors SCO provides an optional LPI-DEBUG which is functional with all the LPI compilers. Each compiler has a front end command structure for each language. To complement the LPI compilers there is an optimiser and run-time library. The function of the optimiser is to modify the code to make greater use of the 80386 internal registers, which has the effect of creating optimised machine language code which executes faster on the 80386 CPU.

The run-time library consists of routines which are called by the application programs during their execution. This minimises the program size and reduces the need for replication since they are not linked in with the executable code.

The Text Processing System has a wealth of options for producing large and complex documents. Provisions have been made to construct mathematical equations (the eqn option) and tables (the tbl option). To add to the appeal of XENIX Text Processing System, the reference manual is available in an on-line format and can be accessed by evoking the man option from the menu.

The SCO XENIX product range is extensive and not too dissimilar to the products offered by INTERACTIVE and include:

SCO VP/ix: Allows concurrent DOS application programs to run within the XENIX environment together with XENIX application programs. Under VP/ix, XENIX and DOS application programs can share and access disk data files. VP/ix has a pop-up menu-driven user interface with various help facilities. VP/ix ensures that the value of prior investment in DOS application programs is maintained. For low-cost multi-user requirements, VP/ix can support terminals which allow users to gain access to the XENIX or DOS resources of the 386 PC. The terminals can be interfaced via extended RS-232 serial ports.

SCO MultiView: A window front end to the XENIX 386 PC where the various options of the XENIX environment can be accessed through pull-down screen menus. During multi-tasking operations each application program or task may have its own window. If there are terminals interfaced to the XENIX 386 PC, then SCO Multi-View will provide a window environment for the terminals as well. The terminals can either be bit mapped graphics terminals or character orientated; SCO MultiView permits window resizing and even the use of printers attached to terminals.

SCO XENIX-NET: Supports a local area network (LAN) which has a mixture of XENIX 386 PC and DOS 386 PC (and other PCs). The LAN resources, distributed among the DOS and XENIX 386 PCs servers, can therefore be accessed by the other users on the LAN. SCO XENIX-NET is a convenient technique for merging the services of combined XENIX and DOS environments and in addition offers support for Micro Channel Architecture (MCA) based 386 PCs. Included in SCO XENIX-NET is an option, known as SCO ASYN-NET, which can be used to great effect to construct a star topology LAN (Section 8.1.3) with a XENIX 386 PC server at the core connecting to other PCs via RS-232 serial links.

SCO uniPATH

Once a XENIX LAN is in place, there is a likelihood that a communication gateway will be required between the PCs on the LAN and a mainframe computer. In the event of the mainframe being part of an IBM System Network Architecture (SNA), then uniPATH SNA-3270 can be used to link the XENIX 386 PC or LAN to the mainframe. The SCO uniPATH gateway task can function concurrently with other XENIX or DOS tasks and offers the full facilities of the SNA-3270 terminal standards.

SCO TCP/IP

If there is a need to link a XENIX 386 PC to a network of dissimilar computers, all working under different operating systems, the SCO TCP/IP may be used. Further details of TCP/IP can be found in Section 8.1.4. To implement either the SCO NFS or X-Windows products then SCO TCP/IP will have to be in place on XENIX 386 PC or server.

SCO NFS

This product is necessary to link a XENIX 386 PC to the SUN Microsystem compatible Network File Server (NFS). It is especially useful for integrating SUN high-resolution graphics workstations to a standalone or a network of XENIX 386 PCs.

SCO Xsight

This is based on Version 11 of X-Windows (X11) and provides the networked graphics windowing system. It is particularly appealing for users involved in computer-aided design, manufacture and engineering where high-resolution graphics and rapid data transfer is essential. SCO Xsight gives the user the opportunity to access, via the LAN, concurrent XENIX processes operating on remote XENIX 386 PCs. Xsight also enables DOS PCs, furnished with TCP/IP facilities, to act as network servers to XENIX clients.

SCO System V UNIX/386

Another product from the SCO System V range is UNIX V/386 which is a full implementation of the AT&T UNIX System V Release 3.2 and encompasses all of the features of the SCO XENIX 386. It is designed to run on the 386 PC which has the Extended Industry Standard Architecture (EISA – Section 7.3.4), but also runs on 386 PCs with the Industry Standard Architecture (ISA) or Micro Channel Architecture (MCA) expansion buses.

SCO UNIX System V/386 possesses the Streams protocols which conform to the Transport Layer Interface (TLI – Section 8.6.1) for networking needs. In fact the complete SCO Streams System protocols, with accompanying development library, are a standard feature of the Development System which is important for handling input/output procedures.

SCO has included the File System Switch (FSS) which makes access to DOS application programs and data on DOS partitions on disks quite transparent to the user. This enhances the ease of mixing UNIX and DOS programs on the same system, be it a single UNIX 386 PC or a network of machines. To compliment the SCO UNIX System V/386 support for a wide range of peripherals, there are many device drivers from SCO which can be installed as required. With the Device Drivers Development Kit, users can compile their own peripheral or device drivers and due to their modular construction existing drivers can be augmented to provide new features.

System V Development System is a platform primarily intended for developing application programs for either UNIX System V/386, XENIX, MS-DOS or OS/2 operating systems. For the development of application programs sourced in C, the AT&T C Compiler and the Microsoft C Compiler have been made product features. MS-DOS and OS/2 software libraries and linkers are supplied with the Development System together with CodeView which is an interactive source code debugger for correcting software errors.

With the additional range of compilers from Language Processors Inc (LPI), the System V Development System therefore represents a comprehensive multi-user software development platform. Another feature included in the Development System is the SCO Computer Graphics Interface (CGI) which is a graphics development package designed to be device independent. CGI provides a selection of features which enable programmers to create software for graphics-intensive applications such as computer-aided design (CAD). With CGI, graphics programming can be performed using either the bit-mapped – where every graphics pixel element can be individually addressed, or the vector graphics technique – where images are defined in terms of lines and relative coordinates (Section 6.3).

SCO has an impressive range of UNIX application programs for business requirements which come under the title of the SCO Office Portfolio. It forms a comprehensive integrated package of software applications which meet many of the needs of an active business environment.

Open Desktop

To complement its range of UNIX and XENIX products and to meet the demands for an integrated graphics workstation environment, SCO has issued Open Desktop which is a graphical operating system. With this product, graphical-intensive application programs can run concurrently, each occupying a dedicated window. Open Desktop allows easy exchange of data between the individual windows and is based on the standards of X-Windows and OSF/Motif from the Open System Foundation of Cambridge, Massachusetts. In appearance it is not too dissimilar from the IBM Presentation Manager (Section 5.6.1) and has several features in common with it. It is available with Ingres/386, from Relational Technology Inc (RTI) which contains an structured query language (SQL) for efficient use of database resources.

5.5 Multi-tasking DOS Software

The major aspect of the 386 PC is its ability to execute several programs at the same time, referred to as multi-tasking. This is seen as a significant improvement over the previous generations of personal computers. To be precise a 386 PC can only execute one program at any one time, however it has the ability to switch from program to program very quickly and this gives the appearance of executing several programs concurrently. One way of achieving this is for the 80386 central processing unit (CPU) to operate in its Virtual 86 mode (Section 2.2.2) where it can simulate several 8086 microprocessors operating simultaneously. A DOS application program will run on the 8086, therefore a 80386 CPU can run several MS-DOS application programs at the same time. The 80386 CPU, in effect, time slices each application program and this is illustrated in Figure 5.5 overleaf.

The advantage of this facility, in allowing several application programs to be active at one time, is increased efficiency. With one program operating as the foreground task, other tasks can be running as background tasks. It is easy to swap a background task to a foreground task and permit data to be exchanged between them if necessary. These are often referred to as virtual machines since they behave as separate PCs within the multi-tasking environment. The 80386 CPU is well designed to accommodate switching from task to task (context switching), and has a low latency – the time taken to effect the switch – in the order of 45 micro seconds for a 16-MHz device.

In practice multi-tasking can be achieved by augmenting DOS with an enhanced operating system which retains the character of the DOS kernel but enlarges its functionality. This will allow many of the advanced architectural features of the 80386 CPU to be used; principal among these is the Virtual 8086 Mode. Each 8086 DOS application program is allocated its own 640K of memory which cannot be breached by other 8086 DOS application programs. To support this the 386 PC should be furnished with at least four Mbytes of extended memory. Each virtual 8086 has its 640K of logical address space (LAS) mapped into a different physical address space (PAS) in the extended memory. Difficulties do arise when a number of the DOS application programs attempt to access a common resource of the 386 PC. Writing to the video screen display is an example and the DOS-enhanced operating system must partition the screen into separate regions to prevent screen overwriting.

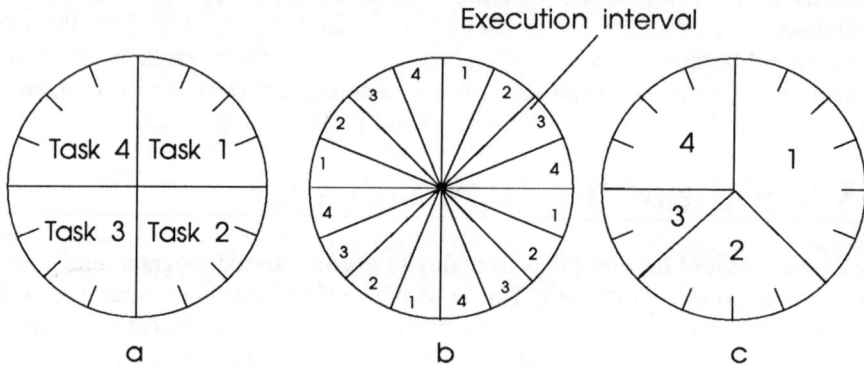

Figure 5.5 Time slicing

Instead of attempting to enhance DOS for 386 PC multi-tasking some vendors have chosen the route of the DOS-Compatible Replacement Operating System (DOS-CROS). This is based on the design principle, developed in Section 5.1, of an operating system kernel which is by far the most effective method of scheduling tasks in a multi-tasking environment.

However it is difficult for a DOS-CROS to support all DOS functions since they are not all documented and this can lead to the system failing to execute all DOS-based application programs. However the move towards DOS-CROS has yet to result in products which capitalise on the full features of the 80386 CPU – page demands, virtual memory and the various protection modes.

5.5.1 Windows/386

One of the first multi-tasking software packages for the 386 PC was Windows/386 released by Microsoft. It makes extensive use of the front end graphics mode based on a Graphics User Interface (GUI) with strong WIMP (Windows, Icons, Mouse,

Pull-down menus) features. In Windows/386 each DOS application program runs within its own virtual machine and has its own window. The 386 PC screen is therefore divided into application program windows which allow the user visual access to each running program. The strong graphical emphasis demands a minimum of an enhanced graphics adaptor (EGA – Section 4.3.2) or a video graphics array (VGA – Section 4.3.3) accompanied by a suitable mouse. The installation of Windows/386 provides a wide choice of the mouse and graphics options. For moving/resizing each window on the screen and accessing the menu bar, a mouse is considered essential.

Windows/386 is memory intensive and a comfortable minimum is four Mbytes of extended memory, but it will run on less. It has the ability to convert a portion of the extended memory into LIM 4.0 standard Expanded memory, if required by an applications program.

The window characteristics of Windows/386 are constructed from its simulation of the video memory for each application program which calls it. Data is therefore transferred to the real video memory from the simulated video memory and subjected to remapping during transit in order to realise the multi-window display. Some application programs, which do not conform to the normal video screen calls, via the BIOS (Section 2.8), will not be accommodated by a window and will consequently require the whole screen. In general application programs can executed in one of three modes:

❏ A window with other application windows

❏ A full screen foreground task

❏ A background task with no window refresh activity (an icon).

Calling an application program directly via the pull-down menu will result in it becoming a full foreground task. However to control the display characteristics of an application program a .PIF (program interface file) can be created which provides information of its screen usage and memory allocation. The program is then started from the .PIF file. Several .PIF files may exist for the same program, each containing different performance parameters. The user can specify with the .PIF whether the application program is to occupy a window, whether it is wholly graphics or a mix of graphics and text.

Data transfer between two windows can be achieved by one of two methods: common hard disk files or using the Windows/386 clipboard. When using the clipboard a portion of a screen (graphics or text) from the foreground task can be marked and copied into it. When a different foreground task is evoked the contents of the clipboard can be transferred to the new task. The transfer of graphical data is not always successful using this technique and if this should be the case, the data from the primary task should be written to the hard disk and later read by the secondary program.

To help with several tasks which require intensive use of the printer, Windows/386 has a print spooler (which resides as a background icon). This is particularly good for managing several printing tasks without fear of conflict. Port usage, from within Windows/386, is carefully managed by allowing only one window access to a given port; the window must be closed before another application program can use the same port. One of the major deficiencies of Windows/386 is its failure to provide the user with an option to adjust the time-slicing and the priority of each application program. It appears that in general background and foreground tasks are allocated equal time-slices, however no CPU time is spent on background tasks which are inactive or have a blocked status. By not being able to adjust the time-slicing, waiting does cause screen intensive application programs to crawl at an inordinate pace. As the number of active foreground windows which involve graphics is increased there is a corresponding slowing up of the 386 PC and when this limit reaches four the system gives a convincing impression of having stopped. This is due to the heavy overheads incurred in graphics processing. However for non-graphical application programs Windows/386 performs adequately as a multi-tasking environment.

5.5.2 Desqview/386

Issued by Quarterdeck of Santa Monica, Desqview/386 is an amalgam of Desqview version 2.2 and QEMM-386 version 4.2 Expanded Memory Manager. Desqview 2.2 enables any PC to run application programs in a background and foreground configuration and permits easy switching between them. QEMM-386, on the other hand, has the normal facilities of an extended memory manager, is able to perform ROM Shadowing (Section 2.8.1) and allows extended memory to be treated like expanded memory. It can also permit terminate and stay resident (TSR) routines to be located and executed from outside the 640K base memory. The Desqview/ QEMM-386 combination supports a multi-tasking environment for up to nine separate screen windows, each operating as a virtual machine with its own application program. Unlike the other multi-tasking software packages, Desqview/386 makes very efficient use of memory by only imposing a 10K overhead space from the base memory and 65K from extended memory for each virtual machine set up in the 386 PC.

After installation, Desqview 386 resides as a background system and is evoked with the Alt key as a pop-up menu to display its options. The menu can be reconfigured according to the user's requirements and it is a straightforward task to add new options to the menu. With several tasks running concurrently, Desqview/386 time-slices each of them and gives a high weighting of four periods of 55 ms to the foreground task. This has the effect of improving the response time of the 386 PC. However this figure can be adjusted by the user via the Advanced Features Menu.

Although Desqview/386 can multi-task application programs, no more than one active graphics program is allowed in the foreground at any one time. The whole screen is transformed into its graphics mode which also simulates the text mode. However the writing speed of the screen addressing diminishes in this mode. Data can be transferred or shared between application programs by using the extensive cut and paste facility of its own application interface. As with other multi-tasking environments, the addition of each application program into the Desqview/386 multi-tasking mode causes a noticeable reduction in performance.

5.5.3 Concurrent DOS/386

Developed by Digital Research, Concurrent DOS/386 is designed to support either a single or multi-user environment. It is in fact a DOS-CROS (DOS-compatible replacement operating system) and is therefore a complete standalone operating system which does not reside on top of or in parallel with DOS. Consequently Concurrent DOS/386 can be installed on to a hard disk as an separate operating system. Concurrent DOS/386 can utilise Expanded Memory (either the LIM or EEMS specification – Section 2.3.3) and the base 640K memory. To optimise the memory resource two instructions, MEMSIZE and LIMSIZE, are available. They exercise control over the limits of base memory required by a particular applications program. The program is therefore limited to the amount of memory it actually requires, the remaining base memory being left available for other application programs.

The maximum number of concurrent tasks is 255 and the screen display can show four application programs in a window format, each window featuring the current state of the program's activity. The windows are not as elaborate as the normal Windows environment but they are adequate for most purposes. By using the Window Manager each window can be resized, repositioned and its colour adjusted to suit the user. However only one window can operate in a graphics mode and only one window can be active at any one time. This is referred to as the foreground task. The operation of each application program can be tailored by creating a .PIF file which contains the parameters necessary for the program to continue execution as a background task.

A 386 PC can be configured as a low cost multi-user option when running under the multi-user version of Concurrent DOS/386 with two terminals (or other PCs running PC TERM) connected via the two RS-232 serial interface ports. The terminals must conform to the American national system interface (ANSI) standard. However most DOS application programs that are expected to run under this condition will probably have to be multi-user versions. If there is a requirement for graphics work stations then the Concurrent DOS/386/Multi-user Graphics Edition (MGE) should be used. This can support SunRiver Fibre Optic Workstations and common resources such as disk storage and laser printers. It is worth remembering that since Concurrent DOS/386 only emulates DOS, compatibility problems may arise.

5.5.4 VM/386

Taking full advantage of the Virtual 8086 mode of the 80386 CPU, VM/386, from the Intelligent Graphics Corp., is a multi-tasking environment which allows several concurrent DOS virtual machines to be active and operate independently of each other. The independence is further highlighted by permitting each DOS virtual machine to have its own terminate and stay resident (TSR) programs installed. Therefore each virtual machine can carry its own set of device drivers if required. To enable this configuration, VM/386 makes heavy demands upon system memory; for four DOS application programs of 640K each, 3.5 Mbytes of extended memory will be required. Each segment of 640K cannot be accessed by other DOS application programs and remains dynamically fixed while the DOS program is running. In the event of an application program crashing only the host virtual machine will go down leaving the rest of the system intact. A soft boot with Ctrl-Alt-Del is sufficient to recover the VM.

VM/386 also caters for the needs of application programs which require LIM standard Expansion Memory by converting Extended Memory into Expanded Memory, making it available to the application program. Since the demands on memory are quite heavy, in practice, the number of concurrent programs is limited. However the switch from each virtual machine is smooth with very little delay. What may be considered as a disadvantage is visibility of only one virtual machine at any one time. This may present a problem if the user wishes to visually monitor the progress of two or more applications simultaneously. Only the foreground task has exclusive access to the screen while the activity of the background task remains hidden.

An attractive feature of VM/386 is the Resource System Manager (RSM), which when evoked, displays its options via a small menu insert. Through the RSM, profile files can be created which contain the relevant information for a virtual machine to function. The RSM allows the user to adjust the priority access of each application program running on a virtual machine, to the system's resources. This can allow controlled access to printers and communication ports from each virtual machine. Changes can also be made to the time-slicing allocation of each application program. The RSM is also used to allocate memory to each program application. However this is not as straightforward since it is often difficult to estimate how much memory a particular program requires. To optimise the response of the 386 PC, the RSM will respond to the priority of the foreground task by suspending the inactive background tasks. It achieves this by monitoring the background task interrupt activity – if this is low the task suspension occurs freeing the 80386 CPU to concentrate on the foreground task.

Since each virtual machine is a stand-alone system the exchange of data between concurrent application programs is performed by means of common disk files. These can be accessed by each virtual machine thereby providing an effective means of data exchange. Disk cacheing can improve this process and VM/386 has the provision for a 32K disk cache routine. This can be used to great effect to limit the number of physical accesses to the hard disk.

An extension to this product is VM/386 MultiUser which allows several users, on other terminals or PCs, to access the resources of the 386 PC and this is covered in Section 8.9.3.

5.6 Operating System/2 (OS/2 v2)

When IBM introduced its series of PS/2 personal computers it also introduced, in conjunction with Microsoft, an operating system referred to as OS/2. Some of the PS/2 range of PCs are based on the Intel 80286 16-bit microprocessor and one of the innovations behind OS/2 was to exploit the protected mode of the 80286 thereby enabling multi-tasking. To match the range of PS/2 PCs based on the 80386, IBM issued OS/2 v2 which makes greater use of the features of the 80386 microprocessor than the previous OS/2 Extended Edition. OS/2 v2, with its Presentation Manager, provides a graphics interface for the user through the use of a WIMP front end and this is certainly more friendly and easier to use than DOS. The pull-down menus, scroll bars and so on give the user an easy access method to the facilities of the PC. OS/2 v2's organisation of hard disk space is quite different to the file allocation table (FAT) method as adopted for DOS. It is based on the High Performance File System (HPFS) (Section 2.5.1) which supports free-form file names and disk volumes up to 2,000,000 Mbytes. With HPFS, files can be as large as 2,000 Mbytes spanning a number of hard disk drives and the file names can be up to 254 characters long. Floppy disks however are still formatted with a FAT to allow DOS data to be transferred to a PS/2 operating under OS/2.

The amount of memory which any one application program can occupy is 16 Mbytes. However OS/2 v2 does provide virtual memory management (Section 2.2.4) which means that large application programs can run without having an equivalent on-board RAM to hold all the program. Referred to as memory over commitment, only part of the application program will reside in RAM and when the CPU reaches the end of the code it is momentarily suspended. A new page is fetched from the hard disk and loaded into the RAM and the CPU continues processing the new code.

One of the key features of OS/2 v2 is its support for multi-tasking. A number of tasks and application programs can be active, some of which can operate as background tasks and can be scheduled according to their priority. Concurrent tasks and active application programs are referred to as sessions. OS/2 v2 can support up to 16 sessions, however four of these are given over to system operations, leaving 12 sessions for user tasks and application programs. The essence of multi-tasking is to give the impression that each application program or session has it own set of resources. OS/2 v2 therefore provides the management for each session to have its own logical set of resources. These include keyboard, mouse and a video display. To aid the multi-tasking, OS/2 v2 has an inherent disk cacheing facility (Section 2.7) for the efficient transfer of data between RAM and the hard disk drive(s). The exchange of data between concurrent sessions is accomplished by means of dynamic data links, referred to as named pipes, which allow sessions to transfer data in a controlled manner. A pipe can be created by one session and the same pipe can then be accessed by another session which may choose to write or read data to or from the pipe.

There is also provision to minimise the size of application programs which rely on library routines. Normally when an application program is compiled and linked, the library routines are included in the linking phase and this can produce an unwieldy, large executable application program. To avoid this, OS/2 v2 implements Dynamic Link Libraries (DLLs). The library routines are resident on the system hard disk and are linked into the application program as and when they are required by the program. This dynamic linking keeps the size of application programs to a minimum and ultimately saves on hard disk space.

DLLs are also used to handle session calls to peripherals or resources. The standard resources of OS/2 v2 will have service routines in the Application Programming Interface (API) which are written to a set of prescribed conventions. Being equivalent to a set of device drivers, the API will reside in the system library and when the session requires the service of a resource, it will dynamically link the API into its program area and run the routine. Application programmers are therefore furnished with a single mechanism for calling the system resources.

As a peripheral is added to a PC hosting OS/2 v2, it will be accompanied by a free-standing device driver which will be loaded as a new function in the system library ready for dynamic linkage to a session. This will enable application programs to be written without reference to peripheral hardware details. Developing application programs under OS/2 v2 is greatly assisted by a range of products supplied by IBM, which include the Software Development Kit, Programmer Toolkit and the Presentation Manager. These are used in conjunction with the language development tools for producing application programs.

Only application programs specifically designed for OS/2 or OS/2 v2 can run in the latter and more and more are appearing on the market. MS-DOS application programs can be run under OS/2 v2 via the DOS Compatibility Mode (DCM). DOS programs running under the DCM can operate concurrently with other OS/2 v2 tasks. When the DOS program has finished, the DCM can be made into an inactive background task within the OS/2 v2 environment. There is a subset of API, referred to as Family API, which can be used to good effect to create application programs which can be run under OS/2 v2 or DOS 3.3 or 4. When the application program is compiled and linked, the Family API is also linked or bound to produce an executable application program. When run in the OS/2 v2 environment the API calls are dealt with in the usual manner. However when the program is executed in a DOS environment, part of the linked code translates the API calls into their corresponding DOS interrupt procedures. The program therefore behaves as though it is a true DOS program.

The OS/2 v2 operating system is complimented by Communication and Database Managers. The Communication Manager renders support for data exchange across a number of local area network designs, including IBM's System Network Architecture (SNA), for communication with mainframe computers. It also supports internetworking through the LU 6.2 standard (Section 8.1.4) which enables dissimilar computers to communicate with each other. The Communication Manager has provision for coping with asynchronous communication devices such as modems (Section 7.1). The Database Manager is composed of the Database Services and the Query Manager where the former is closely linked to IBM's Structured Query Language (SQL). When the user requests data from a local or remote resource server, the Database Services translates the request into SQL instructions.

One of the key features of SQL instructions is their recognition by other IBM computer hardware which may have different operating systems. The Query Manager permits the user to change the appearance of the PC screen by constructing menus, panels and sub-screens with defined fields which represent the system resources. When the resources are located in remote sites, for example mainframe databases, it is the role of the Communication Manager to establish the routing to the resources.

5.6.1 Presentation Manager

In the grand scheme, IBM has set out to establish the idea of common framework for the user interface among application programs where the guidelines and definitions are found in the Common User Access (CUA) documentation. An implementation of this scheme is the Presentation Manager (PM) which is a feature of OS/2 v2.

Currently when new users are introduced to an application program, they have to progress along a learning curve in order to gain proficiency in its use. The Presentation Manager is a means by which all applications programs will have the same common user interface. Many application programs have equivalent functions and it is the design of Presentation Manager to standardise the evocation of these functions.

To a limited extent, this has been achieved with Windows/386 (Section 5.5.1) for DOS application programs. Windows and PM are very similar in their outward appearance since their creators have drawn inspiration from the Apple Macintosh design. PM resides between the kernel of OS/2 v2 and the application program; resources are allocated to application programs according to predefined guide-lines laid out in the CUA documentation. By this method a user, when introduced to a new application program, will find a shallow learning curve since most program operations will be evoked via pop-up windows, menu bars, pull-down options and scroll bars. These types of screen functions form part of PM and can be used directly by an application programmer when generating code.

When an application program is evoked from within PM, it is assigned its own window referred to as the Client Area. Each client area will have its own pull-down menus and scroll bars which enable the user to move it around the screen. The operation of the application program can be suspended and this results in the client area being reduced to an icon at the bottom of the screen working area (minimising the program). The application program can be vitalised by clicking the mouse on the icon.

Since OS/2 v2 is a multi-tasking operating system there is a necessity to exchange data between application programs. PM makes use of a technique known as Dynamic Data Exchange (DDE). Alternatively, for manual data transfer, an area of data from the source program is marked and copied into the OS/2 v2 clipboard. The target program is activated and the contents of the clipboard are then pasted into it.

The use of the clipboard is a technique found within Windows/386 and a user familiar with this method will adapt quickly to the options offered by PM. An application program written for Presentation Manager should run concurrently with other programs while still permitting the user to access other resources via the mouse and keyboard. This is achieved through the adoption of a set of rules which govern the use of auxiliary program threads to the CPU during application code development.

5.6.2 Systems Application Architecture (SAA)

OS/2 v2 is well equipped for the requirements of a local area network (LAN), and with the addition of the OS/2 v2 LAN Manager and a suitable expansion adaptor (Section 8.1.1) the full resources of a LAN can be accessed. LAN Manager naturally has a windows interface which conforms to IBM's System Application Architecture (SAA). SAA is an integral part of the IBM grand design for program compatibility among dissimilar computers.

The window construction, laid down in the SAA, will be common to IBM mainframes, IBM mini computers and IBM PS/2 PCs. In principle, programs written on a PS/2 computer can be directly ported to an IBM 370 mainframe and run without modification. SAA should also allow resource sharing, for example, disk sharing at directory level and a user on an IBM mainframe should be able to access, via the LAN and gateway, the hard disk drives of a PS/2.

Further reading:

Operating Systems

DOS
1. Running MS-DOS, Van Wolverton, Microsoft.

2. The Waite Group's MS-DOS Bible, S Simrin, Howard W. Sams & Co.

3. Advanced MS-DOS Programming, R Duncan, (second edition), Microsoft.

DOS Version 4
1. The New DOS 4.0, K Christopher, B Feigenbaum & S Saliga, John Wiley (1989).

2. DOS 4 Made Easy, H Schildt, Osborne McGraw-Hill, (1989).

3. The ABCs of DOS 4, A R Miller, Sybex.

UNIX
1. UNIX System V/386 set of manuals by AT&T, Prentice Hall: User Guide, Reference Manual , Programmer's Guide, Network Programmer's Guide.

2. UNIX Programming on the 80286/80386, A Deikman, M & T Publishing (1989).

Windows
1. Programmer's guide to Windows D Durant, G Carlson, & P Yao, (second edition – Windows/386), Sybex.

OS/2
1. The Design of Operating System/2, M S Kogan & F L Pawson, IBM Systems Journal, vol 27/2 p90, (1988).

2. Mastering OS/2, J Robbins, Sybex.

6

Peripherals for the 386 PC

One of the appealing features of the 386 PC is the variety of peripherals which can be attached to the machine and in this respect the 386 PC lends itself to a multitude of applications. Each application will require its own set of peripherals and due to its comprehensive design, the 386 PC can be configured to serve a wide variety of applications. When connecting a peripheral to a 386 PC for the first time, some problems should not be entirely unexpected. This is by no means a poor reflection on the quality of the product and it should be remembered that 386 PCs are complex devices which cater for a many and varied design of peripheral. Careful reading of the user manual, however poorly written it may be, can never be over stressed. If difficulties do persist and there is no communication between the 386 PC and the peripheral then a qualified dealer should be contacted.

Peripherals are interfaced to the 386 PC in one of three ways: through an RS-232 serial port (Section 3.3.2), a Centronics parallel port (Section 3.3.2), or an input/output (I/O) expansion interface card mounted in the 386 PC's card cage (Section 3.2). A thorough reading of the installation procedures is highly recommended to ensure proper and normal operation of the peripheral. Many peripherals are accompanied by a floppy disk containing **device drivers** and these are normally essential for correct operation. The device driver software is normally loaded into the 386 PC during the powering-up phase via the CONFIG.SYS or AUTOEXEC.BAT file. Some device drivers have the option of being loaded into Extended Memory (Section 2.3.4) and this location is preferable to base memory .

A peripheral which has its own interface card will have immediate access to the 386 PC's system data bus. It probably uses the direct access memory (DMA – Section 2.3.5) facility in the 386 PC; this has the advantage of being a very fast method for transferring data directly into and from the computer's memory by by-passing the 80386 CPU. The peripherals discussed in this chapter are essentially external to 386

PC and this has the benefit of allowing other users to use the devices since they are detachable from the 386 PC or alternatively may be allocated as a resource on a local area network.

6.1 Printers

One of the essential peripherals of any 386 PC is a printer, since output records detailing progress, will always be required. There is a vast range of printers to choose from and again the choice is determined by the intended application of the 386 PC and the available budget. The price of quality printers ranges from £200 for the standard matrix printer producing draft copies to in excess of £4,000 for a workhorse, high-quality printer with collated outputs. Since many printers have to work in office environments the current trend is towards the quiet printer design and these operate without having those hideous hoods which are not only unsightly and difficult to use, but also unnecessarily take up valuable space. Any thoughts of investing in a daisy wheel printer, which is inherently noisy, should be tempered with caution.

It is customary to find printers supplied with either the Centronics parallel interface or a RS-232 serial interface (or sometimes both). It is, however, preferable to have the printer linked to the parallel port for two reasons: firstly, the Centronics interface was designed specifically with a printer in mind and the default printer settings for most proprietary application programs running under DOS is LPT1 – the first parallel port. Secondly, using a parallel port for a printer frees the RS-232 ports for other peripherals. Printing is achieved in one of three modes: the straight character print commonly used for text, the more involved bit image dump for graphics printing, and the use of a **Page Description Language** (PDL) process.

A graphics image on the PC screen consists of an array of pixels and, during the bit image dump, each pixel is mapped to a corresponding point on the printed paper. Because it is a one-to-one mapping, the time required to print a screen can take several minutes. A graphics driver is required for this function and the one supplied with DOS is GRAPHICS.COM which requires an IBM or compatible printer to work properly. However many commercial application programs, which require a screen dump of graphics, come with their own selection of drivers for a range of printers and the appropriate driver should be chosen during the installation of the software.

A printer (or plotter) can be easily shared among several users by means of a **buffer switch.** The function of the buffer switch is to allow a number of users to output their print documents to a common printer. The buffer switch will have an internal memory of typically one Mbyte for queuing the documents and printing them in the order they arrive with a page eject (form feed) between each document. If there are two printers, a matrix printer for drafts and a laser printer, then a dual output buffer switch could be used. A typical buffer switch is the SPS Plus from Nighthawk which provides two simultaneous output paths, the appropriate path being chosen through an installed Hot Key program. The SPS Plus supports either parallel or serial links and has up to one Mbyte of buffer storage.

PostScript

The established standard in graphics printing is **PostScript** by Adobe. It is a Page Descriptive Language which is a software interface between the personal computer and the printer. Printing via PostScript has become very popular in desktop publishing and offers a high-quality finished product though the control it exercises over the printer. A printer hosting PostScript builds an image of the page within its memory and when the image is complete it is then printed. Adobe has been very shrewd in its marketing of PostScript and has only made an interpreter available on the grounds of a licensing agreement. A printer hosting the PostScript software interface will be expensive because of the additional Adobe PostScript premium. A number of very high-quality printers are equipped with PostScript, for example Dataproducts LZR-1260 laser printer.

Since the PostScript language is in the public domain a number of compatible PostScript interpreters have appeared on the market which can operate as a background task in a 386 PC multi-tasking environment. Two such PostScript interpreters are GoScript Plus from LaserGo (supplied in the UK by Graphic Sciences) and Freedom of Press from Custom Applications (supplied in the UK by Ctrl-Alt-Del). Their function is to take output PostScript files from application programs and convert them into equivalent files which can be accepted by laser printers to produce PostScript quality printing. The conversion process is CPU intensive and in addition requires a few Mbytes of memory. However it is certainly cheaper than a dedicated PostScript printer, but it does take a long time to prepare each page.

6.1.1 Dot Matrix Printers

The most commonly used, low-cost printer is the dot matrix, duly named because the head is made up of a matrix of small pins which are elevated forward to form a letter or character. These are forced forward onto an inked ribbon which impacts with the paper to reproduce the dot pin pattern forming the character. As each character is passed to the printer from the PC, it is used to address a **look-up table** for the appropriate pin pattern for that character. The look-up table is held in the printer's permanent memory. The printing head is affixed to a carriage which traverses the full width of the paper. Matrix printers are capable of simulating various types of fonts such as italics, Roman, small, large, elite and courier, generated by passing the special control characters to the printer. This type of information can be found in the printer's user manual which will also provide details on the character set options which are selected from switches.

When buying a matrix printer there are a number of factors to consider. The width is either 80 (A4) or 136 (A3) columns and there are two types of paper feeding mechanisms. With the tractor feed the perforations on the paper edges are pulled over cogged wheels and the other mechanism relies on a sheet feed where the paper is drawn around the roller. An example of an 80-column print, which has tractor and sheet feeding, is the Epson LX-850 (Figure 6.1). The 136-character printers, with their broader carriage, are ideal for spreadsheet work and an example of this type is the Epson LQ-1015 which also produces **letter quality** printing. The heads on matrix printers usually come in four sizes: 9 pin, the medium quality 18 pin, the superior quality 24 pin or the super with 48 pins. All modern dot matrix printers have a **near letter quality** (NLQ) feature as standard, which, as the title indicates, is supposed to produce type of near comparable quality to that of a high-quality typewriter. This is achieved by double striking each character with the printer head slightly displaced for the second strike. Printers with heads containing 24 pins usually provide letter quality (LQ) printing. An example of this is the Panasonic KX-P1540 (Figure 6.2 opposite) **which has a print rate of 80 characters per second** (CPS) in its LQ mode.

Figure 6.1 Epson's LX-850 9-pin dot matrix printer. (Photo: Courtesy of Epson)

If the printer is to be used for producing graphics then it is important to determine its dots per inch (dpi) specification as this is an indication of the printer's resolution. In general 11-pin matrix printers are not going to offer very good quality graphics. Often when performing a graphics dump the printer output may have a different aspect ratio to the PC screen and if this should occur then image compression will occur in the vertical plane. The printing rate is also an important characteristic and this value varies from printer to printer. The greater the CPS value the greater the throughput of information. However there will be a reduction in the printing rate if NLQ output is required. The Fujitsu DL-3400 for example will print at a rate of 60 CPS in its letter quality mode and 240 CPS in its draft mode. Some matrix printers are able to print colour by using a number of coloured ribbons. However the colour range is limited by the number of ribbons and in general the printing is not really very spectacular.

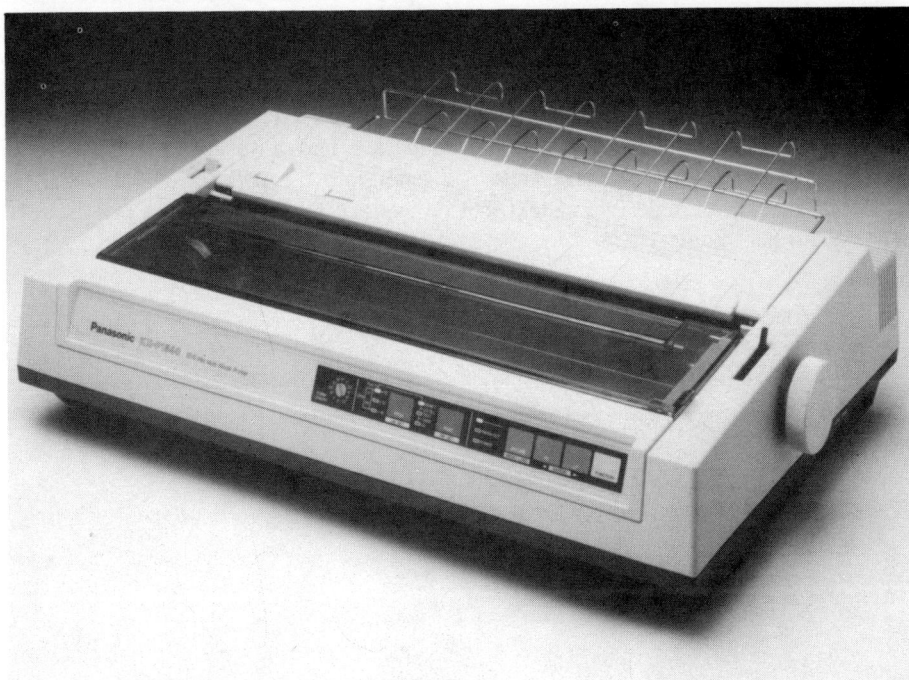

Figure 6.2 Panasonic's KX-P1540 24-pin printer. (Photo: Courtesy of Panasonic)

6.1.2 Laser Printers

In order to achieve high-quality printing and professional looking finished documents a laser printer will be required. The availability of laser printers has raised the standards of document presentation well above the boring typescript which has been endured for so many years. Many of today's laser printers have many interesting features such as printing on both sides of the paper and printing on envelopes. Laser printers can also be easily integrated into networked 386 PC systems. The technological achievement of the laser printer has led to a bewildering choice in fonts and graphical characters which, in turn, has led to the explosive growth of desktop publishing (DTP). Recognition of laser printers is now widespread among proprietary application programs and it is normal to find the inclusion of laser printer drivers. It is in fact rare to find a well furnished office without a laser printer as they have become indispensable printing tools.

In a laser printer, light from a semiconductor laser passes onto a several-sided rotating scanning mirror (normally an octagon prism – Figure 6.3). The reflected light from the rotating mirror falls onto a photosensitive drum and creates a very localised, electrostatically charged region. By switching the laser on and off very quickly a line of microscopic electrostatic dots appears on the drum as the light sweeps across it. When the drum comes in contact with the toner powder, the powder only sticks to the parts of the drum which are charged. As the paper rolls over the drum the powder is transferred onto the paper. The paper then passes into a fusing mechanism with heated rollers which presses and melts the toner into the paper. Several scans are required to create a single line of text, but on average laser printers can print several pages of A4 per minute.

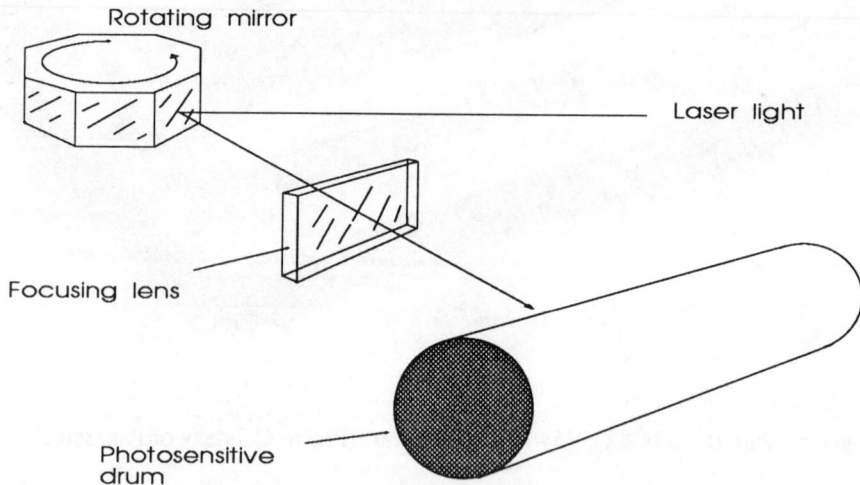

Figure 6.3 The principle of laser printing

Laser printers are supplied with memory buffers which should be a minimum of two Mbytes. This is especially useful when creating a graphics image on a printer, which will be the case for desktop publishing. A single screen image requires a lot of memory and to use the 386 PC's resources efficiently it should be possible to dump the image data into the printer's memory. This eliminates the need to tie up the 386 PC while graphics printing is taking place. The resolution in laser printers is measured in dots per inch (dpi) and this should be of the order of 300 dpi for typescript and in the range of 75 dpi to 300 dpi for graphics printing. For very high-quality printing a resolution greater than 300 dpi should be sought. In general the smaller the dpi value the grainier the final image.

The best known laser printers are the Hewlett Packard LaserJet Plus and the LaserJet Series II (Figure 6.4 opposite). Indeed the former has now become a standard among laser printers. Hewlett Packard has sold over a million of its laser printers and this indicated the extent to which they have penetrated the personal computer market. It is commonplace to find the manufacturers of other laser printers supplying their products with HP LaserJet Plus emulation software. To accommodate the large number of fonts HP supplys a variety of removable font cartridges and these augment the fonts already resident in the printer.

Figure 6.4 LaserJet Series II. (Photo: Courtesy of Hewlett Packard)

Third parties also produce cartridges for the HP LaserJet Series II. An example is the Hewlett Packard Graphics Language (HPGL) Emulation cartridge from Pacific Data Products of San Diego, which enables the HP LaserJet to emulate one of the HP Plotters. Another example is the PacificPage, also from Pacific, which is a PostScript language compatible cartridge. This cartridge converts the HP LaserJet into a PostScript compatible printer. The availability of these third party options for the LaserJet Plus II greatly enhances its capabilities.

The memory for the LaserJet Series II is also a flexible feature and can be expanded to 4.5 Mbytes. For users involved in desktop publishing a **Jet Script Accessory Kit** is available from HP for the Series II printer. It consists of a full length I/O expansion card which slots into the 386 PC's card cage and provides, among other things, on-line scaling of fonts, enhanced graphics and typescript manipulation.

Another laser printer which is growing in popularity is the Canon LBP-8 Mark III. It has a printing rate of eight ppm and a standard 1.5 Mbytes of memory. One appealing feature of the Mark III is the scalable font control which allows characters to be enlarged, rotated or and reduced as required. With the addition of a **Canon Virtual Device Metafile**, more complex character control can be exercised such as image clipping and variable angle transformations. In principle it is possible to achieve many of the desktop publishing functions without having to resort to PostScript.

For a 386 PC networked system where there is likely to be heavy use of the laser printer a typical workhorse printer, such as the Dataproducts LZR-1260, should be considered. It has a high print rate of 12 pages per minute (PPM) and its own intelligence is built on the Motorola 68020 16-bit microprocessor. It has dual bin 250-sheet feeder trays and a facility for handling up to 100 envelopes.

There are other printers based on technology which use light emitting diodes (LEDs) as light sources instead of lasers and liquid crystals as shutters. They work on the same principle of using an electrostatic drum and powder toner. Their introduction into optical printing technology should result in lower priced high-quality printers. An example of a printer based on this technology is the CrystalPrint from Qume which is furnished with PostScript to provide high-quality printing suitable for most desktop publishing applications.

6.1.3 Colour Printers

A number of colour printers are based on thermal-transfer technology and these produce hard-copy high-quality and high-resolution images. They are very attractive for desktop publishing, graphic art, textile design and solid modelling for CAD applications. Thermal transfer printers offer a wide choice of colours (of the order of 4000 different shades) and this is achieved with internal video processing techniques. Much of the early work on colour thermal printers was pioneered by Mitsubishi with its designs in thermal transfer technology.

A key feature of the design of a thermal printer is the ink ribbon which is fabricated from polyester film. The film, which is several microns thick, is coated with a wax-based ink which has a low melting point. As the ribbon comes into contact with the paper it passes between a platen roller and the thermal printing head (TPH). The TPH is an array of individually heated elements mounted in a ceramic housing and these cause localised melting on the ribbon. The molten wax ink is then squashed into the paper from the action of the roller. The three basic colours for thermal printing are cyan, yellow and magenta. To generate the wide array of colours, a technique known as **subtractive colour mixing** is employed. This involves the successive overprinting on the paper with additional colours, blue, red, black and green.

To achieve good quality, paper alignment during the overprinting is critical. Not only must the colour ribbons have good contact with the paper but the their offset must be carefully controlled to prevent mis-registering. This is achieved by ensuring that the TPH is maintained in a parallel position with respect to the platen roller. In the design of the TPH it is important to have the heating of each element isolated from adjacent elements. This produces sharp edges and good colour definition. In addition the thermal capacity of each element must be low to ensure fast printing.

Having established a method for producing discrete colour pixels on a sheet of paper, a question arises on how to distribute the pixels to form what appears to the eye to be a continuous colour range. A technique known as dithering is frequently used which calls on one of two algorithms: the direct and the magic square. Figure 6.5a shows the order of colouring for an element made from 3 x 3 pixels, using direct dithering. In the magic square algorithm the order number for each row and column adds up to 15. With an array of 3 x 3 pixels there are nine possible shades for the three basic colours as can be seen in Figure 6.5b. Any one of the eight shades is built up from filling in pixels in the numerical order of the array with each colour defined in a pixel map. The overall effect of dithering the pixel positions in this manner is to convince the eye of a smoother range of colours than actually exists. To increase the colour range an array of 4 x 4 pixels can be used, at the expense of the resolution.

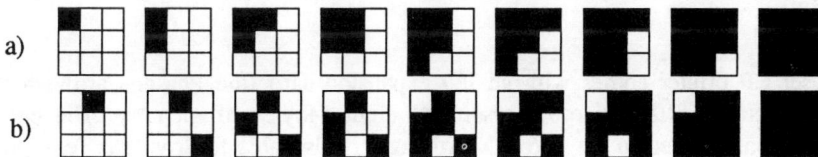

Figure 6.5 Dithering techniques: a) direct b) magic square

One commercially available thermal transfer printer, that incorporates many of these features, is the Mitsubishi G650 (Figure 6.6 overleaf) which has a magazine quality resolution of 300 dpi. To accompany the G series printers there is the MGC-10 controller I/O expansion card which has emulators for several commercial plotters. It is also furnished with half a Mbyte of memory which holds the drawing data thereby relieving the 386 PC of the printing overhead.

An alternative thermal transfer printer is the Phaser CP (Colour Printer) from Tektronix which is armed with a PostScript-compatible page description language. It has a resolution of 300 dpi and either three or four colour wax ribbons – yellow, cyan, magenta and black. Printing is performed in single colour horizontal lines, which is repeated with overprinting for the other colours.

Figure 6.6 The Mitsubishi 6650 Thermal Colour printer. (Photo: Courtesy of Mitsubishi)

The Phaser CP printer comes with an I/O expansion card (the Phaser Card) which hosts a Motorola 68020 microprocessor and eight Mbytes of memory. The card, which is accommodated in the 386 PC card cage, is also able to drive the Tektronix laser printers. The function of the Phaser Card is to convert PostScript and HPGL instructions which can be recognised by the Phaser CP. Images or drawings can be dumped into the card and the printing becomes a separate task from the main PC operation.

6.1.4 The DeskJet Plus and PaintJet Printers

Hewlett Packard has always been innovative in the design and development of printers. Two products worthy of mention are the DeskJet Plus and the PaintJet printers. The DeskJet Plus (Figure 6.7) has many of the features of a laser printer at a fraction of the cost. The printing mechanism employs a thermal technique whereby the ink is heated in minute quantities and the created pressure forces the ink out of a nozzle onto the paper. The so called **drop-on-demand** design has 50 ink cells which constitute the print position and the resulting quality is very close to that of the laser printer.

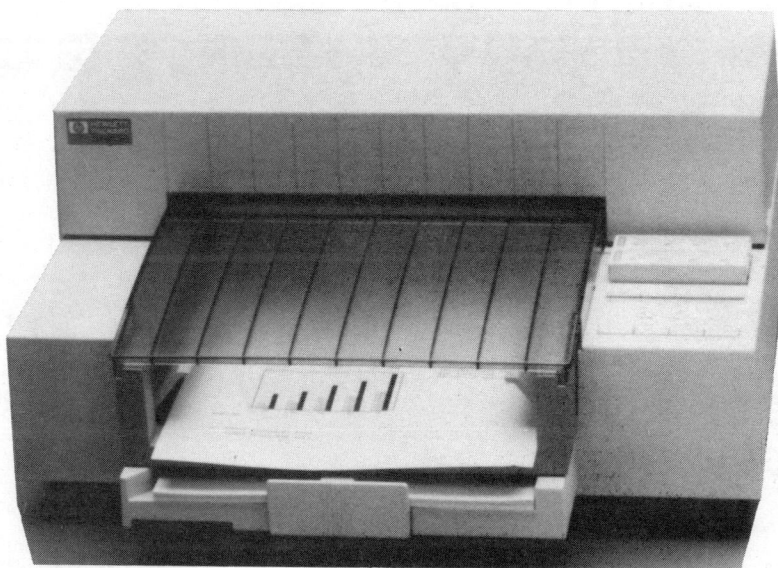

Figure 6.7 The DeskJet Plus. (Photo: Courtesy of Hewlett Packard)

The DeskJet Plus comes with a serial RS-232 and a parallel interface and can therefore be configured for either LPTn or COMn. Although the printing rate is low, 45 seconds for a 55-line page, it does offer a reasonable graphics resolution of 300 dpi. The DeskJet Plus comes with a number of fonts as standard – six portrait and four landscape fonts – however this number can be increased with additional cartridges. Used to enhance its facilities, there is a whole variety of cartridges which can be plugged into the DeskJet Plus. These include two sizes of RAM cartridge (128K and 256K), an Epson FX-80 emulation cartridge and a number of Times Roman font cartridges. With RAM cartridges, the total memory of the printer can be increased to half a Mbyte of RAM. To capitalise on the features of the DeskJet Plus, when using commercial application programs special printer drivers will have to be used. The range of drivers available include Microsoft Word, MultiMate, Lotus 1-2-3, Harvard Graphics and Word Perfect.

The Hewlett Packard PaintJet printer (Figure 6.8) also works on the ink drop-on-demand principle and is capable of providing seven main colours with a resolution of 180 dpi. However, through software control several thousands of colour shades can be generated. The printing rate is 167 NLQ characters per second spaced at 10 per inch. The mechanism for printing relies on two cartridges (black and colour) and there are 60 nozzles in each, 30 for the black and 10 each for the other primary printing colours, cyan, magenta and yellow.

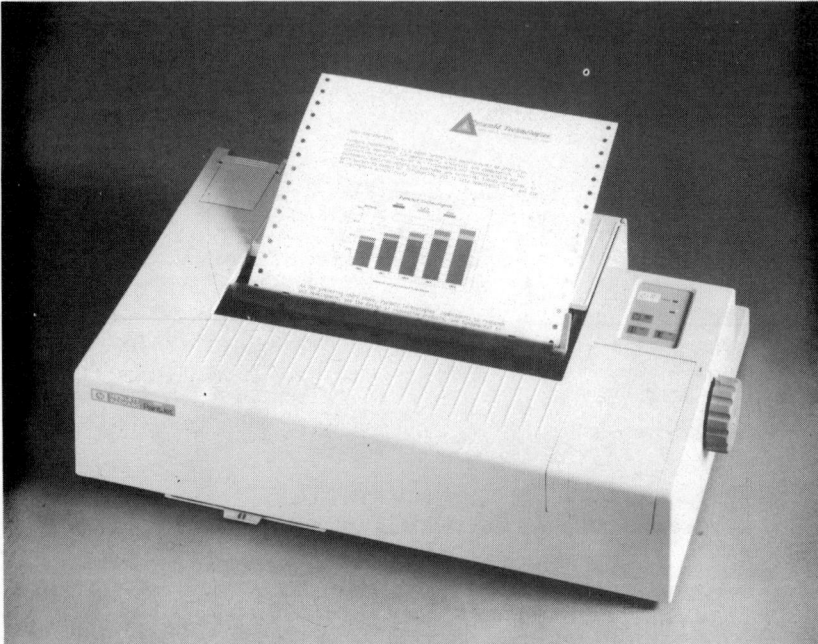

Figure 6.8 The PaintJet. (Photo: Courtesy of Hewlett Packard)

The character set for the PaintJet includes Roman8, the normal ASCII and a variety of European options. It has a font range of 10-pitch Courier, 12- and 18-pitch Letter Gothic Bold, underline, superscript and subscript. In addition to the 8K internal memory buffer, there are three options of interfacing: parallel, RS-232 and IEEE-488.

6.1.5 Image File Formats

Computer peripherals which, in one way or another, involve image printing, plotting or capturing, need to use file formats for storing their images. Over the last few years the task of establishing standards for image files has taken many directions. The result is that today there are several image file formats which are recognised by software producers. Image file formats can be broadly grouped into two camps. The first, referred to as the **bit-map** or **raster**, consists of a matrix of data points where every pixel is represented by a data point in the matrix. There is said to be a one to one mapping between the pixels and the data points in the matrix. This type of format, often used in paint programs, allows to some extent textures, different coloured brush strokes and smooth rounded images to be created. However bit-images do suffer when enlargements are made as the jagged edge of each discrete bit becomes visible.

The other method, referred to as the **vector-oriented** format, has feature constructs, such as straight lines which are defined by their two end points. Each construct has anchor and control data points which define its length and the curvature of its line segments. Application programs which use vector files are required to perform intensive calculations in the reconstruction of the image from the file. As the control data points are extracted from the file, the path connecting the points (a Bezier curve) must be calculated.

In addition there will be secondary control points, tangent points, which are used to improve the definition of the path's curvature. A vector file will consist of control points, anchor points and drawing instructions for each feature construct.

One of the key advantages of an application program using a vector file, is its ability to transform the image by manipulating the control points to create any desired size and projection of the image. The technique for storing images in vector files is frequently used by computer-aided design (CAD) application programs. Vector files can sometimes be transferred to intelligent plotters or printers for producing hard copies of the appropriate size. It is a relatively straightforward task, using the technique of auto-tracing, to transform bit-map formatted files into vector orientated files.

The abundance of graphic file format standards often leads to confusion. Some of the more commonly used formats. with their . tags – which act as distinguishing features – are outlined here.

.CGM	Computer Graphics Metafile; in common use and supported by PageMaker (Section 9.2.2) and Ventura (9.2.1).
.DRW	Micrografx DRaW; a format used in Microsoft Windows/386 and generally supported by application programs produced by Micrografx. The size of .DRW files can exceed 64K.
.DXB	Data eXchange Binary file; a binary version of .DXF which requires less storage space,

.DXF   Data eXhange File; a format devised by Autodesk to enhance the appeal of its prime product AutoCAD (Section 9.3.2) by encouraging third party software houses to produce Auto-CAD compatible software. .DXF files can be large and the alternative format .DXB is frequently used.

.PIC   Lotus PICture file; devised by Lotus for the storage of graphs produced from Lotus 1-2-3. Generally supported by many desktop publishing application programs.

.WMF   Windows Metafile Format; initially designed to allow graphics information to be exchanged between applications programs running in the Microsoft Windows environment. It is only used within windows and its file size is limited to 64K, the size of the Windows Clipboard feature.

.PCX   PC Paintbrush; paint program images.

.TIF   Tagged Image File; a standard often used in image files where the tag holds information relating to colour.

.EPS   Encapsulated PostScript; primarily introduced to cater for the image files used in desktop publishing. .EPS is an amalgam of a bit-image format and a vector oriented format. The screen image map is stored as a tagged image file format (TIFF) while the vector portion is taken up in the PostScript language (Section 6.1). This enables devices with the licensed PostScript facility to interpret .EPS files.

.IMG   Graphics Environmental Manager (GEM) Images; Digital Research produced its famous graphical environment GEM and the accompanying format for storing images .IMG, which is now recognised by several application programs.

HPGL   Hewlett Packard Graphics Language; conceived by HP primarily for its pen plotters and is now a well accepted standard (Section 6.3).

IGES   Initial Graphics Exchange Specification; a format used by a number of computer aided design and drafting packages. Although it was originally intended for transferring image files between mainframe systems and workstations or PCs, IGES has suffered from variations in standards. It is however recognised by AutoCAD.

TIFF	Tagged Image File Format; developed by Microsoft and Aldus with great expectation of becoming a standard among image file formats. The tag is a data field within the TIFF file which contains information pertaining to the nature of the image. Colour information is held within the tag and in a monochrome image the tag information would refer to the levels of grey scaling.

Many application programs which manipulate image files are capable of coping with several image files formats and this is especially true of PageMaker, Ventura and other desktop publishing packages. Although there are several image file formats, Graphics Link Plus, by HSC Software, will allow the conversion of raster image file formats into other raster formats which are more acceptable to the application programs which do not display the same choice of input image formats.

6.2 The Image Scanner

One frequent requirement of a 386 PC is the acquisition and storage of images and pictures. Whether it is for archival purposes, image processing or for publishing, transferring an image onto the 386 PC monitor can be achieved with a variety of image scanning systems. Image scanners are finding increasing applications in areas which use picture databases. These areas include desktop publishing (Section 9.2), product design, cosmetic layouts, screen print design, pattern drawing and advertising. In fact organisations, such as estate and model agencies, involved in image manipulation and storage will find the opportunities offered by a picture database based on a 386 PC very appealing.

To achieve a high-quality image representation of the original it is necessary to have the 386 PC equipped with a video graphics array (VGA – Section 4.3.3) monitor with a screen resolution of at least 680 x 480 dots and a maximum colour presentation. High-quality images do take up considerable amounts of memory: one Mbyte per image (680 x 480 x 3 primary colours) for bit mapped storage. If rapid picture processing and manipulation is also needed then memory with a fast access time will be required. Storing high-quality images on hard disks will also require large amounts of space and if this is necessary then a large capacity hard disk (100 Mbytes) should be used.

There are at least three types of image which can be processed, the first being line artwork which is either black or white – engineering drawings come into this category. The production of an image from this type of input is a relatively straightforward task. The second type of image is the black and white photograph which is constructed from many shades of grey. The difficulty arises when trying to represent the range of grey shades. It is these which give the image contrast and by limiting the range of grey shades the quality of the image suffers. The third type of image is text based and there may be a requirement for translating the text-image into actual character text which can be imported into a word processor for further editing.

There are basically two methods used by scanner manufacturers for coping with the grey processing problem. The first method is known as dithering – a measurement is made of the intensity of a grey level and this is compared with a range of threshold values. The outcome of the comparison is used to produce a dot pattern whose density is dependent on the level of the initial grey level. In the scanners which use this dither technique the output is normally stored in .PCX, .PIC or .IMG (GEM files) format. In this format, a limited amount of extra editing is possible by using a paint software package (GEM). The second method is known as grey scaling. The actual magnitude of the intensity of the grey level is measured. The scanner stores the measured values in a file which is representative of the original image. The file format for this type of image storage is usually the tagged image file format (TIFF). The processing of grey scale images can be performed by the CPU or alternatively special purpose I/O expansion cards can be used. Microtek manufactures a coprocessor board which processes the image ready for the HP LaserJet Series II. This performs high-quality grey scale processing which results in magazine standard pictures.

Translating text-image into actual character text is no easy task and to achieve this a form of **optical character recognition** (OCR) must to be used which is usually performed in software. The first task in a OCR process is to re-define the grey-scaled data in the input file into black and white levels according to a pre-defined threshold value. The characters in the image text are then isolated and compared with tables of known characters. Referred to as **font recognition** or **matrix matching**, when there is a match an ASCII character is generated. If there is no match the OCR can take the translated part of the word and run it through a spell checker and make a guess. If there is a need for feature recognition, font types and styles, then greater demands are placed on the OCR software and a number of packages have risen to this challenge. An I/O expansion board, manufactured by Calera Recognition, is known as the TrueScan Model E hosts four Mbytes of RAM to hold the scanned page and is specified to read 100 characters per second. It has a recognition library of several thousand font characters and forms the interface between the scanner and the 386 PC. It is able to convert text bit-image files from a scanner into four types of files:

❑ 32 word processing formats

❑ Eight image formats

❑ Compact ASCII file format

❑ Three spreadsheet formats

The TrueScan is compatible with several makes of scanner including the HP ScanJet Plus and the Cannon Image Scanner IX-12F. An alternative product is the Omnipage OCR system which is a software package and an I/O expansion card which hosts its own memory and coprocessor for the task of optical recognition. It can accept a variety of scanner file formats. OCR systems should contribute greatly towards the paperless office, although the advent of the personal computer has actually made greater demands on the supply of paper. It is anticipated that this demand will now begin to fall with the availability of information input devices like scanners, and low-cost storage media.

There are at least three sources from which images can be derived:

❑ Document scanners

❑ Video or CCD cameras

❑ Camcorders and video cassette recorders.

All of these can have varying scales of image quality. After capturing an image the scanning system will store the image in a format which can be easily imported into the popular desktop publishing packages such as Ventura or PageMaker. The variety of data file formats for storing images include the **raster image file format** (RIFF), the tagged image file format (TIFF), the GEM format (.IMG files) and the PCX format. When specifying a scanner attention should be focussed on the output and optical resolutions, measured in dots per inch (dpi), the scaling facilities and accompanying software drivers.

An example of a commercial scanner is the Hewlett Packard ScanJet Plus (Figure 6.9 overleaf) which is based on a CCD image sensor. It is suitable for producing images of photographs or drawings and has an output resolution of up to 600 dpi, an optical resolution of 300 dpi and a scaling range between 0.07 to 1.58. The grey scaling has up to 256 different levels which provide good quality images and is available with the ReadRight International Optical Character Recogniser (OCR) software. Provided with the ScanJet is the Scanning Gallery software which, in its run-time version, functions under Windows/386. However the ScanJet Plus does require an HP ScanJet Plus interface board which will occupy one of the I/O expansion slots in the card cage.

If an image is required of a solid three-dimensional object then a system such as the Chinon DESKSCAN 3000 (distributed by Firdata) can be used. It has a maximum output resolution of 300 dpi and takes 24 seconds, at this resolution, to cover its scan area of 196 mm by 281 mm. It uses the dither technique with 16 levels of dot size. It connects to the 386 PC via an RS-232 serial port and can transmit at 19,200 bits/sec.

There is an optional I/O expansion card which enables data transfer direct to the 386 PCs memory. Among the other options is a copy of the ReadRight OCR software and

PC Paintbrush Plus which is useful for editing the image once it has been captured from the scanner. There is a choice of standard output file formats: .IMG, TIFF, TIFF-compressed and .PCX.

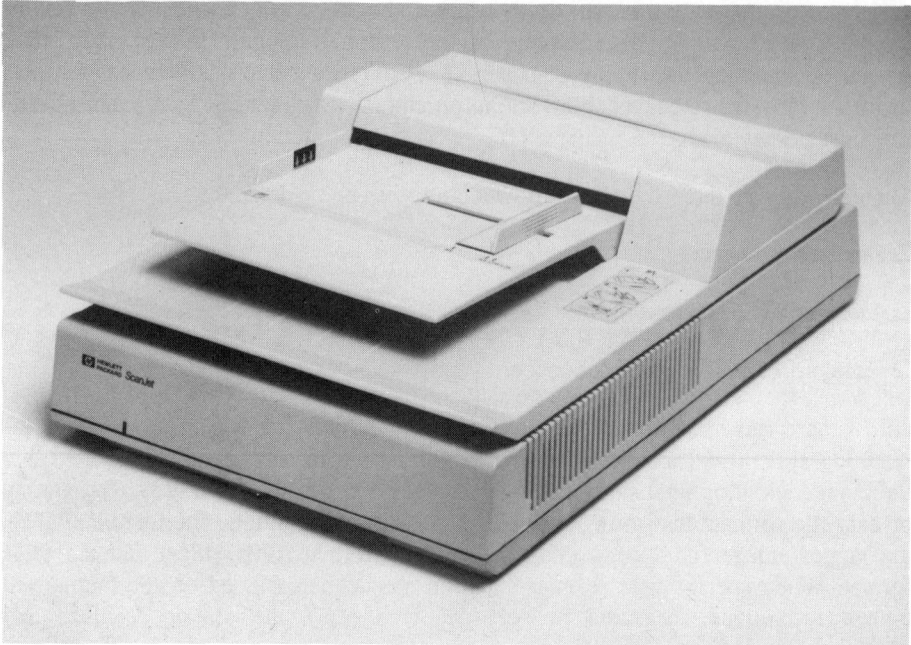

Figure 6.9 The Hewlett Packard ScanJet Plus. (Photo: Courtesy of Hewlett Packard)

Alternatively the Cannon Image Scanner IX-12F, which is a sheet-feed device in contrast with the flat-bed design of the HP ScanJet Plus, also uses the ReadRight OCR software. However in its raw state it is only for character recognition. Only if third-party graphics programs are used can it cope with graphics or picture inputs. Control can be exercised over the scan area which has the advantage of blanking out pictures to prevent the ReadRight software from becoming confounded.

For scanning colour images the JX300 from Sharp is one option. The original image or picture is scanned four times to disperse the colours into cyan, magenta, yellow and black which can then be saved in tagged image file format (TIFF). The resolution of the JX300 is 300 dpi, however it does make significant demands on the processing power of the 386 PC and requires substantial memory – four Mbytes minimum.

An alternative colour scanner is available from Howtek, the Scanmaster II which can digitise A4 colour images and has a maximum resolution of 300 dpi. Also available with the Scanmaster II is an application program, Scan-It, which allows image cropping (hiving off the required part of the image), colour correction and contrast adjustments.

This brief discussion of a few of the many scanners which are available commercially should provide you with enough information to recognise the attributes of a particular design and to be able to determine whether a specific scanner will satisfy your present and future requirements. There are many scanners on the market all having their strengths and weaknesses and you should consider the following:

❑ Compatibility

❑ Speed of scanning

❑ Resolution

❑ Output file characteristics

❑ Image sources, text bit-image, line image or photograph

❑ Future upgrades

❑ Compatibility with OCR software.

The scanner can be a very useful device and is invaluable in desktop publishing applications (Section 9.2). However it should be remembered that a scanner with its own personality I/O expansion card may present difficulties in a multi-user system unless the facility can be accessed through a local area network (LAN).

6.3 Plotters

In many applications for 386 PCs, a plotter is an indispensable peripheral and there are many on the market to choose from. Computer Aided Design/Draughting (CADD) is one particular area where a high-quality plotting facility is required. The choice of a plotter will, to a large extent, be governed by the expected throughput, size of the plots and the quality of the finished product. Plotters are available to accommodate paper sizes ranging from the smallest A4 up to A0. If there are several 386 PCs on a Local Area Network (LAN) and the plotting throughput is likely to be large then it is advisable to attach the plotter to the LAN and allocate it as a plotter server (Section 8.5) on the LAN.

For a single user there are two ways of ensuring that the plotter does not tie up the resources of the 386 PC. The first is to enable the plotting to run as a background task in a multi-tasking environment. The other method is to choose a plotter with upgradable RAM (at least one Mbyte) to allow the whole plot to be dumped into the plotter's RAM. Several plotters have this latter option and the additional RAM can vary from one Mbyte to five Mbytes depending on the plotter size.

Currently there is a standard which has been adopted by many plotter manufacturers, the Hewlett Packard Graphics Language or HPGL. This standard allows simple graphics commands to be translated into actual pen movements. The HPGL software (firmware) is embedded in the control electronics of the plotter and as the plot instructions are passed, they are converted into the pen movements.

6.3.1 Vector Plotter Designs

Currently there several pen plotter designs, also referred to as vector plotters, and there are three designs which warrant discussion. The first is the flatbed or X-Y plotter which holds a flat sheet of paper electrostatically and the drawing pen moves in an X-Y direction over the drawing area. An example of this type of plotter is the Roland DPX-1300, distributed by Number One Systems, which has eight pens and a standard buffer of one Mbyte (Figure 6.10). It is supplied with a Centronics parallel and an RS-232 serial interface and responds to RD-GL I commands which are compatible with the HPGL.

Figure 6.10 The DPX-1300 flat-bed X-Y plotter. (Photo: Courtesy of Roland Digital)

The second type of plotter uses a pinch wheel design with two pairs of narrow gritted drums situated close to the edges of the paper. As the drums rotate, the paper, with its edges sandwiched between them, is drawn along the breadth of the plotter. The writing pen, which resides on a carriage, moves perpendicularly and in conjunction with the motion of the paper. One of the plotters based on this design is the Hewlett Packard 7475A (A3 or A4) which has a six-pen carousel and has proved to be very popular with its self-loading page feed and fast plotting rate.

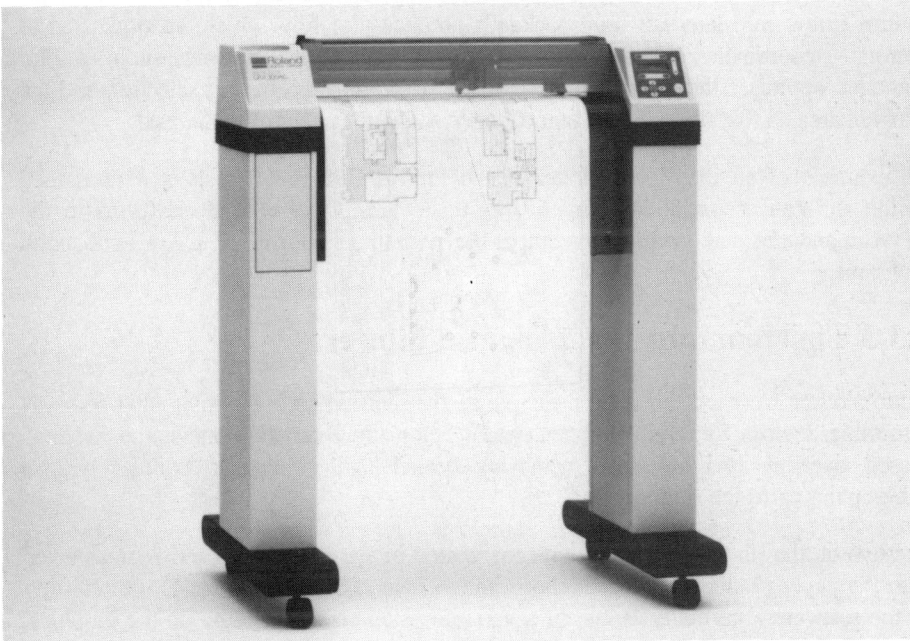

Figure 6.11 GRX-300 Drafting Plotter. (Photo: Courtesy of Roland Digital)

The third type of plotter, suitable for large-area work (up to A0), is the draughting plotter which is able to cope with large batches of complex plots. In this design a roller, extending the full A0 width, supports only a narrow region of the paper. The edges of the paper are held between gritted drums similar to the pinch wheel design. The pen(s) is carried along the width of the drawing area in a brace that moves in conjunction with the movement of the paper. An example of this category of plotter is the Roland GRX-300 Drafting Plotter (Figure 6.11) which is ideally suited for CAD applications. The GRX-300 recognises the RD-GL II graphics language which is compatible with the HPGL and the plotter offers very high-resolution drawing down to 0.00006 inches per step.

6.3.2 Intelligent Plotters

One feature which brings out the quality of a plotter is the firmware within the electronics of the plotter. This firmware has a number of tasks to optimise, such as pen drawing speed, pen travel speed and pen acceleration, and it is therefore responsible for managing the pen and paper motion and should perform the drawing with the minimum number of pen movements. It is now recognised that a plotter with good intelligence will outperform a faster-rated plotter which only has rudimentary control firmware. Many software packages produce plot files which are organised as vectors – coordinates and lines to be drawn. Intelligent firmware, such as Plot Manager, optimises the vectors in the plot file by organising the pen selection and the drawing area so that unnecessary pen changes and pen travel are minimised.

An example of an intelligent plotter is the Philips PM8153, which is of a flatbed design and can accommodate paper sizes up to A3. The PM8153 conforms to the HPGL standards and is directly compatible with the majority of CAD application programs.

6.3.3 Thermal and Electrostatic Plotters

Some plotters work on the same principle as the thermal colour printers and serve as admirable devices for producing respectable plots. In thermal plotters, the paper is passed over an imaging head which is heated and is also in contact with a three-colour cartridge ribbon.

The dye on the ribbon in contact with the heated image head melts and is transferred onto the paper producing a clean, sharp image. The choice of colours is limited only by the software – normally 16 out of a variable pallet size depending on the graphics. An example of a thermal plotter is the ColorView from Calcomp which prints onto A3 size paper.

Electrostatic plotters, also known as raster plotters, offer an alternative technology to the thermal plotter. The black and white or coloured images produced in electrostatic plotters are made up of closely spaced dots and respectable resolutions in excess of 400 dots per inch (dpi) are available on some. With a high-density of 400 dpi, images with near-straight lines can be produced and this is leading to a general acceptance of electrostatic plotters as a viable device.

If fast throughput is essential then electrostatic plotters can offer a 30 times increase over the conventional pen plotter. However, in general they tend to be more expensive. The Hewlett Packard 240D is an example of an electrostatic plotter. It has a resolution of 406 dpi and is suitable for applications which require large A1 plots.

The majority of engineering software packages tend to store their line drawings as a vector plot file which is not suitable for electrostatic plotters operating with raster scans. A vector-to-raster conversion is therefore required which will be a memory intensive operation since each line in the vector file will have to be converted to a series of dots.

On a 386 PC it is preferable to install this vector-to-raster conversion as a DOS task in a multi-tasking environment. Alternatively some electrostatic plotters have their own disk drives and vector-to-raster conversion software. The whole vector file can therefore be downloaded to the plotter without tying up any of the 386 PC's resources.

6.4 Digitising Tablets

There are several applications where a requirement arises to load a two or three-dimension plane drawing into a 386 PC to allow alternative perspectives and scaling. This can be achieved by using a digitising tablet which is a flat surface of standard size (normally A3 or larger) with a movable cursor or puck which has a number of button controls.

Specifically designed to manually input line drawing data into a computer, the majority of digitising tablets are of the flat-bed design and are particularly useful in CAD/CAM, graphic design, animation, and desktop publication work. The tablet itself should be smooth and designed to allow the original drawing to be secured onto its surface. The cursor, which must be free to move over the whole surface of the drawing, must have precision cross-wires to allow accurate alignment with the details on the drawing. The alignment depends on the resolution of the cursor and ought to adjustable; as a guide this could range between 0.025 mm to 25 mm. One of the buttons on the cursor will enter the data point and the remaining buttons are user-programmable.

In essence the working area of the digitising tablet should be a direct map of the 386 PC monitor and it is possible to obtain tablet overlays to scale the screen layout of many design packages. These overlays will feature the icons and the menu options of the software package. The digitising tablet may also be supplied with a stylus pen which can be used with great effect for freehand drawings. A serious user of the GEM graphics software will require a stylus pen to create accurate and well controlled drawings. Very effective use can be made of the digitising tablet for importing three-dimensional plane drawings into CAD software packages. The images can then be viewed in 3-D and rotated to obtain alternative perspectives and solid modelling of the drawings. AutoCAD/386 is one software package which has this option.

Many digitising tablets are interfaced to the 386 PC via one of the RS-232 ports and come with the appropriate software to set up the interface port. The majority of drawing or CAD software packages have installation procedures where the user is asked, via menu displays, for information on the peripherals attached to the 386 PC. It is customary to find the options for the digitising tablets among the mouse support listings.

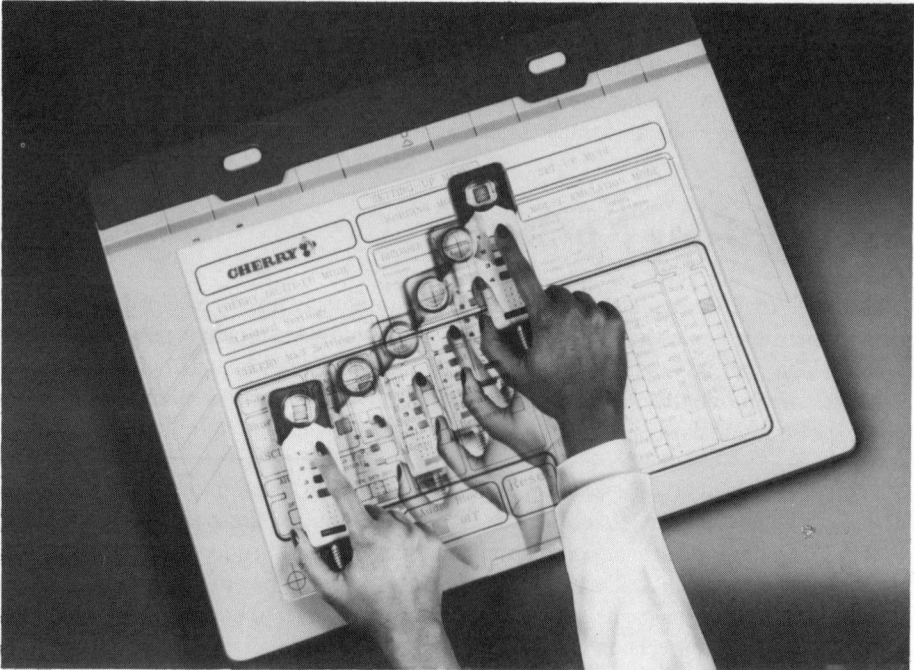

Figure 6.12 Cherry's Digitiser Mk4. (Photo: Courtesy of Cherry Electrical Products)

An example of a commercially available digitising tablet is the Digitiser Mk.4 from Cherry (Figure 6.12); it is supplied with a four-button cursor and a stylus pen. It has maximum baud rate of 38,400 which translates to a remarkable 200 coordinate pairs per second. The minimum resolution goes down to 0.025 mm and the working area is 42 cm by 29.7 cm. An alternative design is the Puma Sketch 1 from Hitachi. This product consists of a 12 x 12 inch digitising tablet with a stylus pen. The design uses induction technology and has an accuracy of .025 mm. Also included in the package is a variety of mouse drivers and emulators.

Further Reading:

1. Hewlett-Packet Laser Printer Power Pack, S J Bennett & P G Randall, Brady (Prentice Hall).

2. The Laserjet Handbook, S J Bennett & P G Randall, Brady (Prentice Hall).

7

Enhancements for the 386 PC

There are many enhancements that can be made to the 386 PC and this chapter will deal with several of the devices which can be accommodated in the input/output expansion card cage. Enhancing the 386 PC with expansion cards has the effect of enlarging its functionality for new applications. Each application will have differing needs and the comprehensive design of the 386 PC will allow it to be configured for an impressive range of applications. This chapter will review the range of expansion cards which are currently available for the purposes of PC enhancement. However network adaptor cards are covered in Chapter 8.

When inserting an expansion card into a 386 PC some problems should not be entirely unexpected. Most expansion cards have default settings and these may be incompatible with other cards which may exist in the 386 PC. The importance of reading the user manual cannot be over stated. The manual should provide sufficient information to avoid possible contention problems between neighbouring cards. As an illustration, many expansion cards use the direct access memory (DMA – Section 2.3.5) facility in the 386 PC. DMA has the advantage of providing a very fast method for transferring data directly into and from the 386 PC's memory by by-passing the 80386 microprocessor. Careful attention should therefore be paid to the DMA default setting to avoid the risk of possible contention problems.

7.1 Modems

If there is a requirement to transmit information between personal computers which are located at remote sites then modems can be used. The modem (short for modulate – demodulate) uses public subscription telephone lines and is available as either an external unit or an expansion card which fits into the 386 PC. It is a very effective device for implementing communication between a 386 PC and on-line commercial services such as bulletin boards. Alternatively the user may want set up a communication link between two remote personal computer and this is referred to as a **point-to-point** application. Modems are by no means simple devices to understand and the breadth of technology which surrounds them can be quite bewildering. When using high-performance modems it is not an easy task to achieve a proper operation of a point-to-point system and great care must be taken to ensure they are compatible.

Using the **Public Switched Telephone Network** (PSTN) as a communication medium for computers does present problems. The PSTN was naturally designed for transmitting the human voice in an analogue format and the frequencies that can be transmitted range from 300 Hz to 3 kHz. This is referred to as the bandwidth and any modem design is limited to work within this PSTN frequency range. The effect of this 'small' bandwidth is to limit the rate of data transmission or throughput between personal computer systems.

To add to the difficulty, the PSTN has various filters, amplifiers and equalisers to suppress echoes, and maintain intelligible speech over long distances. The accumulative effect of this is to render digital transmission over the PSTN almost impossible. Therefore before transmission of the serial digital signal, from the computer, it must first be converted into an analogue equivalent signal and after transmission, the original digital signal must be recovered. These are the principal functions of the modem and this two-phase conversation process is called modulation and demodulation which is the essence of **broadband transmission** (Section 8.1.2).

There is an additional effect which is evident in the PSTN and that is background noise. The strength or amplitude of the transmitted analogue signal can vary and as this becomes contaminated with noise the demodulation process will have difficulty in recovering the original data. In general, the greater the transmission rate the greater the effect of the background noise and this places practicable limitations on the transmission speed of modems. However high-speed modems, which employ clever processing techniques, can comfortably cope with an equivalent digital transmission rate of 9,600 bits per second (BPS).

7.1.1 Baud Rate and Modulation

In communication systems, there is often confusion between baud rate and bits per second (BPS). In a digital systems, where information data is represented in binary logic levels 0 and 1, the BPS is a measure of how many binary changes (0s and 1s) can be transmitted in a second. In analogue transmission systems, a carrier tone frequency (or a number of carrier tone frequencies) is used to impress the data (see Figure 7.1a opposite). The mechanism for impressing data on such a carrier frequency is known as a **modulation** and the **modulation rate** is known as the **baud rate.**

There are a number of modulation techniques which are commonly used and in low-speed modems (300 BPS) **frequency-shift key** (FSK), a type of frequency modulation, is normally employed. In FSK modulation two frequencies are used, a low frequency to represent a 0 and a high frequency to represent a 1. The transmission from an FSK modem is therefore a sequence of high and low-frequency bursts which reflect the data flow (Figure 7.1b). In this case, the baud rate and the BPS are identical. An alternatively modulation method is **phase-shift keying** (PSK), which is a form of phase modulation. In PSK a single carrier frequency is used and the logic levels are assigned to different phase positions of the carrier. However the receiving modem can only detect a phase transition and a technique known as **differential phase-shift keying** (DPSK) is used. In a two-state PSK regime, within each carrier cycle the logic level 0 corresponds to a null phase transition and logic level 1 corresponds to a 180° phase transition (Figure 7.1c). The transmitting modem therefore sends out a single tone which has a sequence of phase transitions impressed upon it.

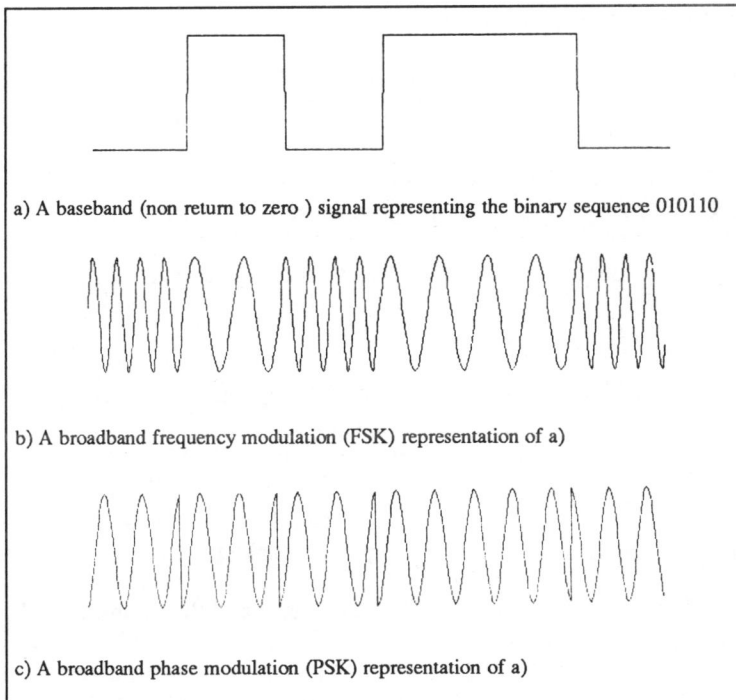

a) A baseband (non return to zero) signal representing the binary sequence 010110

b) A broadband frequency modulation (FSK) representation of a)

c) A broadband phase modulation (PSK) representation of a)

Figure 7.1 Methods of modulation

To achieve higher bit transfer rates, using the same carrier frequency, one of many **multi-level PSK** modulation methods can be used. With these techniques a single carrier cycle may contain several phase transitions each one representing a logical value. This means that each baud or carrier cycle can carry several digital bits. In practical terms a baud rate of 600 can accommodate a bit rate of 2,400 BPS. By combining multi-level phase modulation with analogue modulation a technique known as **Quadrature Amplitude Modulation** (QAM) can be realised The overall effect of using QAM is to increase the information carrying capacity of PSTN. The information capacity of QAM is normally denoted by 2-bit, 4-bit or 6-bit QAM and this signifies the number of bits carried on each baud. However in the context of modems, what is important is the transmission rate of digital bits passing through the system which is the BPS.

Modems normally have options for their operational baud rate: 600, 1,200, 2,400, 4,800 and so on and it is usual for them to work at the highest rate. However if the quality of the local PSTN does not permit operation at the highest rate the modem performs a **fall back** to a baud rate which can be used without appreciable transmission errors.

7.1.2 Transmission Methods

Many modems are capable of performing **synchronous** and **asynchronous** data transmission. Also referred to as start-stop transmission, asynchronous data transfer occurs when the period between the transfer of data characters is of random length. The character is embedded in a packet which also contains start and stop bits. While the receiving modem is waiting for a character it is held in a marking condition (high-level). The beginning of the packet occurs with a mark to space (low-level) transition and when the receiving modem detects this transition it begins sampling the line. After receiving the character it detects the stop bit(s) and then passes into its marking condition waiting for the next character.

Synchronous data transfer does not use start or stop bits as characters follow in immediate succession. This is far more efficient than asynchronous transmission and the characters are placed in blocks and transmitted in bursts. The **Xmodem** protocol (Appendix 7B) is designed for synchronous data transmission with data blocks containing 128 characters. If there are fewer than 128 characters to transmit then ASCII character 0 (NUL) is added to make up the 128 block.

When two modems are communicating with each other and they transmit and receive alternatively then they are said to operate in a **half-duplex** mode – only one transmitting at any time. The time taken to switch from a transmission state to a receive state or vice versa is called the **turnaround time** and this limits the performance of the modem. Alternatively, if both modems can operate in a transmission and receive mode simultaneously this is referred to as **full duplex**.

7.1.3 High-Speed Modems

Modem classification has been laid down by the **Consultative Committee for International Telegraph Telephone** (CCITT) and they are classified by their V numbers. Most high-speed modems conform to the CCITT standards and these include the V.22bis, V.29, V.32 and V.42. Modems in these categories transmit data as blocks or packets in a synchronous fashion. Modems which conform to the V.22bis standard have a maximum transfer rate of 2,400 BPS and use a 4-bit QAM modulation technique. However for higher speed modems there is a need to have advanced echo cancellation electronics which tends to be expensive. With echo cancellation, a full duplex modem can isolate its own transmission signal from its own receiver. This permits the modem to receive and transmit over the same frequency range which is equivalent to having overlapping bandwidths.

High-speed data transmission still suffers from the effect of noise which results in errors appearing in the transmitted data. There are a number of schemes for the detecting errors in the transmitted data and then performing an error correction. Both software and hardware correcting schemes are used and two of the well known software protocols are **Xmodem** and **Kermit** (after the infamous Muppet frog).

Although software error checking and correction techniques are reasonably effective, they tend to be slow and it's not usual to find modems with hardware based protocols. Modems of this design can afford good throughputs and operate at medium baud rates. A series of operational protocols have been established, referred to as the **Microcom Networking Protocol** (MNP) (Appendix 7C), and these are given different classifications depending on the nature of the transmission, their baud rates, the schemes used to correct errors and maximise data throughput. One well known error checking protocol, found in modems built to the V.42 standard, is a combination of MNP Class 4 and **Link Access Protocol** (LAP) type M. V.42 can achieve a 99% error free transmission. This high degree of error free transmission is accomplished by the repetitive sending of data blocks until they are accepted by the modem and then passed onto the system. V.42 is favoured by British Telecom for its **Packet Switch Stream** (PSS) network.

In general, because of the way MNP deals with data transfer, negating framing bits and adding its own bits, a modem based on MNP can only communicate with other MNP modems of similar or lower class. The MNP protocol conforms with the **Open System Interconnection** (OSI) network reference model (Section 8.6.1). OSI is a networking protocol which is partitioned in standardised link layers which help the manufacturers of communication equipment to build to standards.

For high-speed modems a hardware error checking technique known as **Trellis Coded Modulation** (TCM) is often used. Full-duplex modems built to the V.32 specification incorporate TCM. In these devices two carrier frequencies are used and five digital bits are carried on each analogue modulation at the 2,400 baud rate. Although this would give a BPS of 12,000, one of the bits is used for error correction which leaves a data transmission rate of 9,600 BPS (4-bit QAM). V.32 modems are far less susceptible to PSTN noise than the V.22bis QAM modems. The TCM modem itself detects the errors in the transmission and implements automatic error correction before the data is passed on the computer. This protocol removes the ill effects of background noise on the data and can support transmission rate between 9,600 BPS to 14,400 BPS on the PSTN. We can illustrate this with an example: in a V.22bis QAM modem there would be a need to retransmit one data block in every 10, however in a good quality TCM modem this would be reduced to one data block in every 10,000.

An alternative high-speed modem called Trailblazer, and pioneered by the Telebit corporation, uses the **Packetised Ensemble Protocol** (PEP) and is based on the **Dynamically Adaptive Multicarrier Quadrature Amplitude Modulation** (DAM-QAM) technique. PEP works on the principle that the quality of the bandwidth on each telephone link can be a variable. With PEP, 512 carrier frequency tones are generated by the originating modem. The receiving modem performs an analysis on the tones to determine which ones have the lowest noise and are therefore best suited for the transmission of data. The receiving modem then informs the originating modem of the tones which are unsuitable for transmission. On receipt of this information, the originating modem selects an ensemble of tones and decides which modulation technique to use.

On the low-quality tones a 2-phase DPSK may be used. Alternatively for higher-quality tones 4-bit or 6-bit QAM technique may be used for impressing the packets of data on the PSTN. If 400 tones were available, then with a 6-bit QAM a packet size of 2,400 bits could be constructed. With a tone modulation of four Hz a data transfer of 10,000 BPS could be achieved. The PEP also attaches a 16-bit **cyclic redundancy check** (CRC) on each packet to improve the quality. If during the course of the data transmission the telephone link should change in character then the tone ensemble can be readjusted to find the optimum configuration for the new condition. The FASTLINK modem from Digital Communications Associates (DCA) uses the PEP protocol and is marketed as an expansion card.

7.1.4 Hayes Standard

The operating characteristics and configuration of a modem are determined by the contents of its **register set**. Older modem designs had dual in line package (DIP) switches and these would be adjusted manually to change the contents of the register set. However in today's modems, the register set is stored directly in memory and changes are effected in software. The advantage of this design is to allow the communication software to reconfigure the modem's parameters during operation. The modem is also expected to respond to a set of instructions, or command set which will determine its mode of operation and how the modem is to be used. The established standard of the register set format and the command set in modem design has now come to be known as the Hayes standard. Most modem makers now manufacture to the **Hayes Smartmodem Register Set** (Table 7.1 opposite) standard with either the Hayes command set or an extended command set. When communication problems do occur they normally stem from an incompatible register set configuration.The Hayes command set consists of primary commands and extended commands. The primary commands deal with placing the modem off the hook, dialling the number and other basic functions. The extended command instructions deal with the operational configuration of the modem, baud rate and so on. The Hayes Smartmodem has a command buffer which can hold 40 characters and the syntax for issuing the commands is:

```
AT Command[parameters] Command[parameter]...
```

where the first instruction code AT is used to initialise the modem for the commands to follow. The command parameters are normally 0 or 1: for example to switch the loud speaker off the instruction M0 is issued.

Register	Function	Default value
S0	Select ring	0
S1	Ring count	0
S2	Escape sequence character	ASCII 43 +
S3	Carriage return	ASCII 13
S4	Linefeed	ASCII 10
S5	Backspace	ASCII 8
S6	Dial wait time (blind dial)	2 sec
S7	Wait time for carrier dial tone	30 sec
S8	Length for pause for , in number	2 sec
S9	Carrier detect response time	6/10 sec
S10	Delay between carrier loss and hangup	7/10 sec
S11	Touch tone period/space	70 msec
S12	Escape sequence guard time	1 sec
S18	Select test timer	0 sec
S25	Data terminal ready change detect	50 msec
S26	Select RTS to CTS delay	10 msec

Table 7.1 The S-Register Set of the Hayes Smartmodem

The Hayes command set is given in Table 7.2 overleaf, with the appropriate parameters. When commands are issued to the modem it responds with **Result Codes** enabled with the command instruction Q1. The codes for the Hayes Smartmodem are:

0	OK	Command line executed without error
1	Connect	Carrier detected for transmission
2	Ring	Ring signal detected
3	No carrier	Carrier lost or not detected
4	Error	Error in command line

Command	Function
A	Answer the call
A/	Repeat the last command
C	Switch modem carrier off(0) or on(1)
D	Dial a telephone number
E	Enable(0)/disable(1) echo characters to screen
F	Change duplex, half(0) full(1)
H	Suspend call(0) or start call(1)
I	Request checksum(1) or identification word(0)
M	Change loud speaker to off(0) or on(1)
O	Put modem on-line
P	Pulse dial
Q	Request to send(1)/stop sending(0) result code
R	Modem mode to originate only
S	Set modem S register
T	Touch tone dial
V	Request result code as words(0) or digits(0)
X	Use basic(0) or extended(1) result code set
Z	Modem reset

Table 7.2 The Hayes Smartmodem Command set

The Result Codes can be used in developing control software for handling the various conditions which may arise during the operation of the modem. Although the command set is suitable for the Hayes Smartmodem and compatible modems which operate at a maximum 9,600 BPS, for higher performance modems it is quite likely that the command set will be enlarged with special purpose instructions.

Modems are designed in two types of package, external units to the 386 PC and as expansion cards. Both types usually conform to the Hayes standard and the expansion card design does have the attractive feature of integrating into the 386 PC system. An external modem will probably require one of the RS-232 ports and may be slower at transmitting or receiving data.

However the external modem will probably have an array of light emitting diodes (LEDs) to indicate to the user the state of the transmission. Some modems may have up to eight LEDs indicating the following status conditions:

HS   High-Speed – modem operating at maximum baud rate.

AA   Auto-Answering – the modem will automatically respond to any incoming calls.

CD	Carrier Detect – the modem has detected a carrier tone on the remote modem.
OH	Off Hook – indicates that the modem is using the telephone line.
RD	Receive Data – data is being received by the modem.
SD	Send Data – data is being transmitted by the modem.
TR	This indicates that the PC is ready to receive or transmit data via the modem.
MR	Modem Ready – the modem is operative.

Having these LEDs does give the user immediate knowledge of the operation of the modem and some people find this reassuring.

The attractive feature of having a modem integrated into a 386 PC is the ability to assign its operation to a background task in a multi-tasking environment (Section 5.2). Foreground tasks can continue as normal and the modem can be treated as a system resource. If the 386 PC is part of a local area network (LAN), then it is possible to assign the modem a general service on the LAN to be accessed by other users without disturbing the running of the host 386 PC.

7.2 The FAX Card

Another peripheral which can be installed in a 386 PC and employs the telephone network is the facsimile or FAX card. FAX cards come as a single expansion card and are accommodated in the card cage of the 386 PC host. The stand-alone FAX machine has three basic units: a photostatic printer, a scanner and a modem. The functions of a FAX machine can be performed by a 386 PC when fitted with a FAX card and suitable software drivers. A 386 PC with a FAX card, hosting its own modem and control software, can communicate with other PCs with FAX cards or stand-alone office FAX machines. However a 386 PC FAX will have distinct advantages over the office FAX machine owing to its additional intelligence derived from the 386 PC system. This will allow the user to have more control over the operation of the FAX facility than is afforded by the stand-alone machine. The fundamental difference between a FAX unit and a modem is the bit image transmission of the FAX compared to the text transmission of the modem.

The function of a FAX machine is to scan a document in order to generate a bit-image which can be sent as a digital bit stream via the modem to the receiving FAX machine. The original document is then reconstructed by the receiving FAX machine from the transmitted bit-image and printed on thermal paper. All FAX machines and FAX cards must be approved by the **British Approvals Board for Telecommunications** (BABT) before they can be used on the British Telecom system. There are at least four standards for FAX transmission in the UK which have been established by the **Consultative Committee on International Telephone and Telegraph** (CCITT):

Group I   The first standard with a transmission rate of 300 bits per second (BPS). This is equivalent to the transmission of a page of A4 in six minutes and is rarely used these days.

Group II   Transmission data rate of 600 BPS, which corresponds to a page of A4 in three minutes with a resolution of 200 x 100 dots per inch (dpi).

Group III   Official transmission rate of 4,800 BPS but in practice most systems can cope with 9,600 BPS which is equivalent to transmitting a page of A4 in half a minute. The image resolution can range from 200 x 100 dpi to 200 x 200 dpi, but the higher resolution is at the expense of the transmission rate.

Group IV   Used with dedicated, high-quality, leased telephone lines with a resolution of 300 x 300 dpi and is able to transmit a page of A4 in five seconds.

Once the FAX card is installed in the 386 PC the accompanying software drivers will be expected to perform a number of tasks including the conversion of text files and image files into the FAX format ready for transmission. The transmitted data must be acceptable by other PC FAX systems or stand-alone FAX machines. This aspect of the PC FAX facility is relatively straightforward and only a few problems ever arise. However converting text files into FAX formatted files is quite CPU intensive and the operation makes frequent disk accesses and this burden can be lightened to some extent by using a disk cacheing routine (Section 2.7). In the event of a need to transmit an external document then an image scanner can be used (Section 6.2). Most scanners produce files to the tagged image format file (TIFF) standard and the FAX software can convert TIFF to the FAX format ready for transmission.

However receiving FAX transmissions and processing the information is a little more difficult. It is preferable to have the FAX operating as a background task in the 386 PC which can be called as a foreground task at any time. All incoming transmissions will be in the FAX image format and these can be displayed, after minimal processing, on the screen or sent to a printer as a graphics dump. When operating as a background task the incoming transmission can be stored directly on the hard disk drive for processing later. Since FAX formatted files are image files they will rapidly devour disk space and frequent purges will have to be exercised to prevent unnecessary disk clutter. To obtain a text file from a FAX transmission, **optical character recognition** (OCR) software is required and several FAX card manufacturers supply this software as standard. This converts the character patterns in the image file into actual ASCII characters which can be loaded into a word processor for further editing.

The software provided with the FAX card should have a provision for performing several tasks and some of the functions to look out for are:

❑ Immediate transmission of a text file from the DOS prompt

❑ An easy method for receiving a transmission and converting it into a screen display

❑ The ability to maintain an activity log – essential for determining if the transmission was successful and the time of transmission

❑ The presence of a telephone directory otherwise the user will have to enter the number by hand each time the FAX is used

❑ An automatic redial on those occasions when the line is engaged

❑ A time delay facility to allow the user to take advantage of cheap period transmission times (after 6.00pm)

❑ A queuing mechanism to prepare several FAX messages for transmission without the user intervening

❑ Pull-down, drop-down or pop-up menus for accessing control commands

❑ A command language with instructions which can be added to a batch file

❑ An option which allows the FAX facility to become a task icon in a Windows environment

❑ A memory resident software driver which may be loaded into extended memory

❑ Resident FAX software drivers which are compatible with the front end working environment on the 386 PC, eg. Windows/386.

Having discussed the features one might expect to find on a FAX card it is instructive to consider a couple of the commercially available products. The Panasonic FX-BM89 is well suited to a 386 PC owing to its specific background mode of operation. It features a mouse controlled graphics editor, based on the Z-Soft PC Paintbrush, which allows the user to access its facilities in a well organised, proficient manner. The FX-BM89 can convert text from the majority of the popular word processing packages into FAX format files. It will also recognise images files from the HP ScanJet, the Canon IX-12 and the Microtek MS-300. For permanent records the FX-BM89 has drivers for a large variety of printers including the HP LaserJet II.

Another FAX card is the GammaFax-CP (Communications Professional) from Comwave which offers over 50 commands from its array of pull-down menus. The CP derives its intelligence from an Intel 80186 microprocessor and is supported by 256K of memory situated on the FAX card itself. This interfaces with the user via the memory resident queue manager which can be installed during the boot-up phase of the 386 PC. The processing for the file conversion (ASCII to FAX format) is performed on the FAX card which relieves the host 386 PC of the burden. Support for scanners is limited to the HP ScanJet and the Cannon IX-12, however the CP is capable of accepting files in the TIFF and .PCX format. It also supports several laser and a few matrix printers. Before choosing a FAX card, the user should ensure that it is available with, or at least compatible with, an OCR software package.

7.3 Expansion Cards

One important aspect of the 386 PC is the card cage for accommodating input/output expansion cards. This feature allows the 386 PC to be customised for a particular set of applications by fitting appropriate expansion cards in the cage. The variety of expansion cards on the market is quite bewildering and they perform a very wide spectrum of functions. However the main task of any expansion card is to enable data to be transferred to and from the 386 PC. A number of peripherals come with their own expansion card and do not rely on the RS-232 or parallel port interfaces. The advantage of the expansion card over the communication ports is speed, due to many cards having their own processor and memory which is dedicated to a particular peripheral function. Several expansion cards are customised to transform the 386 PC into a specialised piece of equipment. As an example the Compuscope card from Contax converts the PC into a two-channel oscilloscope with a sampling rate of 40 MHz.

The expansion connectors (Section 3.2.1) or slots in the 386 PC vary in size from the XT 8-bit compatible, the AT 16-bit compatible, to the Extended Industry Standard Architecture (EISA – Section 7.3.4) bus on some 386 PCs. Standard on the IBM range or PS/2 386 PCs is the Micro Channel Architecture bus (Section 3.8.1). The majority of expansion cards are of the XT or AT variety, but an 8-bit card can be fitted into a 16-bit connector and function normally. The expansion cards derive their power from the 386 PC's voltage rails and are either full length, stretching the full width of the 386 PC card cage, or half size. Peripheral systems are therefore connected via the expansion card to the internal bus system of the 386 PC. In order for a peripheral to request attention from the 386 PC an **interrupt mechanism** will probably be installed on the expansion card. Most expansion cards have adjustable interrupt level settings via a row of small DIP switches or jumpers. The choice of setting is covered in greater detail in Appendix 6A.

Expansion cards which are available for the IBM PS/2 series of personal computers, based on the MCA, are not compatible with other 386 PCs unless the MCA has been specified. However a number of the newer expansion boards are based on EISA which is supported by a number of 386 PC manufacturers. EISA is the alternative to the MCA and is an open design which does not require licensing, unlike the MCA, with the attractive feature of being compatible with existing expansion card designs.

7.3.1 The IEEE-488 Interface Card

An extensively used expansion card for interfacing the 386 PC to a wide range of electronic instrumentation is based on the IEEE-488 standard and a schematic for its system configuration is shown in Figure 7.2.

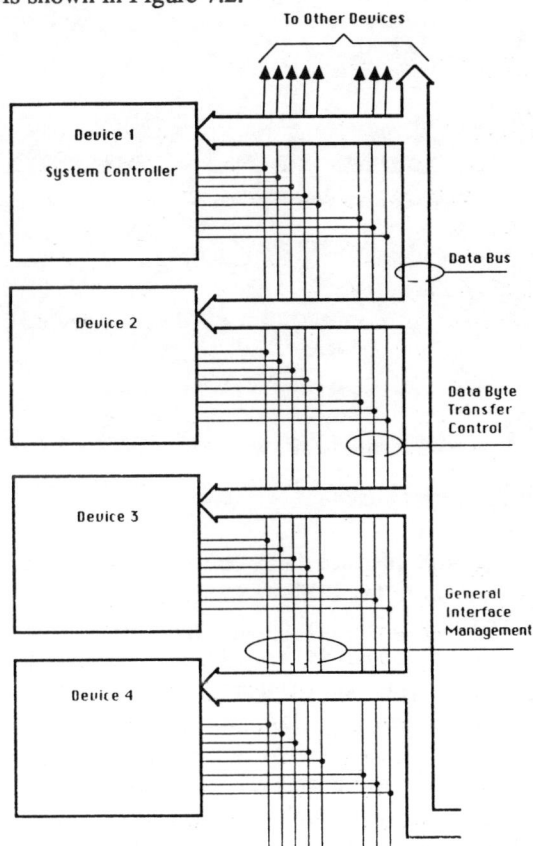

Figure 7.2 IEEE-488 Interface System configuration

It is a parallel interface and has become the recognised standard. It was first established by Hewlett Packard and is also referred as the **General Purpose Interface Bus** (GPIB); it is also known in Europe as the **IEC-625 standard** (the connector is different). The attractive feature of the IEEE-488 interface is the ability to link up to 15 instruments on the same connector, mounted in a piggyback fashion with only one cable leading to the PC. Each instrument has its own address and is easily recognised by the controller (the 386 PC). The interface allows the controller to exchange data between instruments on the bus via a simple protocol. It is very fast – it can transfer data up to one Mbyte/sec, and it is comprehensive enough to allow any instrument on the bus to generate an interrupt. To illustrate the importance of the GPIB, there are very few instruments among the hundreds that Hewlett Packard makes that are not fitted with the interface. All electronic instrumentation manufacturers now provide the IEEE-488 with their products or at least as an option.

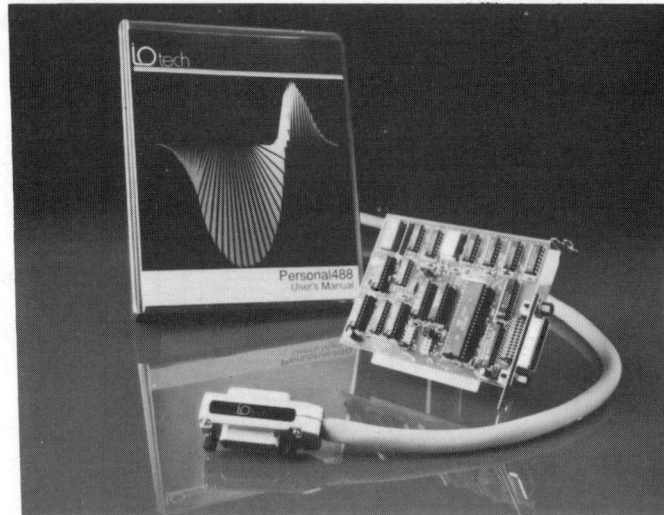

Figure 7.3 The IOTech Personal448

There are many IEEE-488 interface cards on the market which basically perform the same functions laid down in the IEEE-488.2 specification. Some of these have their software drivers resident in ROM and others require the drivers to be installed via the CONFIG.SYS file. The Personal488 from IOTech of Cleveland Ohio, comes as the GP488B half-length expansion card (Figure 7.3) with DOS driver software and is compatible with the standard AT (ISA) internal bus. It is furnished with direct memory access (DMA – Section 2.3.5) and is able to cope with **service request** (SRQ) vectors from the bus instruments. The software drivers for the IEEE-488 cards can be called from a variety of high-level languages, including Microsoft C and QuickBASIC 4.5. IOTech also makes a version of an IEEE-488 interface expansion card for the IBM range of PS/2 computers featuring the MCA (Section 3.8.1).

There are a number of IEEE-488, menu-driven, mouse-compatible program development tools which ease the process of data transfer of data to/from the PC to the instruments on the bus. PM 2240 TestTeam from Philips is an example which has many exciting features. These include drivers for many Philips and Fluke instruments, options for integrating application programs written in C or MS-QuickBASIC and an analysis library to allow further processing of the data imported from the instruments. Alternatively there is the WaveTest application program from Wavetek which operates under Windows/386 (Section 5.5.1). Part of this program is the Library Generator which can be used to define and control the functions of instruments on the IEEE-488 bus. It also contains Program Generator which can be used to automatically write instrument control programs. This works on the principle of integrating predefined operational modules into a string of functions. These modules are visually represented by screen icons and the user combines them in the desired order. Lab Windows, from National Instruments, has many similar features and can also be used to great effect to construct automatic test equipment software. There are a number of dedicated dat analysis application programs which are also able to import data via an IEEE-488 interface card and an example is DADiSP, marketed by Adept.

7.3.2 Special-purpose Expansion Cards

Many manufacturers make special-purpose cards which perform functions which either complement the 386 PC or just use the 386 PC as a platform. Figure 7.4 shows an example of a card – the PCIP-DLA from MetraByte (distributed by Keithley) –

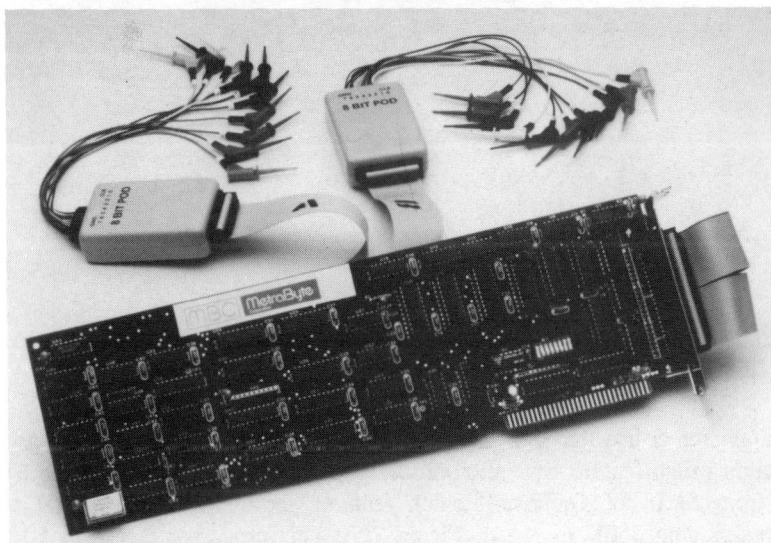

Figure 7.4 MetraByte's PC1P-DLA 16-channel logic analyser expansion card. (Photo: Courtesy of Keithley Instruments)

which expands the functionality of the 386 PC allowing it to be converted into a low-cost logic analyser for observing waveforms in digital electronic systems. There are expansion cards which provide voice recognition systems and these are growing in number and popularity.

Analytical chemistry is another field which has been found to have a wealth of opportunities for 386 PCs fitted with expansion cards. Analysis on spectral data from infrared spectrometers, passed to a 386 PC via an expansion card, is now a commonplace technique. The chemical identification is performed by searching a database for spectra which match the characteristics of the acquired spectra.

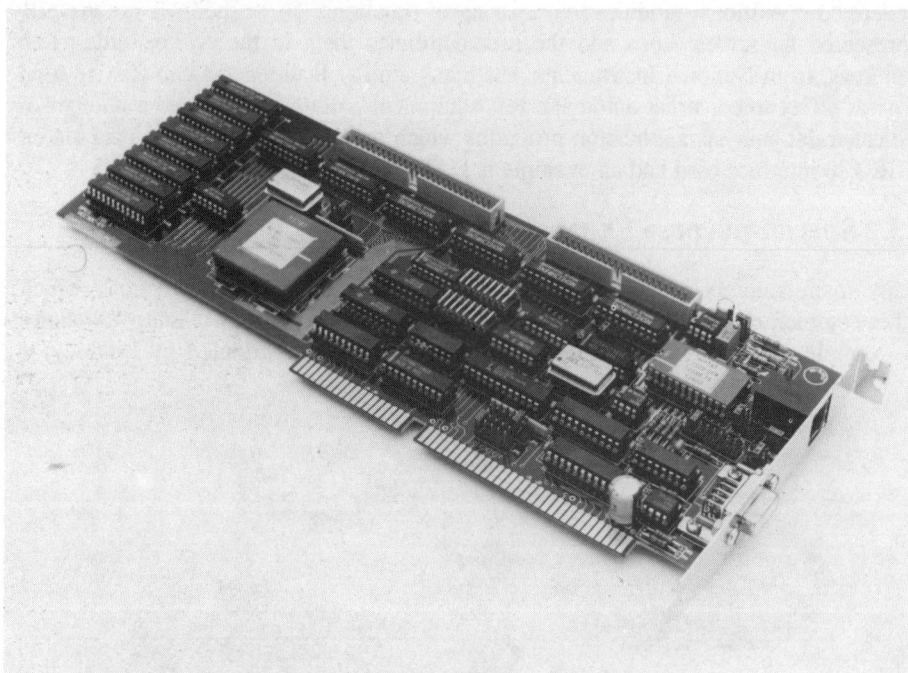

Figure 7.5 The Vector 32C/256 expansion card featuring the AT&T DSP32C which performs 25 Mflops. (Photo: Courtesy of SMIS)

Many manufacturers use the 386 PC as a host for their cards and this is especially true for cards which feature new microprocessors. An example of this is the Vector 32C/256 from SMIS of Guildford which features the AT&T 32C digital signal microprocessor with 256K of RAM (Figure 7.5). This processor clocks at 50 MHz and performs over 25 million floating point operations per second (MFLOPS). The Vector 32C/256 board is particularly convenient for testing digital signal processing algorithms by converting the 386 PC into a development platform.

The much heralded transputer can be found on several expansion cards and Transtech Devices of High Wycombe manufactures a card (the TSB178) with no less than 19 T800 floating point transputers (Figure 7.6).

Figure 7.6 The TSB178 card hosting 19 transputers. (Photo: Courtesy of Transtech)

Since the 386 PC is been accepted as a reliable system controller (Section 9.4.2), data acquisition expansion cards have featured very strongly in the marketplace. The majority of expansion cards have either an 8-bit data bus or the Industry Standard Architecture (ISA) AT bus with 16-bits; the edge connector of the latter is longer. However there is a growing number expansion cards which have the IBM PS/2 MCA interface and others with the alternative EISA (Section 7.3.4).

There are many expansion card manufacturers and Burr Brown of Tucson Arozona, MetraByte of Taunton Massachusetts, Analog Devices of Norwood Massachusetts and Data Translation of Marlboro Massachusetts are market leaders in this field, offering a wide variety of signal acquisition and signal output expansion cards. With a wide spectrum of applications for expansion cards, it is therefore not surprising that standards have emerged regarding the electrical characteristics on expansion cards.

7.3.3 Small Computer Systems Interface (SCSI)

A number of peripheral manufacturers have realised that the existing RS-232 ports on the 386 PC are too slow for their devices creating a bottle-neck for data transfer. A solution to this problem was for the manufacturers to build their own expansion peripheral cards or host adaptors. In order to standardise on the protocol for data transfer between the expansion cards and the PC bus, the **American National Standards Institution** (ANSI) set up a standard to which many card manufacturers now conform. Referred to as the Small Computer Systems Interface (SCSI) specification (ANSI document X3.131-1986) it contains information on permitted delay times in the card's electronics for synchronous and asynchronous operations.

In practice the maximum asynchronous data transfer rate is in excess of 1.5 Mbytes/sec and five Mbytes/sec for synchronous transfer. SCSI is therefore an expansion card standard and is implemented on the card itself or in the peripheral and not on the 386 PC motherboard. One of the first applications for the SCSI was for hard disk drive controller (Section 2.5.4). SCSI is intended to replace the ST-506 disk controller standard which can muster a maximum transfer rate of 10 Mbits/sec using the **run length limited** (RLL) coding. On the other hand, hard disk drives with embedded SCSI controllers can provide average disk seek times of 20 msecs with a transfer rate of 1.5 Mbytes/sec. However, it is unlikely that the SCSI host adaptor card will accommodate a floppy disk drive.

The SCSI standard also contains a **Common Command Set** (CCS) for software interfacing for a wide variety of peripherals and can accommodate as many as seven peripherals on the 386 PC. It has subsequently been adopted by many manufacturers who produce purpose-built expansion cards for their peripherals. The SCSI standard is therefore not confined to the specification of disk drives but for a broader range of possible peripherals including tape drives, optical disk drives, printers, scanners and communication controllers.

7.3.4 Enhanced Industry Standard Architecture (EISA)

With greater demands for higher transfer rates, a number of manufacturers clubbed together to establish a new standard for handling input/output (I/O) from expansion cards. Known as the Enhanced Industry Standard Architecture (EISA), it was intended to address some of the deficiencies of the Industry Standard Architecture (ISA) bus found on the early generations of personal computer. EISA, in many respects, is a competitor with the IBM Micro Channel Architecture (MCA – Section 3.8.1) and has the advantage of being compatible with expansion cards using ISA. Incidentally this is not compatible with MCA thus rendering the first and second generation expansion cards obsolete for the PS/2 (Section 3.8) range of computers.

The IBM PC/XT and their respective clones, carry the 8-bit ISA bus, whereas the

IBM AT, hosting the 16-bit Intel 80286 microprocessor, has a 16-bit ISA bus and the EISA design is a logical extension to the ISA bus. The EISA is therefore intended to be built into the motherboard of the 386 PC. By increasing the data bus to 32 bits, EISA has become a compatible environment for the 80386 microprocessor. It is however still compatible with expansion cards designed for the ISA bus which initialise communication with the CPU by generating a pulse-driven interrupt. Also implemented in the EISA standard are facilities for accommodating **multi-bus masters**. This allows intelligent disk controllers to take control of the system buses for the purposes of efficient direct memory access (DMA – Section 2.3.5). Alternatively, in a networked multi-user 386 PC system, several users may want access to shared hard disk drives and this can be effectively implemented under the EISA standard.

To support the EISA standard, Intel developed a specific set of integrated circuits. Referred to as the **82350 EISA Bus Chip Set,** they can be designed into a product without the need of a licence. The Intel 82350 chip family also has the **Integrated System Peripheral** (ISP) 82357 and the **EISA Bus Controller** (EBC) 82358. The EBC chip has an integral DMA controller and other necessary components to achieve a data throughput of 33 Mbytes/sec for the EISA design and the ISP chip implements the multimaster arbitration scheme.

The EBC interfaces directly with the 80386 CPU and provides control for data transfer over the EISA bus and the old ISA bus. Having assumed control over the buses it performs the addressing tasks and marshals the data into a format appropriate for the expansion card: for an EISA card 32-bit – one transfer, for a 16-bit ISA card the 32-bit data would be partitioned into 16-bit words with two transfers, and for an 8-bit ISA card the 32-bit data would be fragmented into four bytes for four transfers. For intelligent expansion cards, the Intel **82355 Bus Master Interface Controller** (BMIC) chip can be used which takes control of the system buses and offloads bus intensive functions from the CPU. The need for this facility arises in systems which support shared disk units and general network resource sharing.

Expansion cards designed on the EISA standard have a two connectors in parallel (Figure 7.7 overleaf). A 16-bit ISA long-edge socket can accommodate an 8-bit ISA short-edge connector, which means that a 16-bit ISA is an 8-bit ISA with a 16-bit extension. In the card cage of a 386 PC hosting the EISA design, the long connector is a 16-bit ISA whereas the shorter connector has two functions: it can act either as an 8-bit ISA or when combined with the 16-bit ISA connector, it forms the EISA connector. The short connector has two levels of contacts. The bottom set works in conjunction with the 16-bit ISA to provide the EISA interface and the top set acts a standalone 8-bit ISA.

When observing an EISA expansion card, you will notice that the short connector is at a different height to the long connector. It also has notches in it so when it is inserted into the socket it sinks further down than an ISA connector would, hence making contact with the EISA lines. The absence of the notches on the 8-bit ISA connector prevents it from being inserted to the full depth of the socket.

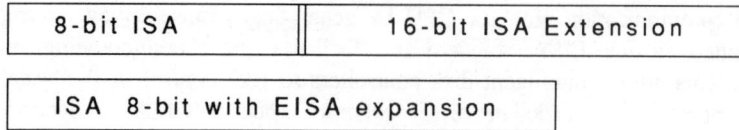

8-bit ISA	16-bit ISA Extension

ISA 8-bit with EISA expansion

Figure 7.7 Configuration of bus connectors on EISA expansion cards

Within EISA, the DMA controllers are limited to a memory address area of 15 Mbytes. However the transfer rate may be as high as 33 Mbits per second which satisfied the design requirements of the high-performance 386 PCs. Since the EISA design incorporates the functionality of the ISA design a number of the older features have been held over. In a 16-bit ISA expansion card, there would be a mechanism to inform the PC bus that 16-bit data transfer could be performed instead of just 8-bit. In addition some 16-bit ISA cards used a wait state line to coordinate the data transfer. Both features have been taken on-board the EISA design and extended to account for 32-bit data transfer.

The expansion card must indicate to the EBC chip the format of the data for transfer. For the maximum data transfer rate of 33 Mbytes/sec, the EBC functions in its Burst Mode where data is transmitted in 1K blocks using the full 32-bit bus width. To initialise this process the expansion card uses the Burst line to indicate to the EBC chip that it can perform in the **Burst Mode.** The EBC requests the bus control from the 80386 CPU and when permission it granted the transfer takes place.

In the specifications of EISA there has been a great deal of controversy surrounding the merits of **edge detection** for interrupt signals. When an expansion card requires the service of the CPU, it generates an interrupt which takes the form of a falling-edge transition on a digital pulse. The support circuitry around the CPU detects this falling edge and the CPU responds in the appropriate manner.

However there are two possible problems with the edge trigger mechanism: firstly a spurious noise signal may be interpreted as an interrupt causing the CPU to go chasing after a spurious service request. Secondly, the edge transition interrupt may not be caught by the CPU support circuitry, leaving the expansion card in a state of limbo waiting for a service which is never going to come. However the likelihood of either of these effects occurring is vanishingly small. The alternative, voltage **level sensing** has been adopted by the main competitor to EISA, MCA (Section 3.8.1).

When buying an EISA expansion card it may be accompanied by an installation floppy disk which might be needed to reconfigure the 386 PC to accommodate the new card. The card can easily be accepted by the system by plugging it into the card cage and running the installation program. Several EISA expansion cards may share the same interrupt level since there are mechanisms for identifying the card which has generated the interrupt from the configuration data.

However when using ISA expansion cards with a EISA 386 PC certain precautions must be observed regarding the interrupt levels. ISA expansion cards do not share interrupt levels and therefore each card is assigned a different interrupt level. Consequently the 386 PC must be configured for each ISA expansion card to ensure that it provides the appropriate service for the card. The interrupt level on an ISA expansion card is set by adjusting the setting of a row of DIP switches and the installation manual for the expansion card should be consulted to set the interrupt to the desired level.

The maximum number of EISA expansion cards that can be accommodated by a 386 PC is 16 and each card will reside in its input/output space of 4K. The addresses are allocated xC80 Hex (hexadecimal numbering) where x ranges from 0 to 15 (F in Hex). When an EISA expansion card installation is performed, the EISA controller addresses xC80 for the identification numbers and the inserted cards will respond with the appropriate information.

Each EISA card will have a configuration file against each identification number and these must match before the EISA card becomes an active part of the system.

In a system which supports bus multimasters there must be a scheme for arbitrating their access rights. In the EISA design, the bus arbitration is decided by the Intel 82357 Integrated System Peripheral (ISP) chip. Three levels of arbitration exist in the EISA scheme of things; the bus users are grouped into three different camps: the Dynamic RAM refresh controller, the direct memory access (DMA) channels and the 80386 CPU with the bus master (Figure 7.8 overleaf).

Once the DRAM refresh controller has relinquished the bus, the first round of arbitration (Level 1) is between DMA channels and the CPU with the bus masters. If the bus control is gained by the CPU and the bus masters, there follows another round of bus arbitration (Level 2) this time between the CPU and the bus masters. If the CPU gains control of the bus, it performs its task and hands the control back to ISP at arbitration Level 1. In the event of the bus masters gaining the bus control, there follows yet another round of arbitration (Level 3) where the bus control is offered to the bus masters sequentially. When the bus masters have finished, control is handed back to the ISP at Level 1.

Alternatively during the Level 1 arbitration the DMA could gain control of the bus. Should this happen, which is quite likely since the DMA has preference over the

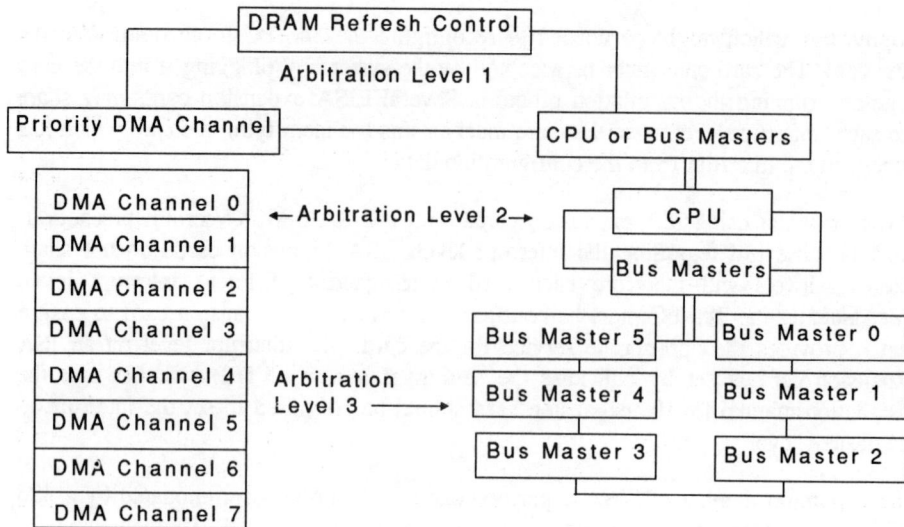

Figure 7.8 The three-level bus arbitration scheme for EISA

others, control is handed to the highest priority DMA channel which requires servicing. On completion of the service task, control would be handed back to the ISP at Level 1. With the various devices bidding for the bus control, the order of servicing would be:

Active DMA highest priority

83086 CPU

Active DMA highest priority

Bus Master 1

Active DMA highest priority

83086 CPU

Active DMA highest priority

Bus Master 2

.

DRAM Refresh

.

The DRAM refresh only occurs every tenth of a second and is threfore a quite rare event in the arbitration scheme.

The EISA standard is becoming well established and many expansion card manufacturers are upgrading their original ISA designed cards with the EISA standard in order to capitalise on the full potential that the 386 PC with the EISA bus standard has to offer.

7.3.5 Accelerator Cards

There are a number of expansion cards which have the ability to perform specific programming tasks far quicker than the CPU in the PC. This is particularly true for highly numerical intensive calculations where even a Weitek coprocessor (Section 3.1.3) would be struggling. The performance of the early IBM XT could be beefed up, for a number of programs, by inserting an expansion card which hosted an Intel 80286 16-bit microprocessor. In a similar manner, accelerator cards are available which give the impression of enhancing the performance of a 386 PC. In reality most accelerator cards only use the 386 PC as a host platform. The 386 PC feeds the data to the accelerator card where it is duly processed, provided the program is in place on the accelerator card. The accelerator card will invariably have a very high-performance processor on board and any program required to run on the accelerator card will have to be compiled for that processor. Once in the card cage of the 386 PC it has in principle access to all the resources of the computer. However the level of control that the accelerator card can exercise over the 386 PC platform will probably be limited. This is due, in part, to the much higher clock speed of the accelerator card processor and the difficulty of software interfacing such a processor with the host 80386 CPU circuitry.

In most cases, a high-level language compiler and cross-assembler will be required in order to enable a program to run on the accelerator card. If the source code is written in a high-level language such as C, Pascal or Fortran, it must be compiled into an object code which can run on the accelerator processor. An example of an accelerator card is the MC30 from Myriad Solutions of Cambridge (Figure 7.9 overleaf). The MC30 hosts the Texas Instruments TMS320C30 digital signal microprocessor and is capable of performing 33 million floating point operations per second (MFLOPs). It is supported by 256K of Static RAM and up to 12 Mbytes of cached Dynamic RAM. This translates into a factor of more than 50 times faster than a 386 PC with 80387 coprocessor, running at 20 MHz. The MC30 can be programmed in either C, assembler, Pascal or FORTRAN and its hardware has a direct memory access (DMA) controller which can work concurrently with the 80386 CPU. To help with program development, the MC30 has a menu-driven, front-end application environment which functions under Windows/386. This serves as a user-friendly interface to the accelerator card and its programming tools.

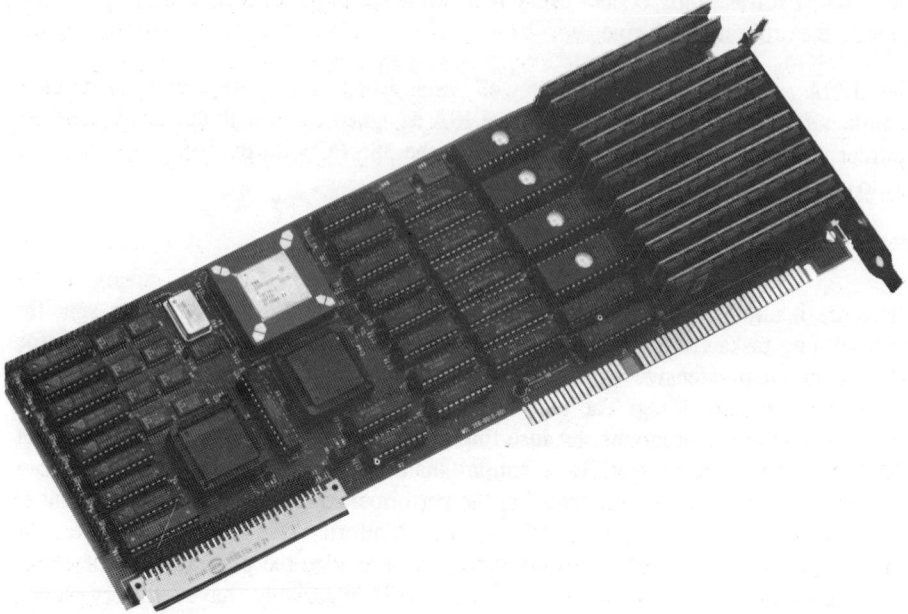

Figure 7.9 The MC30 Accelerator card hosting the Texas Instruments TMS320C30.
(Photo: Courtesy of Myriad Solutions)

7.4 The Compact Disk ROM (CD-ROM)

The storage of information is a key requirement in any computer system and there are several enhancements for the 386 PC which enable it to be customised into an information archival system. One such enhancement is the optical or compact disk and this has become known as the CD-ROM (compact disk read only memory). Its random access, interactive nature and its vast storage potential make it a very attractive personal computer peripheral and consequently it has opened up new opportunities for information processing and retrieval. Added to these benefits are the ease of searching and cross-referencing of the information within this low-cost storage medium. The remarkable feature of the CD-ROM is the information storage capacity, which on average is 500 Mbytes for a 5.25 inch disc. Each CD-ROM is manufactured in a similar manner to the domestic compact disk and the CD-ROM drive uses a laser for reading the embedded data. Not only can CD-ROM technology be used for storing data, printer matter, images and graphics but also sound tracks if required. This is frequently referred to as **Interactive CD-ROM** (CD-I).

However one of the major problems with CD-ROMs is their slow access time which can be as long as 450 msecs, which is irritatingly slow for image transfer applications. In order to standardise the data format on CD-ROMs the High Sierra group of companies introduced a standard which has now been adhered to by CD-ROM manufacturers. This ensures for example that a Nimbus CD-ROM is compatible with a Hitachi drive. The High Sierra standard defines the location of the **disk directory** and the **logical structure** of the data files on the CD-ROM. It is also directly compatible with Microsoft's **CD-ROM Extension.**

To enhance the appeal of the CD-ROM, a full interactive potential of the CD-ROM (CD-I) is being realised. CD-I players work as independent and external units of the PC, although the information (data and images) can be transferred to the PC. The CD-I Starter System from Philips is showing great promise as an educational aid. Microsoft, in agreement with Philips and Sony, have introduced an MS-DOS **CD-ROM Extended Architecture** (CD-ROM XA) standard for the eventual provision of speech, music, graphics and animation as well as ordinary data on CD-ROMs. For graphics requirements the CD-ROM XA standard makes allowance for an 8-bit **Colour Look-Up Table** (CLUT) to produce a resolution equal to that of the enhanced graphics adapter (EGA) standard. Further developments in multi-media CD-ROMs are being actively pursued by Intel, Microsoft and IBM and are referred to as **Digital Video Interactive** (DV-I) technology. DV-I will be an amalgam of high-quality audio, image animation, database storage and the necessary technology to display and access the information.

CD-ROMs are very similar to their audio cousins, the difference being the additional error checking which is required during the retrieval and verification of data. CD-ROMs and their respective drives come in a variety of formats. However, some designs from Hitachi (CDR 3500) and Sony have converged to the half-height unit which occupies a single space in the disk drive section of a PC. A 386 PC fitted with one of these drives composes a fully integrated information archival system. Alternative designs have the CD-ROM drive as an external peripheral and an example of this is the LF5200P Optical Disk Drive from Megstore. This has a maximum data transfer rate of one Mbyte/sec and each optical disk has a capacity of 400 Mbytes (200 Mbytes per side).

In CD-ROMs the digital data is in the form of binary ones (1s) and zeros (0s); the binary zeros are represented as elongated holes or depressions which are melted into the reflective surface of the disk using a laser. This has the effect of changing the reflective properties of the disk. The gaps between the holes represent binary 1s and when illuminated with a light source the reflected light portrays the bit pattern on the surface of the disk. The data on a CD-ROM is held on one continuous spiral track which is read at a constant rate; this necessitates an increase in disk rotation speed as the optical reading head moves closer to the centre of the disk. The continuous design can make the search process rather slow because exact data positions cannot be easily defined. The High Sierra standard lays down the partitioning of the spiral track into

20,000 regions. To add to the confusion these regions are sometimes are also called tracks.

A single CD-ROM can hold in excess of 650 Mbytes of information which is equivalent to 270,000 pages of A4 text. Although the volume of information per disk is impressive, its reasonable access time and the rate of retrieval makes the CD-ROM an attractive storage medium. Search and retrieval software, such as Bluefish from Lotus, is also available and this is required to ensure that the maximum benefit can be derived from the product. To effectively use CD-ROMs Microsoft provides a software routine which patches DOS version 3.3 to enable the 32-Mbyte hard disk limit to be exceeded. This allows the CD-ROM to be treated just like a normal hard disk drive with a very large capacity.

The information base of CD-ROMs is growing month by month and there are now several companies in the UK which act as distributors. Examples of products on CD-ROM are:

❑ PAF-ROM from Silver Platter which has over 23 million industrial addresses and postal codes

❑ The McGraw-Hill Encyclopedia of Science and Technology

❑ Termdok, a multilingual technical dictionary from the Swedish Centre of Technical Terminology Information

❑ US National Technical Information Service database of abstracts and citations, with over 70,000 citations added each year

❑ Lotus One Source, a business and financial database, from Lotus Development

❑ FAME, Financial Analysis Made Easy, a combination of Jordon's database of corporate information, Jordon Watch and financial analysis software

It is customary for the disks to be updated at regular intervals and this demonstrates the organic property of the CD-ROM. This is only a very small selection of available CD-ROMs to illustrate the range of product areas covered by the medium.

7.4.1 Applications for CD-ROMs

As already stated, the CD-ROM is an attractive medium for information storage and retrieval and when combined with the computational power of the 386 PC it provides a powerful tool for statistical processing. One of the key applications for the 386 PC could be in market research. Given that the sizeable amount of sales information for the domestic and industrial market over the last five years could be available on CD-ROM, it would be possible to perform trend analysis, pattern links and recognition, marketing correlation and general multivariant statistical calculations on a single 386 PC. It is therefore constructive to think of the 386 PC as computational engine and the CD-ROM as the information base and, when combined, a fully integrated information processing system. 386-PC-based information systems will effectively represent lower information unit costs which will in turn enable broader access and more widespread use of information. As the demand for information grows there will be a corresponding growth in Information Houses which will specialise in accumulating data and making it available in a readily accessible format like the CD-ROM or through direct transfer.

Artificial intelligence, through the use of **expert systems,** is an area which has great potential for the applications of CD-ROMs on 386 PCs. Expert systems require databases, which have fast access times, to draw on in order to arrive at conclusions. The inference engine, which is responsible for making decisions, would be implemented within the expert system shell on the 386 PC. As information is fed to the expert system from the user, the inference engine would combine this information with data from its knowledge base and documented experience to formulate a set of conclusions. The ability to perform this type of operation quickly and to handle vast amounts of information is a major requirement in operation of expert systems.

7.4.2 WORM Drives

A not altogether different mass storage medium is known as WORM (Write Once Read Many) and is more aligned to personal information storage needs. WORM discs are packaged differently to CD-ROMs and their drives are incompatible. As the name implies, WORM discs can only be written to once but they can be read as many times as required; they are however treated like a hard disk unit by the PC. They are particularly attractive for the critical record archiving of medical, legal and audit information. New files with existing file names are written onto the WORM at the next available area. The old file is not erased and it no longer carries the file name but it can be recovered if necessary.

The technology in WORMS relies on light from a laser creating pits in circular tracks on the surface of the WORM disk which is either metallic or a organic dye compound. Each pit represents a binary 0 and each space represents a binary 1. The access time of WORMs is of the order of 75 msec and the storage reliability is probably better than any other format which consequently leads to a long shelf life provided the disk surface does not have any ink labelling on it.

WORMs are well suited to archives and personal data storage although no clear standard has yet emerged. The capacity of WORM disks varies from 200 Mbytes to 800 Mbytes – for example Panasonic WORMs are double sided and hold up to 470 Mbytes per side. If the DOS version in your 386 PC is 3.3 (or less) then it will be necessary to perform a patch to overcome the 32-Mbyte hard disk limit and the necessary details for doing this are supplied with most WORM units. A word of caution about Compaq's 386 PCs with their version of DOS: there may be problems when installing the DOS patch and an experienced Compaq dealer should be consulted if difficulties arise.

Most WORM systems are peripherals to desktop computers and are housed in separate units which are interfaced to the PC via a suitable control card fitted into the card cage. An example of a WORM product is the Panasonic LF-5000 which comes with a half-size adapter card to the Small Computer Systems Interface (SCSI – Section 7.3.3). The LF-5000 can use 5.25 inch WORM disk, for example Plasmon optical disks, with a storage capacity of either 200 Mbytes (single-sided) or 450 Mbytes (double-sided). It also comes with the Corel software utilities which can be used for back-up and retrieval purposes. The Corel software also contains a utility called HISTORY which keeps a record of the history of each file as it re-copies on the WORM, thereby allowing the user to access previously made versions of the file.

An alternative WORM drive is the Hitachi OD101 which accommodates 600-Mbyte WORM disks and with its SCSI interface can support data transfer rates up to 690K/sec (continuous). It requires the OF101S Format Controller which can support up to four OD101s.

7.4.3 Magneto-optic Erasable Disks

The limitations of the CD-ROM as a read only medium and the WORM as a single write-only medium has prompted development into CD devices where the write-once restriction can be relaxed. In a magneto-optic erasable disk (MO) the data bits are held as the orientations of magnetic domains which are frozen within a thin plastic layer.

During a write operation, a magnetic field is applied to a domain which is subjected to localised heating from a laser. This results in the domain aligning itself with the magnetic field and, as it cools, the new alignment (new data pattern) becomes frozen. Changing the alignment of a domain also changes the way it reflects or transmits light. The domain on the disk is read by illuminating it with a polarised laser light; as the light is reflected (or transmitted) its polarisation is rotated and this can be detected. A 5.25 inch MO disk can have a storage capacity of 650 Mbytes and this is obviously appealing for many archiving applications where the information is required to be updated from time to time. The expected life time of the MO is at least 10 years, however there is no guarantee – if it fails after this period, no one can guarantee your replacement data.

The available MO systems on the market include the Sony Microsystems SMO-D501 which is an integral disk drive and SMO-C502 controller card. It uses 5.25 inch removable MO disks which have a very low wear rate and a sustained data transfer rate of 7.4 Mbits per second (error free). The access time of the disks is 90 ms but this decreases to 20ms for the innermost 64 tracks. Emphasising the compatible aspect of its design, SMO-D501 disks can be used with a whole range of Sony News Unix products. Dilog also makes an optically erasable MO, the MO600 (Figure 7.10). Each disk holds up to 600 Mbytes of data and has a maximum data transfer rate of 7.4 Mbytes/sec. Its half-height footprint makes it ideal for integrating into the disk drive area of a 386 PC.

Figure 7.10 The MO600 Magneto-optic erasable drive. (Photo: Courtesy of Dilog)

7.4.4 Digital Paper

An exciting innovation from ICI is digital paper which has a substrate polyester base (Melinex) coated with a thin metallic layer. On this layer is deposited an infrared absorbing dye polymer. The mechanism of writing on the paper requires illumination of very small regions on its surface with a laser whose emission wavelength exactly matches the absorption wavelength of the polymer. This has the effect of deforming the polymer into a depression through a process known as **pyroplasticity.** The overall result is to change the reflective properties of the polymer. Laser light is used to read the paper. The reflectively altered bits represent binary 0s and the unaffected bits binary 1s.

Digital paper has many attractive features; it has an estimated memory retention of at least 15 years and is very low-cost – a few pence per Mbyte. Expected data transfer rate should exceed 10 Mbytes per second. It can be prepared as disks or tape and lends itself to original design. The extraordinary feature of digital paper is the huge storage capacity of the medium. It is estimated that a 2,900 foot half-inch tape can hold a phenomenal 600,000 Mbytes of data, which is little more than the human mind can comfortably cope with.

At the time of writing, a digital paper drive from Bernoulli Optical Systems of Boulder, Colorado was under development. It consists of the aerodynamic Bernoulli plate mounted close to a rotating disk of digital paper. There is an air flow through the side of the hub and then between the plate and paper. This stabilises the system so that the plate and paper never come into contact. The writing head protrudes through the Bernoulli plate and creates a moving depression in the rotating digital paper disk. The separation of the stationary writing head and the paper is one micron and at this separation a 10 mWatt laser can write directly onto the paper. Expected data transfer rates should be 1.5 Mbytes/sec.

Appendix 7A: Interrupts

When the user of a 386 PC installs expansion cards into the card cage it is sometimes necessary to have an appreciation of the interrupt switch setting on the card. An interrupt is a mechanism used by a peripheral to indicated to the CPU that it requests attention. However with several peripherals, each peripheral interrupt is prioritised. This is achieved through the design of the CPU and the operating system and each interrupt is given a priority level.

For example, a disk unit would be expected to have higher priority than the keyboard since it requires a faster response from the CPU. Each peripheral to the CPU is assigned a priority level, however it is quite possible for several peripherals to share the same interrupt level and this is common practice in microprocessor design when there are more peripherals than interrupt lines. An example of this is shown in Table 6A-1 where in order to obtain 16 levels of interrupts IRQ2 has eight sub-levels attached to it. IRQ8 to IRQ15 are assigned the same priority and if two or more interrupt at the same time it will be up to the operating system to sort out the priority.

Many expansion cards act as peripherals and can be assigned to an interrupt level, however many of the levels will be in use by the 386 PC system. In the example shown in Table 7A-1 opposite, interrupt levels IRQ3, 4, 5 and 7 could therefore be shared by installed expansion cards without causing problems for the system.

Interrupt Level		Function
Non Maskable (NMI)		Input/Output check
IRQ0		Timer Output 0
IRQ1		Keyboard buffer full
IRQ2		Augmented Interrupts – IRQ8 to IRQ15
	(IRQ8)	Real Time Clock Interrupt
	(IRQ9)	Software redirect
	(IRQ10)	Reserved
	(IRQ11)	Reserved
	(IRQ12)	Reserved
	(IRQ13)	Coprocessor
	(IRQ14)	Fixed or Hard disk Controller
	(IRQ15)	Reserved
IRQ3		Serial Port 2
IRQ4		Serial Port 1
IRQ5		Parallel Port 2
IRQ6		Floppy disk Controller
IRQ7		Parallel Port 1

Table 7A-1 Interrupt level map with IRQ8 to IRQ15 attached to IRQ2.

Appendix 7B: The Xmodem Protocol

This protocol is used for the synchronous communication between modems. In this protocol when the **receiving modem** (RM) is ready to receive data it starts by issuing ASCII character 21 (**Negative Acknowledgement – NAK**). In response to the NAK, the **transmitting modem** (TM) leads its transmitted data with ASCII character 1 (**Start of Header – SOH**) followed by two characters: the **block number** and its complement (255 - block number). This is followed by the actual data block of 128 characters, and tagged onto the end is the **checksum** value which is used for error detection.

The RM performs its own checksum on the data block and if there is a match it is accepted. The RM then issues an ASCII character 6 (**Acknowledge – ACK**) to indicate to the TM modem that the data block was accepted. The TM responds by issuing ASCII character 4 (**End of Transmission – EOT**) followed by the RM sending an ACK to the receiver. This completes the transmission of a data block containing 128 characters. In the event of the data block being corrupted during transmission it is highly probable that the checksum calculation performed by the receiver will be different to the checksum tagged onto the data block. If this does occur the receiver issues a NAK character.

On receiving this the TM retransmits the whole block and continues as normal. If this should fail on 10 successive attempts the process is effectively aborted by the TM. Figure 7.B1 shows the normal protocol and the protocol for corrupted data. Xmodem is a stop-and-wait protocol since the (N+1)th data block cannot be transmitted until the Nth data block has been accepted and this limits its application for high-speed data transfer.

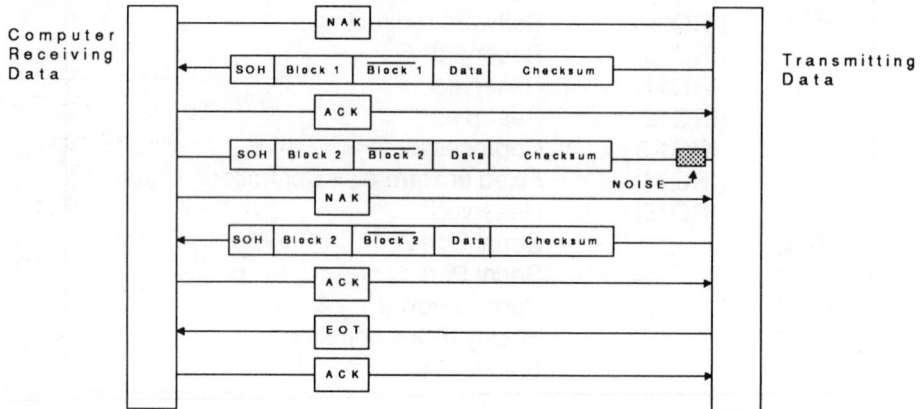

Figure 7.B1 Xmodem protocols for normal and corrupted data

Appendix 7C: MNP Classifications

Class 1   Uses bit-orientated, asynchronous, half-duplex – maximum transfer rate 1,700 BPS.

Class 2   Uses bit-orientated, asynchronous, full-duplex – maximum transfer rate 2,000 BPS.

Class 3   Uses bit-orientated, synchronous, full-duplex, block or packet transfer. No longer requires start and stop framing bits – maximum transfer rate 2,600 BPS.

Class 4   Uses **Adaptive Packet Assembly** (APS) and **Data Phase Optimisation** (DPO). In the APS scheme the error rate on the received data is continuously monitored. If the error rate is low the packet size is increased thereby reducing the overheads incurred through error checking. However for poor error rates, the average transmission rate is low since frequent block re-transmissions are requested. DPO uses one of the bits in each analogue modulation for error correction. Maximum transfer rate, 2,900 BPS from a 2,400 baud rate.

Class 5	Uses a real-time adaptive algorithm which results in **data compression** and an increase in the BPS rate. The algorithm monitors the transmission data and adjusts the compression ratio to maximise throughput. The effectiveness of the compression depends on the pattern content in the data and ratios between 1.3:1 to 2:1 are normal. With this protocol a performance of 4,800 BPS can be obtained from a 2,400 BPS modem.
Class 6	Uses the features of **Universal Link Negotiation** (ULN) and **Statistical Duplexing**. When the link is set-up the MNP modems communicate as low-speed 2,400 baud V.22bis modems. After negotiation the modems switch to a full Class 6 V.29 depending on the line quality. Through the statistical duplexing, error checking methods have been extended to allow non-compatible modem modulation schemes to be incorporated within the protocol. Throughput rates of 19,200 BPS can be expected.

Appendix 7D: Checksum Error Checking

When data is transmitted over the **Public Switched Telephone Network** (PSTN) the noise background can cause the data to become corrupted and errors occur in the transmission. There are many error checking algorithms used for determining if a block of data has been corrupted during transmission.

One of the more well known algorithms is the checksum. This is a calculation which is performed by the transmitting system on the content of the data block and the result is tagged onto the end of the data block before transmission. The receiving system performs the same calculation and compares its calculated checksum with the one sent by the transmitter. If they are equal there is a high probability that the transmitted data block has not been corrupted. If they are different then data corruption has occurred.

In the checksum algorithm the ASCII values of 128 characters are added together and the sum is then divided by 255 (an odd number). The fractional part of the result is then multiplied by 65,536 to form a 16-bit number which is used as the checksum tag. The checksum algorithm is used in the Xmodem protocol.

Further Reading:

Modems
Communicating with the IBM PC Series, G Held, John Wiley & Sons (1988).

Expansion Cards
The Handbook of Personal Computer Instrumentation, Burr Brown, (4th edition).

IEEE-488
IEEE-48, A J Caristi, Academic Press (1980)

CD-ROM
The Brady Guide to the CD-ROM, L Buddine & E Young, Prentice Hall (1987).

8

Networking and Multi-user Systems

Among the exciting features of the current generation of personal computers are the facilities for linking several of the machines together to form a loosely coupled network or **Local Area Network** (LAN). If you have several 386 PCs, then at some point the question will arise: What criteria should be considered when deciding whether or not to integrate the PCs into a network system? There are many and a number of these will be discussed.

At one time the main reason for networking PCs was to share resources, however today the dominant reason is the need to share common data. Business and commercial applications of PC-networked systems depend strongly on efficient data storage, access and exchange. With a multi-user network system, where data file sharing is a paramount need, careful attention must be paid to the appropriate file security to ensure that data integrity is maintained. Security mechanisms must therefore be part of the network to provide controlled file access and this should be part of the system specification.

Many applications for personal computers require several users working with the same application program. The users may be using the same program but processing different data with it. A network is attractive for this type of function since only one copy of the program need exist and the users can access the single copy on the system. Alternatively, a team of several users may not only be using the same application program, but also accessing the same information. This is often the case in archiving applications where an information or database needs to be amended and updated by several concurrent user sources.

The result of allowing several users to access common databases will be to enhance the overall productivity of the users as a working group. A network system will provide a fast channel of information transfer which is essential for multi-user applications. Most peripherals – printers, plotters, CD-ROMs, modems and mass storage devices – can be regarded as hardware resources. One of the attractive features of a networked system is the ability to make these resources accessible to all users. In the environment of the network, the hardware resources and application programs become common services at the disposal of the network users.

Many of the well known application programs have versions specifically designed for running on networks with several users. They are characterised by a degree of file protection which is often required when a number of users are accessing the same data files. These programs usually come with a site licence for multi-user applications. With only one copy of an application program on a network, the introduction of upgrades or new versions is made easy since only one copy is required. This ensures that everyone is using the same edition of the application program.

The subject of networking personal computers has become an expansive area of interest and it is beyond the scope of this book to deal with the subject in any significant depth. Several very good references are given at the end of this chapter and they should be consulted for information of a more specific nature. However, the areas covered in this chapter not only refer to network technology in general, but more specifically to the application of 386 PCs in network structures. This should enable the user to gain a preliminary insight into network technology and the specific functions which can be played by 386 PCs in network systems.

8.1 Local Area Networks

The minimum number of personal computers which can be gainfully integrated into a Local Area Network (LAN) is three. LANs have become established methods for linking personal computers together in order to enable users to share common system resources and to permit the rapid transfer of data. Once a requirement for an LAN has been established, a number of questions regarding the following areas are likely to arise:

❑ Hardware configuration and requirements

❑ Network software

❑ Which LAN technology?

❑ Consideration of future needs

❑ Data transfer speed

❑ Distance between PCs

❑ The number of PCs supported

❑ Links between the LAN and a mainframe computer

❑ Cost

❑ Commercially available network systems for 386 PCs

❑ Upgrading.

As various technical aspects of LAN technology unfold in the following sections, the reader will be in a better position to answer these questions in the context of 386 PCs. The important consideration to keep in the foreground is the future needs and demands which are likely to be made on the LAN. This will require planning and a good appreciation of the current state of LAN technology.

8.1.1 Network Hardware

The method of linking several 386 PCs together is to use LAN expansion cards or **network adaptors** which are also referred to as **Network Interface Circuits** (NIC). The network adaptor card is accommodated in the card cage of the 386 PC and special cables are used to link the PCs together. The purpose of the network adaptor card is to form the network interface to the 386 PC and it has several important functions to perform in order to ensure the smooth operation of the 386 PC within the LAN. The network may not consist exclusively of 386 PCs so the general term 'device' will be used to refer to an active network element.

The LAN will have one communication channel which will be shared by all the devices on the LAN. Devices can be talkers and/or listeners and at any one time there can only be one active talker. There are various methods for a talker to become active and access the LAN. For one access method, to become an active talker there must be a sufficient gap in the LAN traffic which indicates that no other device is transmitting information. Once a gap has been detected, a talker can become active.

The process of listening for a gap in the network traffic is known as **Carrier Sense Multiple Access** (CSMA). It is quite possible for two potential talkers to have detected the same gap and try to become active talkers; this would normally lead to a **collision**. However the adaptor cards are furnished with **collision detection** circuitry to detect the presence of other talkers on the channel. When this happens the active talkers cease and idle for a random length of time before searching for another transmission gap. The random period reduces the chances of the talkers becoming active at the same time again. CSMA which has the addition of the collision detection is referred to as CSMA/CD. The CSMA/CD access method is used by the Ethernet design and is part of the IEEE 802.3 standard (Section 8.6.3). CSMA/CD is admirably suited to LANs which have intermittent transmission and the data traffic is not too high.

An alternative method to CSMA/CD is the inclusion of a technique for estimating when a collision is likely to occur. When the likelihood is high, transmission is avoided until the traffic subsides. This procedure is referred to as **Carrier Sense Multiple Access with Collision Avoidance** (CSMA/CA) and is cheaper to implement than CSMA/CD since no circuitry is required to detect collisions on the network. However, many LAN adaptor cards use the CSMA/CD technique which is generally accepted as the standard. Alternative expansion cards for LAN communication use the Token-Ring Protocol which is covered in Section 8.7.1.

CSMA/CD adaptor cards may also have some DIP switches or jumpers to allow the card setting to be changed. Typical settings involve:

❑ The station number or address of the PC in the LAN.

❑ The memory address which the card will occupy in the I/O map of the 80386. (The 80386 CPU will address the adaptor card in the same way as it addresses memory.)

❑ The interrupt level for the network I/O (Appendix 7A). If there is a conflict, then change the LAN adaptor IRQ2 to IRQ3.

❑ The direct memory access (DMA – Section 2.3.5) channel.

The speed of the LAN can be derived from the data transfer rate. A LAN which can support one Mbit per sec (MBPS) can transfer a maximum of a 125K file every second. However when taking into consideration the overhead duty and the traffic due to the other PCs on the network this rate cannot be achieved for a one MBPS link.

8.1.2 LAN Transmission Methods

The mechanisms of data transmission along the LAN cables can be broadly divided into **baseband** and **broadband**. In baseband transmission the digital data is transmitted directly as binary voltage pulses (Figure 8.1).

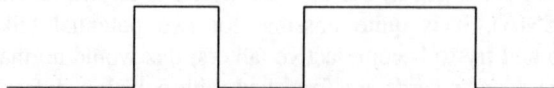

Figure 8.1 Baseband digital transmission representiing the binary sequence 010110

The attractive feature of baseband is its low-cost and minimal circuitry to implement. Broadband transmission on the other hand is more involved since it involves the generation of several sub-carrier frequencies (Figure 8.2 opposite) which is similar to radio transmission techniques. The binary data is then impressed onto one of the sub-carrier frequencies by using a modulator.

However there is an additional hurdle: although data is transmitted on one sub-carrier it is received on a different one. A frequency translation process is therefore required and this performed by a remodulator which moves the data from one sub-carrier to another. The frequency translation process is carried out on the LAN adaptor card and is quite transparent to the user. However this all adds to the cost of implementing the broadband transmission method, but the transmission rate can reach 10 MBPS with suitable coaxial connecting cable.

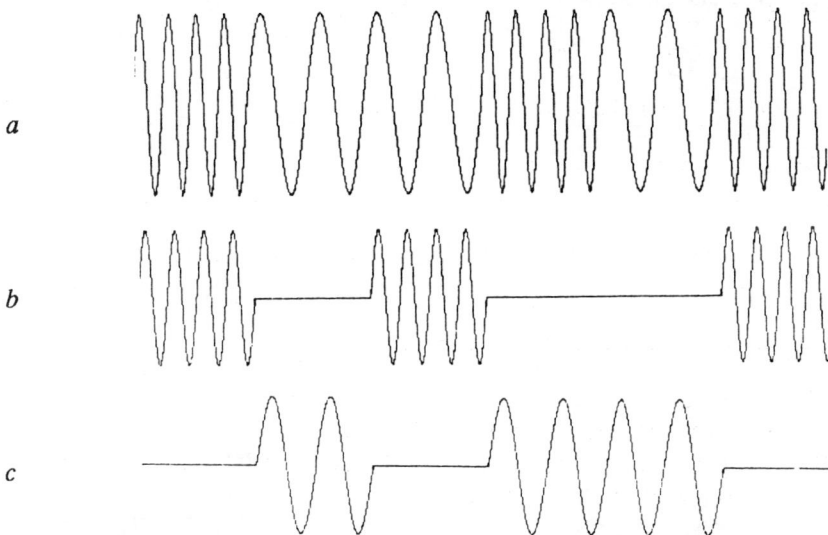

a

b

c

Figure 8.2 a) is a frequency modulated broadband signal representing the sequence 010110. The frequency components would be detected by passing the signal into two parallel band pass filters. The outtput from these would appear as b) and c)

8.1.3 LAN Topology

LAN topology refers to the geometric configuration of devices or nodes on a network. Three of the most popular types of LAN topology are the **bus,** the **ring** and the **star**. These are shown in Figure 8.3 overleaf. It is not always clear which topology has been adopted by some LAN manufacturers. IBM's Token-Ring LAN for instance is a mixture of ring and star topologies. In the bus topology a single backbone cable, which acts as the data highway, stretches over the area where the network devices are distributed. Each device is connected to the backbone cable via a transceiver which permits communication between the device and the network highway.

In the bus topology, when a device transmits a block of data, the address of the target device is attached to the block. As part of the operational protocol, the data will only be accepted by the device holding the relevant address. In the ring topology a single cable is also used as a data highway and branches are attached to the ring perimeter in order to make the device connection. The ring topology could be considered as a looped bus topology with the data propagating around the ring visiting each LAN device in turn. Since data is passed from device to device, in the event of a cable break or a device failure occurring then the network will come to a standstill. IBM's provision of a ring-star design in its Token-Ring, addresses this problem (Section 8.7.6) and has resulted in a system with a high degree of reliability.

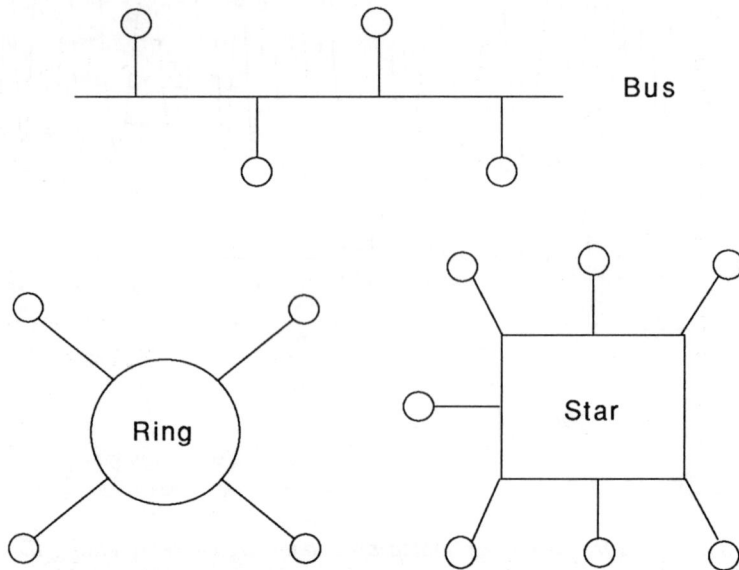

Figure 8.3 Bus, Ring and Star topologies for LAN configurations

With the star topology, each LAN device is connected directly to a network controller. For data to transfer from one device to another, it must pass through the controller. This design does have the disadvantage of the whole network coming to a standstill if the central controller should malfunction. However it is easy to implement, since every office has a telephone system which could be used as LAN medium with twisted pair cable. However this technology is not suitable as a high-speed network data link.

8.1.4 Internetworking

To extend the versatile nature of the LAN, it is possible to connected different LAN systems together; for example there may be a need to integrate a bus LAN and a loop LAN (Figure 8.4 opposite). This can be achieved by means of a **bridge** and the subject of integrating LANs is referred to as internetworking. Bridges are a combination of hardware and software elements. For physically close LANs, bridges can be constructed by configuring a 386 PC as a bridge server which contains two adaptor cards, one for each respective LAN system. If the LANs are on different sites then it may be necessary to adopt an internetworking communication based on the X.25 **Wide Area Network** (WAN) (Section 8.6.2), which can use leased lines from a telephone company and affords data transfer rates of 64K bits/sec.

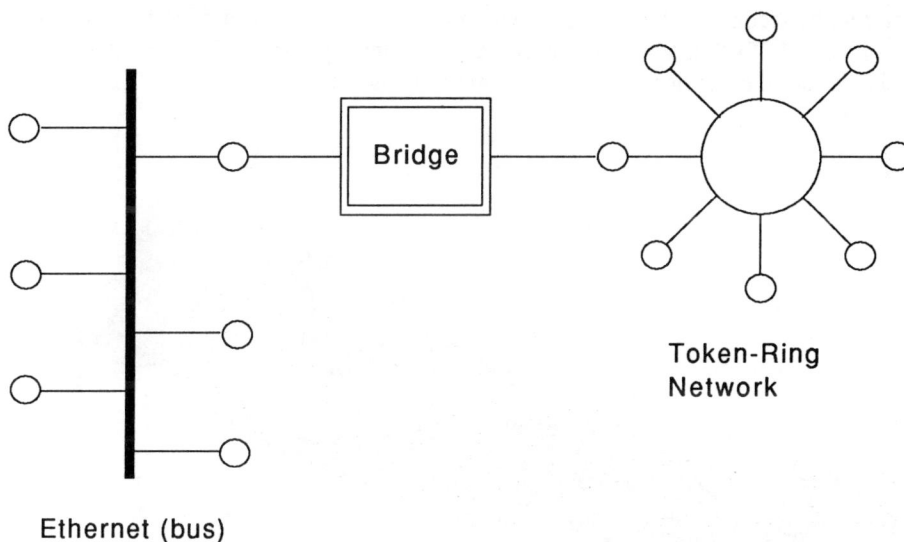

Bridge

Token-Ring
Network

Ethernet (bus)

Figure 8.4 Internetworking two different LAN systems by means of a bridge

If a requirement arises to integrate a LAN to a mainframe computer or to other types of workstations such as Apollos or SUNs then a **gateway** has to be established. For connecting a LAN to a mainframe a 3270 Gateway could be used; 3270 is the name assigned to terminal controllers which are linked to IBM mainframes. This comes in the form of a communications adaptor expansion card which is accommodated in one of the 386 PCs on the LAN, the 386 PC then becomes a mainframe server. Each 386 PC on the LAN can run IBM 3270 emulation software and is connected to the mainframe via the mainframe server like a normal 3270 terminal.

An expansion card suitable for this task is the Information Retrieval Management Adaptor or IRMA3 which is distributed in the UK by Computer Marketing. The clever design feature of the IRMA3 expansion card is the dual bus. Along one edge it has the Industry Standard Architecture (ISA) bus connector and along the opposite edge it has a Micro Channel Architecture (MCA) bus connector (Figure 8.5 overleaf). It can therefore be accommodated in a PC hosting either bus architecture.

There are a number of standard protocols used for internetworking. For example SUN's **Network File System** (NFS) is a standard for file exchange between computers running different operating systems. This is eminently suitable for multi-tasking 386 PCs which can act as file servers (Section 8.5.4).

Another well known protocol which is used for networking different types of computers is the **Transmission Control Protocol/Internet Protocol** (TCP/IP). The TCP/IP has been defined in order to satisfy the requirements for data exchange between dissimilar computers, via a network. Information sent under TCP/IP must therefore be recognised by any computer and to achieve this, each must have its own customised TCP/IP module to match its operating system. TCP/IP modules are available for all computer makes and designs ranging from mainframes to PCs.

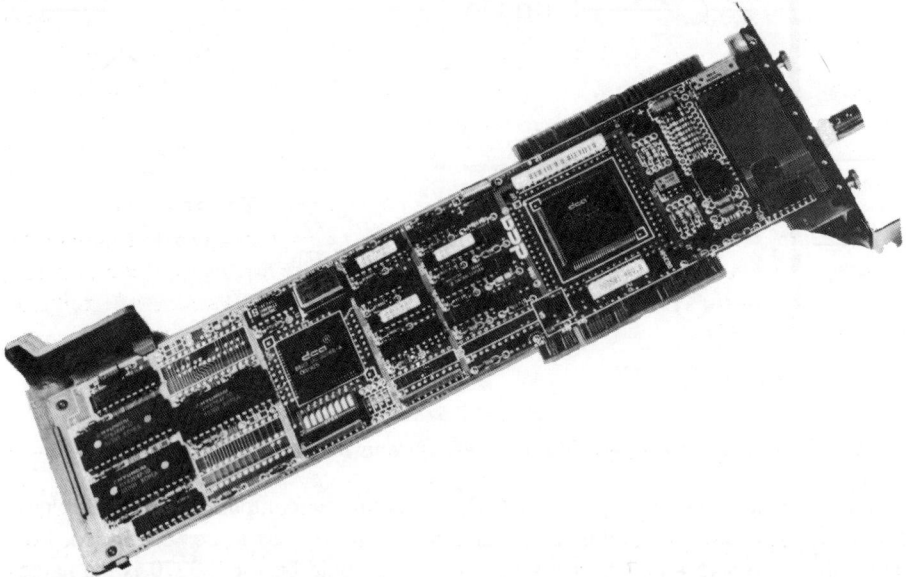

Figure 8.5 The IRMA3-3270 adaptor card with dual ISA and MCA buses. (Photo: Courtesy of Computer Marketing)

When 386 PCs, employing TCP/IP, communicate with other computers via a LAN they must be furnished with an intelligent adaptor expansion card and suitable TCP/IP software. Intelligent adaptor cards and corresponding software are available for either Ethernet or Token-Ring based LANs (Section 8.2). A TCP/IP facility can be implemented on a network of 386 PCs as a network resource and this facility would act as a **gateway** for the other 386 PCs. In this case only one 386 PC would be furnished with the intelligent adaptor card and the TCP/IP software.

The purpose of the gateway is to translate the data, originating from the 386 PC with its own network protocol, into a protocol acceptable by the TCP/IP environment and vice versa. It is the Internet Protocol (IP) portion of the TCP/IP which will contain the internet address of the destination node on the network. In addition, the IP will also contain information relating to the gateways and paths along which the information can be routed to reach the destination node. A TCP/IP block of data, once it has reached the destination, will be ascribed to a specific layer according to the OSI Model (Section 8.6.1). In order for the TCP/IP data block to reach the appropriate layer, part of the IP protocol, which is known as the **User Datagram Protocol** (UDP), will be attached onto the data block during the final routing.

After the TCP/IP has delivered a data block to the appropriate destination node on the network, a number of protocols can be used to make the data accessible by the destination node. There are three associated with TCP/IP: **File Transfer Protocol** (FTP), **Simple Mail Transfer Protocol** (SMTP) and a communication program called **Telnet.** Software running on dissimilar remote machines, which recognise FTP, can be used to exchange data and establish general communication. It can even translate between ASCII characters and IBM EBCDIC characters. SMTP on the other hand acts as convenient method for implementing electronic mail (email) on dissimilar computers.

To access the services of TCP/IP a user may use the Telnet protocol. For example if a 386 PC is to serve as a terminal for a DEC mainframe computer across a network, then it is likely that the Telnet protocol will have DEC VT-100 terminal emulation software. The range of terminal emulators will be found in the product specification for the TCP/IP package.

There are several TCP/IP software products on the market at present. A typical example is the TCP/IP for DOS by the Communication Machinery Corp. distributed in the UK by Anglia Technology. This product features the ENP-66 Ethernet expansion card with the TCP/IP software embedded in the card. The ENP-66 hosts its own Motorola 68000 16-bit microprocessor which relieves the 80386 CPU from the TCP/IP tasks. The DOS software for TCP/IP contains a suite of FTP, SMTP and Telnet programs, the latter having provision for emulating the DEC VT-series terminals. Alternatively, a family of TCP/IP products is the LAN Workplace for DOS by Excelan and distributed in the UK by Dataguild.

The LAN Workplace software module, called the TCP/IP Transport System, contains software drivers for the Excelan Exos 205 Ethernet intelligent adaptor card. The Exos 205 has its own 80186 processor for performing the TCP/IP tasks and also supports the NETBIOS (Section 8.4.1) on top of the TCP/IP. Another member of the LAN Workplace family is the HostAccess software which has FTP, Telnet and terminal emulation utilities. HostAccess will also act as an MS-NET redirector which enables the user to access resources on an MS-NET server.

8.2 Token-Ring

An alternative network technology to the Ethernet design is the Token-Ring which has become a great favourite with IBM. The transmission rate of the system is 16 MBPS and up to 260 nodes or devices can be accommodated by the LAN. Token-Ring has in fact a star ring topology which is uni-directional. Each device is connected to the Ring by means of a 8228 multi-station access unit. Each 8228 can support eight network devices and several 8228s can be daisy-chained together to realise the Ring. The token Ring system uses the baseband mechanism (Section 8.1.1) for transmitting data which lends itself to a variety of cabling systems.

The essence of the Token-Ring is a token which is a 24-bit packet of information which circulates the ring. Data can only be transmitted around the ring with the token and when a PC needs to transmit data, it must first wait for the token to arrive from its neighbour. Provided the token is free, the device sets a flag on the token to indicate that it has command of the LAN.

The adaptor card in the device impresses its own address and the target address on the token. The token is then retransmitted followed by the data stream coupled with a checksum (Appendix 7D) for error checking. The token is then passed from device to device on the ring until it reaches the target device, at which point the data stream is buffered in the adaptor card's memory.

The checksum is recalculated and tagged onto the end of the data stream and re-transmitted on the ring until it reaches the source device where the checksum is verified. If there is a match, the token is reset and sent to the next device on the LAN. On the rare occasions when the checksum is different the token and the data stream are re-transmitted for a second time.

The management of the token is controlled by a PC or workstation which is referred to as the **monitor**. On start-up of the LAN the first device will assume the role of monitor and will generate the token. It will thereafter ensure that the token is circulating the ring in the appropriate manner. It will even generate a new token in the event of the old token becoming corrupted.

In principle any PC or device on the LAN can act as the monitor since each adaptor card has the necessary software and hardware to perform the monitoring task. In the event of the monitor being switched off or developing a malfunction, the task of the monitor will be taken up by another device which may generate a new token if necessary. This ensures that if a fault occurs with one device on the LAN, even if it is the monitor, it will not cause the whole network to come to a standstill.

8.3 Network Cable

So much LAN technology is based around the design of cables which carry information around the network. When planning a LAN system, it is of great importance to realise the variation of cable options in order to match the intended data traffic and the number of devices (nodes) which are likely to be connected to the LAN. The transmission media used in LAN designs fall into three groups, twisted pair cable, coaxial cable and fibre optic cable. The twisted pair consists of two wires, one carrying the signals and the other being an earth lead. Their are three major draw backs with the twisted pair design: its high susceptibility to electrical interference which degrades the data rate transmission, low transmission rates (2 Mbits/s at best) and only short cable lengths. For high-performance LAN systems the twisted pair option is not a viable solution and only has limited application. However much development has been made in the alternative options which has resulted in their pricing has become competitive.

8.3.1 Ethernet Cabling

One of the standard LAN cables is the **Thick Ethernet** which in general is expensive. The cable itself is of a 1.03 cm diameter, double braided coaxial design (Belden 9880 for example). The data transmission speed is 10 MBPS and each PC or LAN device is connected to the Ethernet cable via a drop cable to a coaxial **transceiver.** Some transceivers have a number of light emitting diodes (LEDs) to indicate status conditions on the LAN. An example of a transceiver is the ANC-20 from Cablelines, which has ports for two drop cables.

There are at least two methods of connecting a transceiver to a Ethernet cable: **-N Series Connectors** or the **intrusive tap.** To use the -N connector the Ether cable is cut and the connectors are attached to the cable ends which are then screwed into the transceiver unit. The intrusive tap relies on drilling a hole into the Ethernet cable through to the core. A clamp connector is then attached to the cable which has a pin to penetrate the hole to make contact with the core. The drop cable connecting the transceiver unit will have a 9-pin D-connector which mates with the Ethernet adaptor card in the PC. Although the Ethernet cable segment should not exceed 500 metres (set by the IEEE 802.3 standard – Section 8.6.3), it can be extended by using a multi-port **repeater** between cable segments. These repeaters usually require **Remote Access Programs** (RAPs) in order to exercise control over their switching.

One problem which frequently arises is that of signal **reflections** in the Ethernet cable. The Ethernet cable has to carry high frequency signals and an important parameter of the cable is its **impedance.** Providing this remains constant along the length of the cable then the signal propagation will be uniform. However if there are breaks or sudden changes in the cable's impedance then the signals reflect back along the cable, from the breaks, giving rise to unwanted reflections. It is therefore important to use 50 Ohm terminations to ensure that the cable impedance matches that of the termination. This will minimise the effects of the signal reflections.

8.3.2 Cheapernet

Since the cost of Thick Ethernet cabling is high, an alternative cable product is Cheapernet which transmits data at the same rate of 10 MBPS. Cheapernet does not use Ethernet transceivers so that PCs can be linked together directly. The cabling for Cheapernet or **thin cable Ethernet** is also different, using the standard 50 Ohm, single braiding coaxial cable (for example Belden 9907) with BNC connectors. Several PCs can be chained together using separate lengths of cable with BNC T connectors which connect directly onto the adaptor cards. The first and last PC in the segment have 50 Ohm terminations which minimises the signal reflections. Although it is acceptable to remove a BNC T connector from an adaptor card while the network is active, the 50 Ohm termination must not be removed otherwise the network will go down. A word of caution: the BNC T-piece must also be 50 Ohm – a 75 Ohm BNC T-piece looks exactly the same. The maximum length of a cable connecting the PCs (a segment) is 300 metres, however up to three can be linked using two repeaters.

8.3.3 Optical Fibres

The latter half of the 1980s has seen a growth in application programs which require graphical front ends. The transfer of graphics information via a LAN makes substantial demands upon its information carrying capacity. Once this becomes the norm, with the growth of application programs which involve high-resolution graphics, LANs will be expected to carry greater amounts of traffic. For very high-speed data transmission, optical fibre is the appropriate choice. Although the technology is a little more involved than coaxial cable, the installation techniques and procedures are now well understood.

Optical fibres are well matched for point-to-point applications. This arises from the design of a fibre link, with an optical source (a semiconductor laser or a light emitting diode) on one end and an optical detector on the other. The light source produces binary light pulses and the photodetector responds to the pulses. Among the commonly used optical fibres there is a class of fibre referred to as **multimode** which can support several propagating optical modes. When there are several modes propagating in the fibre an effect known as **dispersion** arises which limits the data transmission rates.

When an optical pulse is launched into the fibre, it generates several modes and these travel along different paths in the fibre. The consequence of this is the broadening of the pulse width as it arrives at the other end of the fibre since the different modes arrive at different times. However the data transmission rate for multi-mode optical fibres can exceed 500 Mbits/s. An alternative fibre design, the **single mode fibre**, only supports one optical mode. Consequently there is no modal dispersion and the transmission rate can exceed 3,000 Mbits/s.

With this information-carrying capacity it is not only possible to have computer data but also voice and video data flowing along the same fibre. Optical fibres have the distinct advantage over coaxial cable of being immune from electrical interference, therefore the maximum distance of LAN cable lengths is greatly increased. They are also reasonably secure since it is very difficult to tap into them. Long cable runs can therefore be implemented without the restrictions imposed on coaxial cable.

One of the standards governing the use of fibre optic cables in LANs is called the **Fibre Distributed Data Interface** (FDDI) and the specifications are being developed by a committee of the American National Standards Institute. The FDDI standard is a token ring structure with a maximum transmission rate of 100 Mbits/s and a maximum LAN cable length of 100 km. The separation between any two nodes should not exceed two km. In the FDDI standard, a dual-fibre ring is attached to one of three types of device. Only one of the rings will carry the traffic while the other is a standby in the event of primary ring failing. Should this happen, the system can detect the primary ring failure and reconfigure itself with the secondary ring.

The first type of LAN device, Class A, will be linked to both fibres and will serve as a network attachment point in the event of the primary ring failure. The second type of device, Class B, is only linked to the primary ring. The third type of device is a modified Class A called a **wiring Concentrator** which contains the necessary bypass circuitry to ensure that the system remains operative in the event of a Class B device going down. These devices would therefore reside between the Class B devices and the primary fibre optic ring.

In the FDDI X3.139 standard there are four sections which deal with management of each node on the LAN. The **Physical Medium Dependent sublayer** (PMD) specifies the nature of the optical signals, their respective waveforms and the connectors used in the terminations. The **Physical layer protocol** (PHY) is concerned with two functions: clocking and coding. Of every five bits transmitted along the fibre only four will carry data, referred to as four of five code, which reduces the transmission rate to 125 Mbits/s. However provision for error checking can be incorporated using the fifth bit. Typical frame sizes will be 9,000 code symbols which will be equivalent to 4,500 bytes. The **Media Access Control** (MAC) layer will be responsible for:

❏ Scheduling data on/off the ring

❏ Packet framing

❏ Station address recognition

❏ Token passing

❏ Verification of frame checking

The last layer, the **Station Management** (SMT) will account for:

❏ The initial ring configuration

❏ The bit error monitoring

❏ Reconfiguration of the LAN during a bypass operation

❏ The general management services during normal ring operation.

Although the X3.139 deals with a token ring structure, it is only one standard. Considerable efforts and investments are continuing with Ethernet technology which incorporates fibre optic technology. It is interesting to note that in an Ethernet LAN which uses optical fibres, a transceiver is still used, but the drop cable is replaced with a fibre pair which connects to a fibre optic adaptor card. Implementing Ethernet on optical fibres should result in a transmission rate of 10 Mbits/s and this has become known as the **10baseF** standard.

8.4 Network Software

The purpose of the network software is to enable communication between a PC on the network and the network resources. This is achieved by exercising control over the devices on the LAN and on the manner in which they gain access to the LAN.

One well known LAN software package, which will be considered for illustrative purposes, is MS-NET from Microsoft. It is very similar in operation to IBM's PC LAN. MS-NET incorporates a hard disk sharing method with a common directory which means that directories are shared as well as the disk storage. Each device on the network is given its own identity by MS-NET together with its functional definition, **server, messenger, receiver** or **redirector**. This is achieved by using the NET START command. MS-NET also supports a message passing facility which is equivalent to electronic mail (email).

This is an important aspect of a LAN facility, transferring information to individuals or a list of people for general dissemination purposes. When setting up the network, the system manager would make extensive use of the MS-NET commands for configuring the resources on the LAN. This configuration file would be resident in the AUTOEXEC.BAT file of the file server which will be brought into effect when the system is booted up.

Table 8.1 opposite, gives a list of MS-NET commands which are commonly used in configuring a LAN. This very brief examination of MS-NET should provide an indication of what to expect from a LAN software control package and what features to look for when assessing other LAN packages.

NET	Network start using menu
NET ERROR	Display list of errors
NET CONTINUE	Restart network after pause
NET FILE	List files, current users and locks
NET FORWARD	Forward messages on network
NET LOG	Log incoming messages
NET NAME <name>	Receive message from <name>
NET PAUSE	Pause network operation
NET PERMIT	Permit exclusive use of resource
NET PRINT	Network version PRINT
NET SEND	Send a message on network
NET SEPARATOR	Page separator between spooled files
NET SHARE	Enable remote access to resource
NET START <name type>	Network start as name and type
NET USE	Use a shared resource device

Table 8.1 A number of MS-NET commands

8.4.1 NETBIOS

Embedded in the IBM adaptor card is a software module known as the NETBIOS which plays a similar role to that of the BIOS (Section 2.8). The BIOS handles system calls to the utilities on the 386 PC such as the disk units, the keyboard and monitor. Likewise, the copyright protected NETBIOS forms a low-level software interface between the 386 PC and the network adaptor card input/outputs (Figure 8.6).

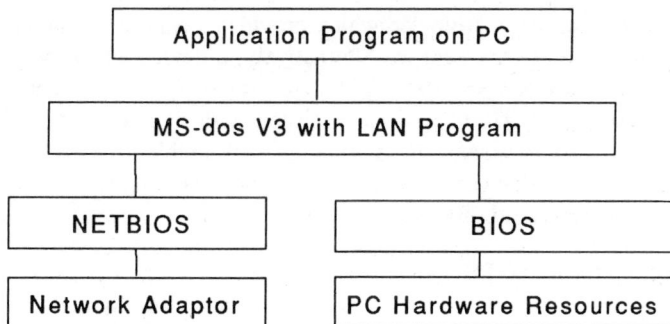

Figure 8.6 The operation of the NETBIOS relative to the BIOS

The operations for controlling data flow through the adaptor card are called through the NETBIOS. Many commercial adaptor card manufacturers have an imbedded NETBIOS which standardises the interface between the PC and the network. However the NETBIOS is not essential since many of its operations can be performed by MS-DOS 3.3 and 4 (Section 5.3). MS-DOS, which implements the Presentation Layer 6 of the OSI Model (Section 8.6.1), provides a service to interface an application program and the LAN via the adaptor card. It can be said that there are two levels of connectivity between the PC and network resource: through the NETBIOS or through MS-DOS.

MS-DOS has a provision (known as Interrupt 33) which can be called by the network to aid the process of data transfer to and from files. The importance of Interrupt 33 is the relationship it has with MS-DOS and the NETBIOS in the Presentation Layer. When a request arises from an application program running on one PC, to access a file on a file server, it issues an Interrupt 33. This is recognised by MS-DOS as a LAN request and is passed to the redirector on the LAN. The redirector constructs a **Server Message Block** (SMB) which is passed via the NETBIOS to the server. Since a unique relationship exists between the SMB and the NETBIOS, manufacturers of adaptor cards have either to use a licensed version of NETBIOS or devise a method of emulating its functions.

However to enhance the compatibility aspect of LAN application programs with LAN systems, the importance of using the NETBIOS with Interrupt 33 as an MS-DOS to NETBIOS gateway cannot be over emphasised. It must be stressed that MS-DOS 3.3 and 4 are not networking operating systems. When IBM introduced its Token Ring Network (Section 8.7.7) the NETBIOS was removed from the adaptor card and implemented a stand-alone module which is loaded alongside the operating system.

8.5 Network Servers

A network may have a number of devices on it and these devices are classified according to their function(s). A device which provides a service for other devices to use is referred to as a **network server.** Alternatively, a device which only requests a service is called a **client** or **requester.** A resource server can be resident in any 386 PC on the network and if the 386 PC is furnished with monitor and keyboard it is referred to as a **terminal server.** It is sometimes desirable to have a number of devices acting purely as **dedicated servers** for performing single tasks quickly and efficiently, for example a hard disk unit.

It is quite possible for a 386 PC to have a hard disk which can be accessed by other users on the network, which would be an example of a **non-dedicated server.** It can be used as a PC while serving the storage needs of other users on the network. For small networks it may be advantageous to have all the 386 PCs acting as servers and requesters, referred to as a **homogeneous network.** The resources of the network can be distributed among the 386 PCs without putting too much loading on any one machine.

Alternatively in a **central** or **single server** configuration all the resources are attached to one device which acts as a dedicated server. However in practice as the network grows, the **mixed network** usually emerges where there are PCs acting as requesters and other PCs acting as servers and requesters (**server/requesters**) with duplicate resources. This provides a degree of protection in the event of a server or resource breaking down. A contingency measure of this nature is a wise precaution for a system used by a team having to constantly meet target deadlines.

8.5.1 Device Servers

The most common device server is a shared hard disk unit, either hosted by a terminal server or in a stand-alone unit. The task of allocating disk space to users and scheduling user access is carried out by the **file server** normally residing with a shared hard disk. There are a number of problems when implementing a disk server on a network, partly stemming from the fact that DOS is a single user (task) operating system and allowing several users to write to a disk drive in a concurrent fashion is problematic. If the users only read the hard disk, then disk management is easy.

The problems occur when several users are working on the same data file and making modifications to it. It is common practice to partition the hard disk into individual user areas or **volumes** which can only be accessed by the logged-in user. This entails restricting access to data files to one user only. However there are techniques for extending DOS to enable multi-tasking operations. DOS does have a facility for engaging the Print Spooler as a **background** task while running a **foreground** application program concurrently. A number of network operating systems use the same technique for implementing a multi-user framework.

8.5.2 Communication Servers

To provide a facility for exchanging email and distributing mail among several users a communication server is required. Using this type of server is also an effective way of transferring data files from private volumes to other users on the network. When used efficiently, email can replace the paper memorandum mountain and yet retain the memorandum on the file server for future reference. Communication servers can also be responsible for modem sharing. This is a valuable resource if some PCs are at remote locations and require access to the network via the telephone line.

8.5.3 Management Servers

The function of a management server is divided into three aspects:

❏ to grant users an entry onto the network

❏ to act as a name server

❏ to synchronise the network.

Each PC or terminal on a network must be identifiable by a node or address number. When users log onto the network with a PC, it is the function of the name server to assign the PC address to the users and allow them access to permissible resources. Different users will have different levels of access depending on their needs. System managers will have a high access rating since they will be responsible for the day-to-day operation of the network. The name server will also produce a file listing of the network users and the users currently logged on. Having dealt with the users, the name server must also cope with other device servers on the network. If a PC has been defined as a server, it will login to the network in its own right without a user. This is done in a similar manner to the users except the server names remain fixed and their entry onto the network is via their AUTOEXEC.BAT file.

When data files are updated, the operating system will date and time them according to the latest update. For several PCs on a network, it is important that they have a common time and date. It is the purpose of the synchroniser or **timer server** to ensure that this is the case. As each PC logs onto the network its time and date are set to the timer server setting. In order for the server to maintain a record of the PCs which have logged onto the network and are still active, each PC sends a **heart beat** to the server at regular intervals. If the heart beat is absent, due to lack of activity on a PC, the server takes an appropriate measure to log the PC off the LAN. On some network designs, once the server receives the heart beat, it responds by transmitting the current time, thereby keeping all the active PCs synchronised.

8.5.4 File Servers

Many of the functions outlined above are encapsulated into a single server which is often referred to as a file server. However the function of a file server entails considerably more than those just discussed. One of the prime requirements of a LAN is a device which acts a file server for accommodating application programs which can be called at any time by the users on the LAN and a common data storage facility.

A file server is a device which satisfies these requirements and special attention is paid to the need for several users to access and write to common data files. This would arise when using a database application program such as dBASE IV where a number of users are modifying specific databases.

The file server has to support file functions such as open, close, create, read and write, in addition to a directory file structure. To prevent more than one user writing to a file at any one time a system of **locks** is evoked. This has the effect of controlling access to a common data area to one user at a time. It is also the function of the file server to implement security features by ascertaining whether a user is allowed access to a requested file. To do this an **access list** is checked for the valid entry.

A flag is frequently used by locking mechanisms in a file server and this is referred to as **logical locking.** With this technique the resource controller in the file server sets a resource flag or **semaphore** to indicate that the resource is currently in use. MS-DOS 3.3 and 4.1 have a file locking facility which means that once a data file is open, access is denied to other users until the file is closed. However some applications only open a data file for a short period while its contents are updated. On completion of the updating, the file is closed and in principle is available to other users. A locking problem can arise if single-user application programs are used on a LAN, but for most LAN versions the procedure of locking is well implemented. To secure a data file as read-only the MS-DOS command ATTRIB +R can be used. Alternatively there are commands within the network software for implementing file locking and restricting access; NET PERMIT and NET SHARE are MS-NET examples.

To enhance the reliability of the data storage facilities on a LAN it may be necessary to have more than one file server storing the same data. The question of file replication therefore arises. Reading a common file does not present a great problem. However with several users writing information into a common file how do file the servers keep the most recent copies of the file?

There are at least two methods which can be employed to update replicated files: the first is known as the **primary** copy. On the creation of a file, it is allocated a version number (VN) and each time the file is amended the VN is incremented. A replica of the file is made on each file server. When a user gains access to a copy of the file, with the view to amending it, the accessed file becomes the primary copy. When the access is complete the VN is incremented and this becomes the master version. The file server which has the primary copy makes a replica on the other file servers and this is a background task which is transparent to the LAN users.

The second method of replication is known as **voting** and only comes into play if the majority of files servers are free to access. This works as a **write quorum** where the file servers lock their copy of the file and the quorum effectively becomes a single server. On completion of the file modification, a copy is made on the quorum servers and the VN is incremented. This is followed by the release of the locks and the file is updated on the servers outside the quorum using the primary copy method. In the event of the file being read by a user before the other servers have had time to receive replicated copies, only servers in the quorum can be accessed by the user.

8.5.5 386 PC File Servers

Several manufacturers produce 386 PCs which are well designed to fulfil the function of a file server. There are however a number of features to look for on a 386 PC which will is to be used as a file server. It should have a high clock rate 80386 CPU and the motherboard should have sufficient room to accommodate 16 Mbytes of system RAM. The card cage must have adequate space to house several expansion cards which will be expected to perform some of the following tasks:

❑ Control for the hard disk floppy disk drives which should be based on SCSI technology (Section 7.3.3)

❑ Support the tape back-up device

❑ Provide the necessary interface to the network

❑ Allow bridge or gateway expansion facilities to be incorporated into the 386 PC for communication to other LANs or mainframe systems.

The size of the hard disk will depend on the application, but in general its capacity should be not less that 60 Mbytes. With a view on the future expansion of the network, it may be prudent to consider a 386 PC which has either the IBM Micro Channel Architecture (MCA – Section 3.8.1) or the Enhanced Industry Standard Architecture (EISA – Section 7.3.4) expansion interface bus. The 386 PC file server will also house the appropriate network software for file servicing and general LAN management.

An example of a 386 PC which is well suited as a file server is the Compaq Systempro (Figure 8.7 overleaf) which has its CPU running at 33 MHz. It is supported by 64K of cache memory (Section 2.3.2) and to enhance its performance, coprocessors and a second 80386 system processor can be added. It also has sufficient flexibility to meet the demands of 80486 CPU for future requirements. It does this by being able to accommodate either a 80386 and a 80486 or two 80486s. To achieve a high level of system integration, the Compaq Flex/MP Architecture of the Systempro, couples a separate processor/memory bus with an EISA bus. This permits fast data transfer rates with the necessary protection overhead which is expected from a quality file server. The hard disk access is also impressively fast. Based on **drive array technology**, it is on average only 20 msec.

As an added reliability feature in the disk storage, **data mirroring** is used where a secondary copy of the disk data is made and stored on the same disk. To aid this process, Compaq provides a protocol called Data Guarding which minimises the space taken up by the secondary copy. The software support for the Systempro comes in the form of Compaq's LAN MANAGER 386/486 which is fully compatible with commercial multi-user software such as Novell Netware/386 (Section 8.7.4) and SCO UNIX System V/386 (Section 5.4.1).

Figure 8.7 The Compaq Systempro, well matched to the demands of a LAN server. (Photo: Courtesy of Compaq)

8.5.6 Distributed Applications

It is quite probable that a network of 386 PCs will require a shared or common database embedded somewhere in a file server. For data processing needs, on the outset it may be acceptable to transfer the entire contents of the database to a 386 PC for processing. However it is unnecessary for the 386 PC to perform the analysis when the remote file server itself could perform the processing task just as well. It would be preferable if the 386 PC could send a set of search criteria to the file server and enable it to fulfil the role of an application server by performing the processing. On completion of the processing, only the results would be returned to the source 386 PC. This is sometimes referred to as a **value added process** and its use would eliminate the need to transfer large amounts of data over the LAN, thereby reducing the amount of LAN traffic. This is the objective of IBM's Structured Query Language

(SQL) and several commercial database applications programs claim to support its operation.

Xtrieve, from Novell, operates in a similar manner. It is a database query system which is menu driven with an easy-to-use report writer option. It allow the user to catalogue, retrieve, analyse and update databases. The type of remote data processing it performs includes:

❑ Statistical analysis with results shown in new display fields

❑ Transport data or data sub-sets to ASCII or Lotus 1-2-3 worksheets

❑ Sorts and sifts through a database according to the user-specified criteria

❑ Extensive scrolling to enable the user to view the contents of databases.

8.6 LAN Standards

From the early days of computers a need arose to establish a method for implementing a communication standard between different computers. IBM was among the first commercial companies to recognise this need and promoted a **layered architecture**. Behind this concept was the belief that all communication functions of a system could be broken down into a number of operational layers. Each layer would be responsible for a particular group of communication functions.

The concept of this layer design is broadly described as the **Systems Network Architecture** (SNA) and many network implementations fall under this banner. A number of layers within the SNA are responsible for transmission onto a network, organising data flow and general access management to the network and these are operations fall within the definition of a **Logical Unit** (LU). The LU serves as an interface between the user, in the so-called application layer, and the network. Part of the communication across a network, in the context of a SNA, is concerned with the interface between the application layer and the LU, and communication between LUs.

Each user and LU can be considered as a node on the network and there are strict protocols governing data exchange between nodes. The most widely used protocol is the **LU 6.2 Advanced Program to Program Communication** (APPC). An example of its function: if a user on the first node wishes to use the resources on a second node, a request is made from the first LU to the second LU. The LUs establish a **session** via the SNA and the resources in the second node are accessed by the first node. To ensure that the definition of each layer function takes on a universal understanding, LAN standards have been derived which help to unify LAN products from different manufactured sources.

8.6.1 The ISO/OSI Model

Establishing standards in area network communication systems has focused on the efforts by the **International Standards Organisation** (ISO) with its Reference Model for **Open System Interconnection** (OSI). The OSI standard defines the structure of a network in terms of a seven-layer hierarchy. Each layer is well defined and the objective of this approach is to establish how a network node appears from other nodes. It is intended to define how different aspects of a network should be integrated to form a interconnected structure. Having categorised a LAN in terms of the OSI model, the OSI standard broadly defines how each layer in the network interfaces with the layer below and with the layer above. The standard is not too concerned with the actual events in each layer, only what is presented by each to its neighbouring layers. Manufacturers of network equipment are free to produce competing designs within a layer provided they interface with other manufacturer's products in the adjacent layers. This allows the users to pick and choose layer products which are best matched to their application, with the confidence that they will be compatible.

The seven layers of services for the OSI Model are:

Layer 1   **The Physical Layer** is the deepest layer in the model where all the interchange of signals for data and control occur. There is also a specification for the electrical and mechanical connections.

Layer 2   **The Data Link Layer** is where control over data frames is exercised. Data transmission may be bit or block orientated with defined delimiters. Acknowledgement of received data is carried out with error checking. Data link protocols may reside in this layer, which may include the **Binary Synchronous Communications** (BSC) and the **High-level Data Link Control** (HDLC). The Token-Ring or CSMA/CD format is implemented at this level.

Layer 3   **The Network Layer** is where the logical interface between different networks is defined to allow networks to communicate with each other. It therefore provides services which include switching, receiver addressing, network routing, sequencing, data flow control procedures and gateway functions to other networks. In this layer the data is prepared as packeted data blocks with address and route information and these are transferred to the transport layer. The route is either fixed or adaptive according to the network traffic.

Layer 4   **The Transport Layer** is where control of data transfer integrity is performed. After a communication link has been established between two nodes, various error checking protocols are used to ensure successful data exchange. It is concerned mainly with making the most efficient use of resources to maximise error-free data transfer between the two nodes. This is important if a slow node is receiving data from a high-speed node.

Layer 5   **The Session Layer** is responsible for the interface between a device and the network, ie setting up a connection between nodes on the network. Here the transfer of data between a node and the network is properly established and terminated. LAN synchronism and collision recovery are also organised.

Layer 6   **The Presentation Layer** is concerned with the format in which data is presented for transmission on the network. Being a software function, a number of routines will be available in this layer. These might include data encryption and decryption, data compression and decompression, syntax checking and format conversion for the transmission of ASCII characters.

Layer 7   **The Application Layer** behaves like a window through which access can be gained to the services provided by the OSI model. It accommodates the operating system shell and the user application programs. It also deals with the manner in which user programs exchange data and provides file transfer and terminal services. There are referred to as **Specific Application Service Elements** (SASEs) and form part of the general service of the Application Layer. These in turn are sometimes called **Common Application Service Elements** (CASEs).

Information is transferred through the network in frames and each frame has a header which contains address and control information. As the frames travel from layer to layer, each layer adds its own header and removes the header attached by the lower layer. By the time the frame reaches the physical layer (1) all the lower layer headers have been removed and the frame arrives at its target in its original form.

In principle the OSI Model should cover all network designs whether local area (LANs) or wide area networks (WANs). As far as LANs are concerned the relevant layers of the OSI Model have been further refined and standardised by the American Institute of Electrical and Electronics Engineers (IEEE).

8.6.2 The X.25 Communication Protocol

It may be necessary from time to time to generate a **bridge** between two or more remote LAN systems and one method of achieving this is by using the X.25 protocol which employs leased lines or a **Packet Switched Stream** (PSS). It will also serve at this point, to demonstrate how the ISO model can be implemented in part. Although the ISO model is comprehensive in its structure there are occasions when a reduced structure will be adequate and this can be shown with the X.25 Protocol.

The data to be transmitted is assembled into packets and after transmission it is disassembled to provide the original data. This process is known as **Packet Assembler Disassembler** (PAD) and is particularly attractive in large LAN systems where there are many possible routes to the target node on a network. Since the data packet will carry its destination address it can be switched along alternative routes in the LAN to ensure minimum traffic congestion. British Telecom has adopted the X.25 protocol and provides a service called **PSS X.25.**

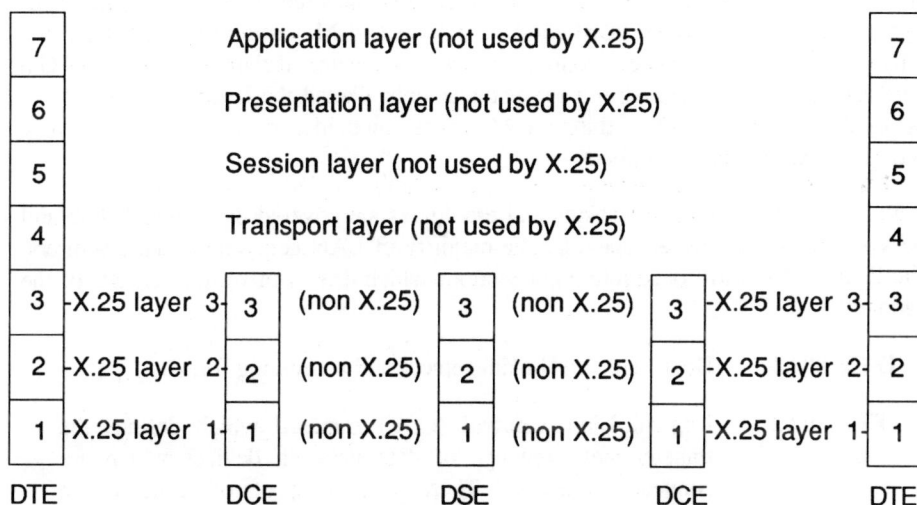

7	Application layer (not used by X.25)								7
6	Presentation layer (not used by X.25)								6
5	Session layer (not used by X.25)								5
4	Transport layer (not used by X.25)								4
3	X.25 layer 3	3	(non X.25)	3	(non X.25)	3	X.25 layer 3	3
2	X.25 layer 2	2	(non X.25)	2	(non X.25)	2	X.25 layer 2	2
1	X.25 layer 1	1	(non X.25)	1	(non X.25)	1	X.25 layer 1	1
DTE		DCE		DSE		DCE		DTE

Figure 8.8 The X.25 Protocol in the context of the OSI model

In the X.25 protocol the 386 PC, furnished with the suitable hardware (modem) and software, will take in the role of the **Data Terminal Equipment** (DTE) and will be interfaced to the network via the **Data Circuit-terminating Equipment** (DCE) which will consist of a modem in the general sense. This will be linked via the network to another DTE through its DCE (Figure 8.8). The connection between the two DCEs (the network) is referred to as the **Data Switching Exchange** (DSE). As can be seen from the illustration the X.25 is defined in three layers.

The Frame Layer 3 (equivalent to the Network layer of the OSI Model) is responsible for reliable data transfer between the DTE and the DCE. It adds bits to the data which is produced from the Packet Layer 2 (equivalent the Data Link Layer of the OSI Model) to make a data frame which has a format known as the **Link Access Protocol** (LAP). Layer 1 of the X.25 deals with the data packet within the frame itself. The data packet is therefore embedded within the LAP frame and there are 15 different sorts of X.25 packets which handle the modes of operation of the standard. These include procedures for coping with collisions and busy target DTEs.

To realise the X.25 protocol it will be necessary to install an appropriate card in a suitable 386 PC server on the LAN. An example of an X.25 expansion card is the PC Xnet from OST of Cedex which is accessible via MS-DOS or the NETBIOS. PC Xnet can also perform the function of a network adaptor card and is compatible with other protocols which include X.32 and X.21.

8.6.3 IEEE 802 Series

In 1985 the IEEE of the USA published a set of standards for the specification of layers 1, 2 and 3 of the ISO/OSI Model for local and **Metropolitan Area Network** (MAN) design. Six working groups with two associated technical groups (TAGs) were set up and this resulted in a set of documents. Called the IEEE 802 standard, it has established, among other things, LAN access methods, transmission cables, data rate and maximum node numbers.

A number of possible LAN designs and topologies are covered by the IEEE 802 and the standards have been accepted by the majority of LAN component manufacturers. The IEEE 802 is partitioned into eight sections which deal with various aspects of the standard:

IEEE 802.1 Deals with LAN management and addressing formats.

IEEE 802.2 **Logical Link Control** (LCC) standard which defines the transfer and exchange of data between devices which are connected to a LAN. There are two aspects of connection in this specification: 1. An unacknowledged connection which permits a user to transmit and receive data without formally agreeing to a connection – used as an emergency or temporary link. 2. Connection-orientated link which appears as a hard-wire connection between devices and is sometimes called a virtual circuit.

IEEE 802.3 This is a description of the physical bus structure which uses CSMA/CD as a method for gaining access to a LAN communication channel and is similar to the Ethernet design with a 10 MBPS data transfer rate. The specifications for Ethernet cable are:

	Thick Ethernet	*Thin Ethernet*
Max Segment length	500 m	185 m
Max Network length	2.5 km	925 m
Max No nodes/segment	100	30
Max No nodes/Network	1,024	1,024
Node separation	2.5 m	0.5 m

IEEE 802.4   Is applicable to a physical bus which uses token passing as a method for gaining access to the bus.

IEEE 802.5   The physical ring network structure is defined in this standard which employs the token passing method for gaining access using baseband transmission. This is equivalent to the IBM Token-Ring Network design which is also known as the **803 Wide Area Network** (WAN).

IEEE 802.6   Specifications for the metropolitan network **MAN** which lies somewhere between a LAN and a WAN.

IEEE 802.7   This TAG provides information relating to broadband (Section 8.1.2) transmission on LANs.

IEEE 802.8   Concerned primarily with matters relating to optical fibre specifications in LAN systems.

There are two examples where the IEEE standards have been adopted: the Technical and Office Protocol (TOP), based on the IEEE 802.3 and the **Manufacturing Automation Protocol** (MAP) which is based on the IEEE 802.4. At the higher levels MAP and TOP are very similar and are intended to be compatible. The purpose of this is to integrate the computer-aided machine (CAM) and other activities on the shop floor (the MAP operations) directly with management control (the TOP operations) via a network.

8.7 Commercial LAN Systems

Currently on the market there are several Network systems which are suitable for implementing on 386 PCs. It is beyond the scope of this book to present a comprehensive review of available network systems. However, a discussion of a few such systems will be instructive in order to gain an appreciation of what to expect from them. The systems which have been designed with the 386 PC in mind will be covered in greater detail.

To implement an LAN on a number of 386 PCs, each PC will require an adaptor expansion card and suitable software drivers. Most commercial network system software is capable of using a wide variety of adaptor expansion cards. The LAN software can be loaded onto one of the 386 PCs which will act a file server, but it must be stressed that the essence of LAN is distributed resourcing. If required, the resources of the network can be spread around the individual 386 PCs and they act as servers in one form or another.

When reading through manufacturers' brochures on LAN equipment and software you will not be alone in failing to understand what they are trying to sell. Network product brochures are particularly bad at explanation and the degree of ambiguity is, to say the least, quite alarming. It is therefore very important to ascertain, not so much what the product is capable of doing but whether it will satisfy your present and planned future requirements.

8.7.1 Expansion Adaptor Cards

The general functions of adaptor cards have been discussed in Section 8.1.1 and these cards fall into either one of two camps: those which implement the CSMA/CD LAN access method and those which use the Token-Ring access method. Ethernet adaptor cards use the CSMA/CD access method and some are furnished with two connectors – a BNC for 'thin' coaxial cable, a D-connector for connection to a transceiver via a drop cable. An adaptor card should conform to the Ethernet and Cheapernet standards laid out in IEEE 802.3 (Section 8.6.3).

When choosing an adaptor card it is important to confirm that it is compatible with the network software, for example Novell/386 or 3Com. To ensure a maximum data transfer rate of 10 Mbits/s, it would be preferable to use an adaptor card which has at least a 16-bit Industry Standard Architecture (ISA) edge connector for interfacing to the 386 PC bus. Such a card, based in the ISA interface, will have jumper settings to adjust the direct memory access (DMA – Section 2.3.5) channels and should have a sizeable memory buffer of at least 16K.

A typical set of Ethernet cards which satisfies most of these requirements is manufactured by Torus Network Products (TNP) of Cambridge. TNP makes Ethernet cards with the 16-bit ISA, 16-bit MCA and 32-bit EISA interface standards as well as a variety of Token-Ring network cards. For networking with fibre optic links the FAT Card from Onelan could be considered. The FAT Card has a 16-bit ISA bus and uses the AMD Supernet Chip Set for implementing the Fibre Distribution Data Interface (FDDI – Section 8.3.3) standard. It has a 256K frame buffer and can be supplied with a variety of utilities to allow the card to be configured as a system service for users on the LAN.

8.7.2 IBM PC Network

In an attempt to establish a standard for LAN communication, in 1984 IBM issued a LAN system which consisted of three elements:

❑ The IBM PC Network Adaptor card

❑ A network program (the IBM PC Network Program)

❑ An updated version of DOS (version 3.1).

The current edition of IBM's network program, called PC-LAN, was written by Microsoft and is basically a tailored version of its network software MS-NET. IBM PC Network is a bus system which employs the broadband (Section 8.1.1) mode of data transmission at a rate of two MBPS.

The adaptor card hosts two microprocessors: the Intel 80186 which executes a set of protocols called LocalNet/PC, and the Intel 82586 which controls the CSMA/CD process for accessing the LAN. Since the IBM PC Network is broadband the adaptor card also has a modem for implementing **Frequency Shift Keying** (FSK) modulation (Section 7.1). In the adaptor card the transmission frequency is 219 MHz (the forward direction frequency) and the receive frequency is 50.75 MHz (the reverse direction frequency). The adaptor card also hosts a **Network Translator Unit** or remodulator (Section 8.1.1). The function of this device is to take the data off the transmission sub-carrier frequency of 219 MHz and impress onto the receiver sub-carrier frequency of 50.75 MHz. This is necessary because an adaptor card transmits at 219 MHz for another card to receive at 50.75 MHz.

There are a few restrictions with the cable lengths allowed in the IBM PC Network. This arises from the attenuation and dispersion that high frequencies suffer when propagating along coaxial cable. IBM has minimised this effect by incorporating a compensation in the adaptor card, however the cable lengths are limited to combinations of 25, 50, 100 and 200 feet. Careful attention must be paid to allowable length combinations which are specified in the IBM PC Network Technical Reference Manual. Since the data transmission rate is only two MBPS the information carrying capacity of the coaxial cable is under used. It is therefore possible, in principle, to transmit other information channels along the same cable, such as video and speech.

Part of IBM's PC Network is the IBM PC Network Program which assists in allowing the LAN users to share the resources. Each device on the IBM PC Network can be configured as a server, a messenger, a receiver, a redirector or a combination of these. The Network Program is used to specify a device in the appropriate manner according to its function. There are over 45 network commands in the Network Program which are used to control the operation of the Network.

8.7.3 3Com

This is a LAN system which supports either Ethernet or token ring; in the latter case 3Com supplys token ring hardware in the form of its own RingTap and Token Plus cabling which permits the token ring to be configured in a bus topology. The choice of hardware is made during the installation of the 3Com software. The networking operating software from 3Com is 3+Open and a core product of 3+Open, called 3+Share, augments MS-DOS 3.3 and 4 and NETBIOS with two additional modules for permitting multi-user operations. The first is a process manager for scheduling the multi-user tasks and the second, a multiaccess disk input/output system referred to as CIOSYS.

Other software modules which come under the 3+Open umbrella include 3+Menu, 3+ OS/2 LAN Manger, 3+Share, 3+Name, 3+File/Print and 3+Mail. 3+Menu sets up the screen in a Graphics User Interface (GUI) format with mouse control to activate the options via pull-down menus. LAN Manager requires four Mbytes of RAM and has provision for PCs bearing the IBM OS/2 operating system which has a disk cacheing facility for disk sharing at directory level. Part of OS/2 is the front end Window graphics display known as Presentation Manager (Section 5.4.2) and LAN Manager operates within this framework.

LAN Manager has an option of a variety of different communication protocols which include **NETBIOS Protocol** (NBP), **Xerox Network Systems** (XNS), **Data Link Control** (DLC) and **TCP/IP.** These are built into the menu structure which conforms to the IBM SAA (Section 5.6.2) standards found in the Presentation Manager. There is a provision within LAN Manager to allow PCs running dissimilar operating systems (OS/2, MS-DOS or UNIX) to exchange data via a network link and this is a form of **Demand Protocol Architecture** (DPA). The 3+Share is a network operating system similar to MS-NET.

Typical functions of 3+Share include disk sharing, a filing system and a centralised name service for network devices. The disk sharing options can be used to partition the resource hard disk storage among the network users and allocate access priority. This can be done for shared, private (these require pass words) or for public access. When a hard disk resource is partitioned by 3+Share, it is divided into volumes which can vary in size from 64K to 32 Mbytes. A number of such volumes can be accessed by a user (from a single PC) at any one time. If a receiver 386 PC had a floppy disk drive A:, a hard disk C: then the available volumes on LAN disk drive would be assigned the logical drives D:, E:, F: and so on.

Another facility on the 3+Open product is the 3+File/Print which is a print spooling routine. It enables files, sent to a printer, to be stored in a queue while waiting for the printer. Between each file printing, EtherPrint produces a divider sheet giving details of the user of the file. With several users on the LAN, this feature is especially useful; when the file is committed for printing EtherPrint takes the file, leaving the user's PC free of the printing process. The email option of the 3Com product is 3+Open Mail and provides the full mail facilities required within a LAN environment.

An attractive feature of the 3Com product is the degree of options offered in its network design. For example, if there are only a few PCs on the LAN, then it is quite possible for the LAN to function without a dedicated server. One of the PCs, with a sufficiently high-capacity disk, could serve as a common storage area for the other LAN users by configuring it as a server and receiver. But it could still be used as a workstation by a user. 3+Open is compatible with the majority of network adaptor expansion cards, however it is always advisable to clarify that the network software is compatible with the adaptor cards of the users choice.

8.7.4 Novell NetWare/386

Among the principal features of the Novell NetWare/386 is the ability to provide product support in four areas: server platforms, open network architecture, open protocol technology and proprietary NetWare services. A network environment will be furnished with many 386 PCs. Some will be expected to act as server platforms and NetWare/386 has a generous provision for accommodating this requirement.

Although the techniques for integrating 386 PC clients/servers into a network are well established, NetWare/386, through its open network architecture and open protocol technology, provides an effective means of integrating dissimilar technology into a loosely coupled system. NetWare/386 is a true 32-bit network operating system which is able to run on the 80386 in its protected mode (Section 2.2.3) and demands a 33 MHz 386 PC as a host to optimise the response time. With its 32-bit performance, the NetWare server has the ability to cope with heavy user loading by supporting a huge storage capacity. This takes the form of up to 250 users and 100,000 open files at any one time where any one user can access 100 open files. It is able to support a disk space of 32 Terabytes (1 Terabyte = 1,000,000 Mbytes) and a file can be as large as 4,000 Mbytes and consequently occupy several hard disk drives.

However to effectively support the data throughput of this memory capacity, the 32-bit network operating system will be best served by 386 PCs which are armed with the corresponding 32-bit EISA (Section 7.3.4) expansion card capability. The architecture of NetWare/386 is essentially modular and each operating component is added as required. The central feature is the **System Executive** responsible for allocating memory to tasks, granting users access to resources and scheduling network tasks.

A key feature of the System Executive is its facility for coping with file systems and this includes support of the CD-ROM High Sierra standard (Section 7.4) as an extended file. The System Executive, which acts as a multi-tasking kernel, can dynamically adjust the amount of memory required by the major network resources. The System Executive can therefore respond to the loading of a server by allocating memory to its needs by removing memory from less exacting resources. The versatility of NetWare/386 lies in the range of **NetWare Loadable Modules** (NLMs) which allow the creation of a powerful integrated network server.

NLMs are software modules for driving and accessing resources on the network and they are connected to the System Executive via the NLM Interface (NLM-I) as shown in Figure 8.9 . NLMs perform a wide range of service functions, for example gateway electronic mail, Btrieve – the file management server and Print Server which supports printers attached to networked 386 PCs. As a new service is added to the network a corresponding NLM will also be attached to the NetWare/386 server. To prevent NLMs from being added which could circumvent the system security, NetWare/386 has a Secure Console option which only allows specified users to add NLMs.

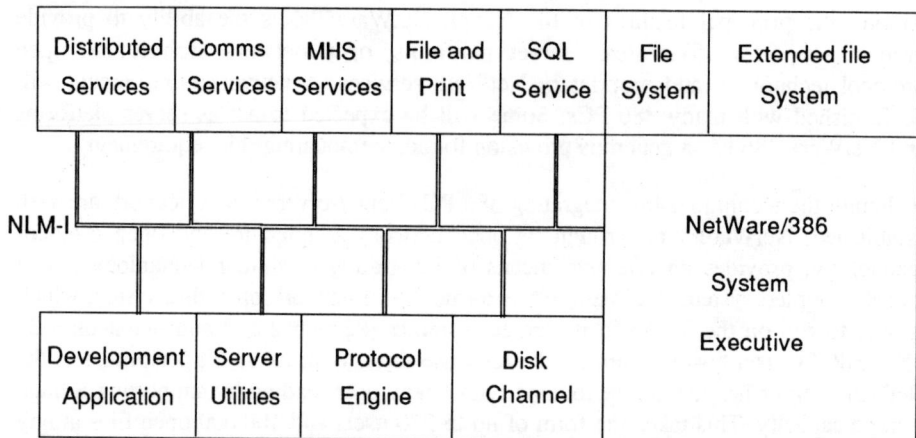

Distributed Services	Comms Services	MHS Services	File and Print	SQL Service	File System	Extended file System

NLM-I

Development Application	Server Utilities	Protocol Engine	Disk Channel	NetWare/386 System Executive

Figure 8.9 Block architecture of NetWare/386

To encourage third-party vendors to create NLMs for their own products, Novell provides the Programmer's Workbench which contains all the software tools necessary for distributed applications to run under NetWare/386. This includes the NetWare **Application Program Interface** (AIP), which is a set of software call procedures used by programmers to implement network services, and the C Network Compiler/386 specifically for the 80386 and NLMs. NetWare/386 has a **Dynamic Resource Configuration** (DRC) which is used when a new application program is added to the system. The DRC will allow adjustments to be made to network routing buffers and the allocation of memory for directory cacheing. The attractive feature of the DRC is the ability to add application programs without having to shut down the network.

As part of the open protocol technology, NetWare/386 supports a variety of internetworking transport protocols and these are advanced in the protocol engine as shown in Figure 8.10. The function of the **Open Data-Link Interface** (ODI) is to allow transport protocols to use a single network adaptor card for gaining access to the network without fear of traffic conflict. The NetWare Streams on the other hand functions as a common interface between the transport protocols and the NetWare Services and server application programs. By incorporating several protocols within the protocol engine, network services appear transparent across the network irrespective of their protocol and source. Novell has taken this one stage further by including in NetWare/386 support for a number of client-server protocols of other commercial products, such as the Apple Macintosh and Sun Workstation.

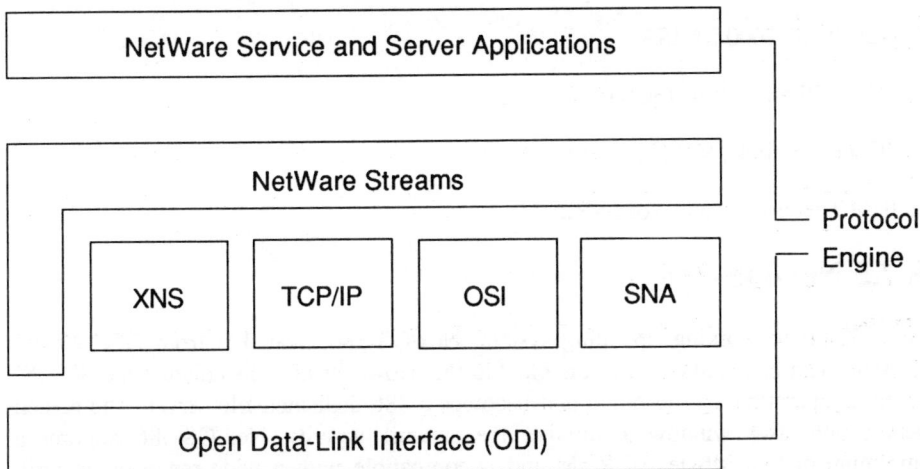

```
┌─────────────────────────────────────────────────────────┐
│        NetWare Service and Server Applications           │─┐
└─────────────────────────────────────────────────────────┘ │
                                                             │
  ┌───────────────────────────────────────────────────────┐ │
  │                   NetWare Streams                      │ │── Protocol
  │                                                        │ │── Engine
  │  ┌────────┐  ┌────────┐  ┌────────┐  ┌────────┐        │ │
  │  │  XNS   │  │ TCP/IP │  │  OSI   │  │  SNA   │        │ │
  │  └────────┘  └────────┘  └────────┘  └────────┘        │ │
  └───────────────────────────────────────────────────────┘ │
  ┌─────────────────────────────────────────────────────────┐
  │          Open Data-Link Interface (ODI)                 │─┘
  └─────────────────────────────────────────────────────────┘
```

Figure 8.10 NetWare protocol architecture

The reliability aspects of NetWare/386 include **disk mirroring, disk duplexing, transaction tracking** and **mirrored servers.** A disk drive which is used for mirroring purposes uses one half for data storage proper and the other half as a copy. To implement a mirrored server, a secondary server keeps lock-step with the primary server and carries a duplicate copy of its data. In the event of the primary server developing a major fault, the secondary server steps in with a minimum amount of disturbance to the network users. These features are part of the comprehensive file system of NetWare/386 which also performs read after write verification and dynamic bad disk area mapping.

Security on NetWare/386 relies on a number of features including encrypted passwords and user profiles. The user profile is a list of resources which a named user may have access to. Therefore each user has varying degrees of access rights to the system's resources. As changes are made to the user access rights, an audit trail is automatically maintained which can be consulted in the event of a security breach. The system manager can use an Inherited Rights Mask with great effect to prohibit a user from gaining access to a directory when they have only been granted access rights to one of its sub-directories. There is also an intruder detection which notifies the system manager that an unauthorised entry has been attempted. To assist network management and enhance system flexibility, a management console utility, which can only run on the network server, can be accessed remotely by an authorised user.

The adaptor expansion cards recognised by NetWare/386 Version 3.1 include Ethernet and token ring cards for various expansion bus architectures, which include:

❑ Novell NE/2 for MCA

❑ Novell NE-2000 for ISA

❑ 3Com Etherlink plus (3C505) for ISA

❑ 3Com Etherlink /MC (3C523) for MCA

❑ IBM Token-Ring and Token-Ring/2.

8.7.5 Nex/OS-386

As a 32-bit networking operating system, Nex/OS-386, available from DSC Nestar Systems, can be installed on a suitable 386 PC. However after installation the 386 PC loses its operation as a terminal and becomes a 386 dedicated file server. The screen serves only as a window to monitor the network activity. Nex/OS-386 requires a minimum of two Mbytes of RAM and is compatible with a wide range of network cards. Owing to the impressive addressing range of the 80386 CPU, Nex/OS-386 uses this to support hard disk volumes up to 400,000 Mbytes. In order to secure file access, Nex/OS-386 uses **Data Entity Security** which permits users to gain access only to the files they have created. This has the advantage of offering a high degree of security at the expense of additional file access management which loads extra processing on the 386 file server.

Among the interesting features of this product is the way the disk directory is displayed: the entries are listed in alphabetical order. This arises because Nex/OS-386 indexes all data by means of the **Indexing Sequential Access Method** (ISAM). Integral with Nex/OS-386 is a database engine which is furnished with an **Applications Programming Interface** (API). This is to promote third-party software houses to write database application programs which encompass the API facilities. These facilities include the normal services provided by a file server in addition to index file operations, record selection, transaction processing and a query service. To enhance the appeal of this database engine, it is compatible with software for the Novell BTRIVE API which has now become a standard for file indexing.

8.7.6 VINES/386

Another example of a commercial product specifically for the 386 PC is the VINES/386, from Banyan of Massachusetts, which is a environment for integrating the resources of a LAN. VINES/386 comes in two sections: a software package and a **Intelligent Communication Adaptor** (ICA) card for the 386 PC. However it also requires a standard Ethernet adaptor card (Section 8.7.1). The VINES/386 software can be installed on an approved 386 PC and converts it into a file server with a virtual networking operating system. This permits the hard disk unit to be accessed for application program sharing. It also uses the parallel ports on the 386 PC for printer resource sharing. VINES/386 provides the standard features of a file server, user access to application program and comprehensive file access with the normal degree of file locking and protection. In addition it offers support for up to four different LANs by permitting transparent LAN-to-LAN bridging and server-to-server integration with the usual high level of file security. Provision is also made to support back-up tape drives for 60-Mbyte or 150-Mbyte data storage.

The ICA is compatible with several commercial network servers and has six high-speed serial communication ports with various protocol options. These include Synchronous Data Link Control (SDLC) for IBM SNA/3270 emulation (mainframe link), High Level Data Link Control (HDLS) for leased lines and X.25 (Section 8.6.2) for server-to-server integration over Public Switched Telephone Network (PSTN) lines. The intelligence of the ICA is drawn from its Intel 80286 microprocessor which is supported by 512K of memory. Achieving synchronous data transfer rate of 64K per second does require quite a lot of fast processing.

8.7.7 IBM Token-Ring Network

IBM has adopted the Token-Ring for its future networking standard which allows several sub-rings to be interfaced into an integrated LAN system. Each device on the network is connected to a central access unit which gives the token ring a star-like appearance. However these units are daisy chained into a ring topology. The Token-Ring can accommodate coaxial cable, twisted pair or optical fibres. With the coaxial cable the data transfer rate is 16 MBPS, however with the optical fibres the rate is greatly increased to 100 MBPS. Each Token-Ring, with coaxial cabling, can support up to 260 devices, however in principle any number of token rings can be linked together without having to worry about device separations. The IBM Token Ring design is well suited for applications where there are likely to be a very large number of device installations.

IBM intends to use the Token-Ring to integrate PC networks with the whole range of other computer systems it manufactures such as mainframes. The standard for communicating with networks is the **Logical Unit or LU-6.2** which is part of IBM's

Advanced Program to Program Communication (APPC). This defines the hardware and software required by two computers to function as commensurate systems. The IBM Token-Ring not only supports NETBIOS but also the APPC for future system integration.

8.8 Alternative Software and Systems

When upgrading from a single 386 PC to a multi-user system of 386 PCs it is important to recognise the change in conditions for using proprietary application programs. Most of these are issued with a single user licence which basically means that only one person should be using that software at any one time. By installing the application program on a network for multi-user usage, the agreement is infringed and the LAN owner can be subject to prosecution. It is possible that several editions of the software could be purchased, but it is common practice to buy a single copy of the application program which has a multi-user agreement for use on networks. When using a database application program on a network it should be specified for multi-user usage. This will ensure that a degree of file protection will be incorporated in the application program itself. Multi-user programs of this nature are usually written to support concurrent file access with appropriate file locking and protection.

There are a number of products on the market which allow the 386 PC to be configured as a mutli-user system. The information provided here should give a good indication of what they have to offer and whether the product is able to fulfil the initial requirements of the user.

8.8.1 Concurrent DOS/386

An operating system designed specifically for multi-user and multi-tasking requirements on 386 PC systems is Concurrent DOS/386 (C-DOS/386) from Digital Research. The multi-tasking facilities of CDOS/386 are covered in Section 5.5.3 and this section will dwell on its multi-user facilities. CDOS/386 is hosted on a 386 PC with a number of satellite terminals which are interfaced to the 386 PC using the CDOS/386 Systems Builder's Kit.

CDOS/386 allows multiple DOS application programs to run on the satellite terminals in a multi-tasking environment where the users on the system share the common resources of the 386 PC, hard disk drives, application programs, common data areas, printers and plotters. It can be described as an enhanced version of MS-DOS 3.3 with additional features. Among these attractive features of CDOS/386 is the File Manager and the menu utilities which allow the menus to be customised to personal requirements.

8.8.2 386/MultiWare

A product issued by Alloy, 386/MultiWare, will enable a multi-user and multi-tasking facility to be created from a single 386 PC acting as a central controller with several attached terminals, graphics workstations and/or other PCs. Each terminal is connected to the central 386 PC via a MultiPort I/O expansion card (IMP2) which permits the terminal user to access the resources on the 386 PC. Alternatively for 386 PCs with the IBM PS/2 MCA bus (Section 3.8.1) there is a IMP2/PS expansion card.

To oversee the proper operation of the system Alloy provide a DOS compatible multi-user operating system, NX386, and this allows several users to share the resources on the 386 PC hosting the MultiPort expansion card. To emphasise the multi-tasking aspect of the system each user can have up to eight tasks running simultaneously in the Virtual 8086 mode (Section 2.2.2) as virtual machines (VMs).

To accommodate the memory demands placed on the 386 PC from several users, the NX386 operating system implements a virtual RAM and demand paging scheme the with hard disk. When the total memory requirement exceeds the physical RAM the virtual hard disk memory, with its allocated space, comes into effect. Pages of programs are drawn from the hard disk and loaded into RAM. Although this operation may slow the system down it is otherwise quite transparent to the user. However this is offset by some extent by the NX386 disk driver in conjunction with an optimised disk cacheing technique which maintains maximum data throughput.

As mentioned, the hardware components of the 386/MultiWare consist of a Multiport expansion card which hosts its own processor for exercising most screen management functions, and this together with a distribution box forms the link to the other terminals on the circuit. Each terminal behaves as a DOS machine and executes its own AUTOEXEC.BAT file on power up thereby providing a customised workstation. To achieve the optimised performance with the 386/MultiWave system, the serving 386 PC should be running at least at 25 MHz with a minimum of two Mbytes of Extended memory (Section 2.3.4) and an extra half Mbyte per user.

A variety of MultiPort cards are available depending on the expected complexity of the system, starting with a minimum of three users up to 21. 386/MultiWare can support monochrome graphics terminals, such as the Wyse 99GT and colour graphics workstations such as the Sun River FOW. It also compatible with Novell's NetWare which permits each user on the 386/MultiWare to become a LAN node and thereby gain access the resources of the network.

8.8.3 VM/386 Multi-user and NetPak

If there is a requirement to link a 386 PC with a small number of user terminals or other PCs running under DOS, without going to the expense of a full LAN, VM/386

Multi-user, from IGC of Santa Clara (distributed by Phasestrong), is an option. It uses the 80386 CPU in its Virtual 86 Mode (Section 2.2.3) where several tasks become concurrent operations. VM/386 Multi-user assigns these tasks for other users to permit multi-user operation. Each user occupies a VM within the 80386 CPU.

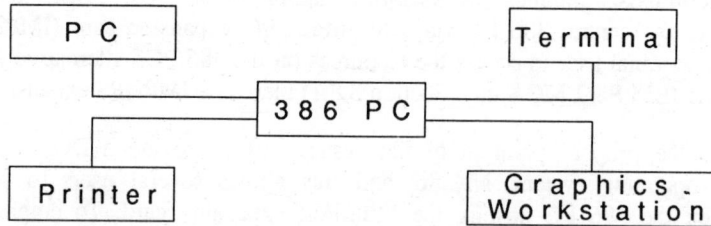

a) The 386 PC as a central host for VM/386 multi-user configuration

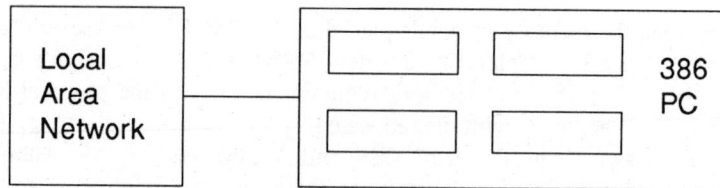

b) A single 386 PC user with LAN VMs and application program VMS

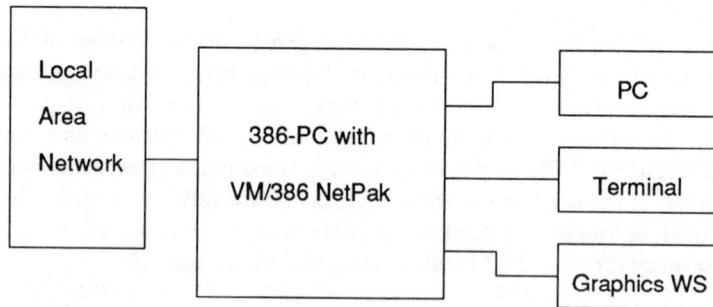

c) Multi-users gaining access to the LAN via a 386 PC

Figure 8.13 Various configurations of a 386 PC in a network

The 386 PC can therefore act as a central host machine providing its resources to other users (Figure 8.13a). There are three ways of linking the PCs together, through the RS-232 ports (COM1 or COM2), through multiport RS-232 cards (Section 3.3.2) or through graphics adaptor cards which have additional ports. Once a link has been established then the disk storage can be accessed by other users and VM/386 Multi-user supports file sharing and record locking. One of the attractive feature of

VM/386 Multi-user software is the support it provides for a combination of PCs, text terminals and graphics workstations. It offers support for a range of terminals including the Wyse WY-60, WY-150 and Kimtron KT-70. As for graphics workstations, the Viewport Technology Hercules VPT1000 and EGA VPT2000 are compatible with VM/386 Multi-user.

VM/386 NetPak is an additional module or extension to VM/386 (Section 5.5.4) or VM/386 Multi-user. For a single user, VM/386 can support one VM to access a network in order to reach the network resources. However VM/386 NetPak, together with a suitable network adaptor card and network software, will allow several VMs to be created for access to the network resources. VM/386 NetPak can be used in one of two ways. As a single user, each of the network resources can be accessed through a dedicated VM on the 386 PC (Figure 8.13b). The user can therefore have VMs for the network resources running alongside other VMs hosting applications programs. This configuration will permit the single user fast access, for data transfer from network VMs to the application program VMs which are running concurrently on the 386 PC. The other way VM/386 NetPak can be used is in a multi-user configuration (Figure 8.13c). This is similar to VM386/ Multi-user except users on the linked PCs, text terminals or graphics workstations gain access to the network through the central 386 PC. Each user and network resources will be configured as an individual VM on the central 386 PC host by means of the VM/386 NetPak software which is compatible with adaptor cards from 3CoM, Novell and IBM.

Further Reading:

1. Systems International: (Monthly), Reed Business Group, Quadrant House, The Quadrant, Sutton Surrey.

2. Datacom: (Monthly), EMAP Business & Computer Publications, Priory Court, 30 Farringdon Lane, London EC18.

Networking
1. Local Area Networking with Microcomputers – A guide for the Business Decision Maker, S R Lehrman, Brady (Prentice Hall).

2. Local Area Network Design, A Hopper, S Temple & R Williamson, Addison-Wesley (1986).

3. Low Cost PC Networking, M James, Heinemann (1989).

4. Local Area Networks and their applications, B Tangney & D O'Mahony, Prentice-Hall (1988).

5. Packet Switching and X.25 Networks, S Poulton, Pitman Publishing (1989).

9

Applications for the 386 PC

The 386 PC is a very powerful and versatile computer and its general-purpose design renders it suitable for an immense spectrum of applications. However in a text of this nature only a limited number of applications can be briefly reviewed, as an in-depth discussion of each area warrants a book in its own right. It is hoped that this brief survey of the possible applications of the 386 PC will be sufficient to enlighten the user as to the potential value of the machine. Some insight will be gained into what is required to customise a 386 PC to perform specific tasks and to give an expectation of the performance of the computer. The following areas of discussion have been chosen primarily for two reasons: firstly the 386 PC is particularly good at these functions and offers distinct and overriding advantages over 80286-based personal computers, and secondly they can perform tasks which are not available to the 286 PC.

9.1 Software Development

Software development for personal computers is a field of intense activity and the employment growth in this area in the Western World remains strong with every sign that it will continue. It is however very intellectually labour intensive and greater demands are placed upon the computer hardware and software tools in order to optimise resources. Comprehensive development facilities are therefore paramount in the practice of software engineering. There is currently a significant opportunity for the application of **Computer Aided Software Engineering** (CASE) tools in the development of products for the 386 PC. In this respect many of the growing number of development tools have powerful front-end user interfaces based on the windows icons mouse pull-down menus (WIMPS) and these offer high levels of system integration. One attractive feature which has arisen from this flexibility is the ease of integrating object modules written in different languages to form standalone executable programs.

Developing software for microprocessors or computers is a multi-stage process and only a brief outline of the overall processes will be presented here. The barest development tools consist of a screen editor, a compiler and a linker. The screen editor is required to write the **source code** and this can be written in assembly language or a suitable high-level language like FORTRAN, Pascal or C. It is common practice to write the source code in several separate modules. Each source code module is then compiled. This is achieved by using a software package called a **compiler** which produces from each source code module an **object code** file consisting of machine code for a specific microprocessor. The application of the **linker** software combines all the compiled object modules and necessary the libraries into an executable file (.EXE file in DOS).

One of the appealing features of a 386 PC is the upward compatibility from the 8088/6 80286 personal computers. Any software development tools which run under DOS for the earlier machines will also run on the 386 PC. All DOS software will execute on a 386 PC but for the efficient use of the 386 PC the source code needs to be compiled specifically for the 80386 microprocessor. There are many high-level language compilers for the 8088/6 and 80268 microprocessors, for example Microsoft QuickBASIC 4.5 or Boland's Turbo Pascal. There is a also a definite emergence of high-level compilers for the 80386 which are suitable for the 386 PC. These include a number of FORTRAN, C and ADA language compilers which generate native 80386 code and accommodate the instructions sets of the 80287/80387 and the Weitek 3167 coprocessors (Section 3.1). As the compilers become available, it is envisaged that much of the source code for earlier commercial software will be compiled for the 80386 and will be repackaged specifically for 386 PCs.

When writing application programs specifically for 80386, in either assembly language, PL/M, ADA or C, a range of DOS compatible development tools from Intel can be used. For assembly language programs, the ASM-386 Macro Assembler may be used to convert the source code – consisting of labels and assembly language mnemonics – into object modules of 80386 code. An alternative 80386 assembler is Microsoft's Macro Assembler (MASM) which has a set of assembly language and macro directives to provide a suitable framework for assembly language program development. Object files derived from MASM can be linked (using Microsoft's LINKer) with object files derived from other Microsoft compilers. Information relating to this task can be found in the text – Microsoft Mixed-Language Programming Guide.

For the high-level languages, Intel supplys a range of 80386 compilers including PL/M-386, C-386 and ADA-386. Once the object code modules have been created, for their linkage Intel supplys its Relocation, Linkage, and Library Tools (or RLL-386). RLL-386 builds executable files from linking the 80386 object code modules and library routines. RLL-386 also has a system builder for configuring protected, multi-tasking systems and a support library for the 80387 coprocessor.

Testing executable programs for software errors can be aided by using Intel's **DOS Resident Debugger** (DB386), which permits 80386 code to be executed and amended directly on a 386 PC. The screen display of DB386 has a window format with drop-down menus. Part of the window display will represent the architecture of the 80386 and this permits the user to observe the progress of a program. The user can observe the contents of registers and browse through memory. There is also a disassembler and a single line assembler for the code instructions. By using the pull-down menus, the user can gain full access to the options of DB386 such as breakpoint setting, trace operations and single line code execution. DB386 also enables the software developer to monitor the progress of protected mode programs via a run-time interface. However attractive these tools are for developing assembly language programs, it is a practice not to be recommended unless absolutely necessary. Since the 80386 is a 32-bit microprocessor, its complexity suggests that it should only be programmed in a high-level language. The temptation to resort to assembly language programming, except for very short routines, should be resisted. It can be a very lengthy and time consuming exercise and careful cost considerations should be made before embarking on such a venture.

9.1.1 80386 FORTRAN Compilers

Over the past few years there has emerged a healthy number of FORTRAN compilers for the 80386. This has added considerable weight to the continuing importance of FORTRAN as the only language for tasks which require mathematically intensive operations. Exploiting the full potential of the numerical memory performance of the 386 PC will require methods of accessing the Protected Mode of the 80386 CPU and these are available to the FORTRAN compilers. With the large memory capacity and computational rate of 386 PCs, it is acceptable to import FORTRAN programs which are currently running on mainframes. There a number of FORTRAN compilers to choose from and needless to say the hosting 386 PC will require a numerical coprocessor. What are the features to look out for in a FORTRAN compiler? This can be partially answered by considering three commercial products which merit discussion.

The Software Marketing Group at Salford University offers an impressive FORTRAN 77 compiler for the 386 PC entitled FTN77/386. FNT77/386 accesses the full potential of the 80386 microprocessor by enabling it to function in its Protected Mode (Section 2.2.3). It accomplishes this by introducing an extra layer of operating system by its DBOS MS-DOS extender program which is loaded via the AUTOEXEC.BAT file. In the Protected Mode, programs are not limited by the 640K DOS boundary and consequently all the additional extended memory is directly accessible.

FNT77/386 requires at least one Mbyte of memory and a numerical coprocessor, preferably a 80387 for executing the 32-bit floating point arithmetic. For this task a library of intrinsic functions based on proven algorithms is supplied with the compiler. The compiler speed is in excess of 13,000 lines per minute and makes full use of the 80386's protected mode instruction set in its object code. With FNT77/386 there is a screen debugger which can display variables in a pop-up window. It also allows break point control, expression evaluation, single stepping various other options which are useful in debugging code.

During the compiler operation the /PROFILE switch can be set which keeps a count of the execution of every line of source code. When viewed from the debugger it provides a visual method of observing the bottlenecks in the code, a well established technique in logic analyser design. As expected in any FORTRAN compiler, FNT77/386 provides facilities for implementing **Dynamic Link Libraries** (DLLs), via the Virtual Memory technique, which are swapped in and out of hard disk memory as required during run-time. This is one method of minimising the size of .exe files. However FNT77/386 does not support virtual memory access for data. The run-time libraries of FNT77/386 support windowing, basic EGA and VGA graphics, command line parsing, low-level I/O operations and a variety of other options. In addition to the compiler, LINK77 (which is a fast 32-bit linker) is also supplied and the Load-and-go option performs the compilation, the linking and execution of the program.

Lahey Computer Systems of Incline Village, North Virginia produces a FORTRAN 77 compiler for the 386 PC, the F77L-EM/32, which is a full implementation of the ANSI X3.9-1978 FORTRAN standard. It has its own powerful **Source On-Line Debugger** (SOLD) and the compiler supports three types of numerical coprocessors: the 80387, the Weitek 1167 and the Weitek 3167. F77L-EM/32 requires either the two DOS-Extender Operating Systems from AI Architects, Cambridge – MA-USA or the Developers Kit OS/386 – which will enable the Protected Mode of the 80386 CPU to be used while maintaining a proper DOS environment. FORTRAN programs compiled from F77L-EM/32 have the attractive feature of being able to call Microsoft C, Borland Turbo C and Lattice C programs. This is an attractive option for accommodating heavy graphics routines which could be sourced in C. FORTRAN does not easily lend itself to graphics programming and it would be preferable to use alternative languages for this purpose.

The MicroWay NDP FORTRAN-386 compiler also produces code which runs in the Protected Mode of the 80386. This compiler can run under one of two operating systems: MS-DOS or UNIX System V/386 (Section 5.4). Under either operating system the compiler produces assembly language code object files which are linked with UNIX System V/386 tools or with the proprietary PharLap Tools if under MS-DOS. To access the Protected Mode of the 80386 through MS-DOS the PharLap DOS Extender software will be required. NDP FORTRAN-386 is a full implementation of FORTRAN 77 with options to port mainframe FORTRAN (ANSI X3.9-1978) into the 386 PC. The compiler produces optimised code by first compiling the source modules into a memory-based operator tree. During the global optimisation the variables used in the code are, if possible, stored in registers as opposed to actual memory. This enhances the execution speed of the code by maximising the use of the 80386/7 register set.

In the FORTRAN compilers discussed, only a few of their respective features have been mentioned, but a good impression should have been created as to the facilities you can expect to be find on them. The 386 PC is certainly a viable platform for developing and running FORTRAN programs. The support offered by a wide range of compiler producers is a clear indication that it has a promising future, and will remain one of the principle languages for computationally intensive applications such as image processing, mathematical modelling and economic forecasting.

9.2 Desktop Publishing

One major application area for the 386 PC is desktop publishing (DTP) and this has seen substantial growth in the 80s following the success of the Apple Macintosh DTP system. DTP offers the opportunity to produce high-quality, professionally finished products at a fraction of the cost of traditional publishing methods. Coupled with the greatly reduced preparation time, DTP has won wide acceptance from the commercial and industrial sectors. DTP software uses the PC screen in the graphics mode where every dot (pixel) is addressable. It is therefore able to produce any type of font and allow pictures to be mixed with text.

DTP on the 386 PC offers fast screen refresh, rapid document retrieval, large storage capacity and when networked to other 386 PCs, prompt communication with other users and peripherals. It is particularly attractive for a single, standalone 386 PC and when interfaced to a suitable printer forms a complete publishing system.

DTP software relies strongly on the graphics capability of the 386 PC and for this reason a high-resolution graphics option is of paramount importance. Although most DTP software caters for Hercules monochrome and EGA standards for intensive DTP work, the video graphics array (VGA), either monochrome or colour, option should be chosen (Section 4.3.3). Having established the most appropriate graphics standard, it is necessary to choose the most suitable design of printer. For many DTP tasks, a laser printer will suffice (Section 6.1.3).

Its relatively low-cost, good choice of fonts and fast speed (eight pages per minute) make it an attractive device for this application. If it has PostScript, this is an added bonus. Although most DTP software packages have options for matrix printers they cannot provide the same professional quality finish as the laser printer. The screen display in DTP software is a graphics image and each pixel on the screen has to be mapped pixel by pixel to the printer.

When choosing a DTP software package a feature to look out for is the option of importing data, image or text files from other software packages. This is now recognised as an important characteristic of DTP software packages and each time they are updated the import option base is usually enhanced. Files created from spreadsheets like Lotus 1-2-3, databases like dBase IV, or word processors like Multimate Advantage-II should be directly importable into the DTP software. This requirement is particularly important for producing monthly costing reports where the latest information is imported directly into the document.

DTP software packages normally run within a *windows* screen display where menu features ease the access to the DTP's facilities. A mouse is essential in order to engage the menus and manipulate the text and drawings in the working area.

Because of the windows format a paper white screen with grey contrast should be chosen in preference to a green monitor which can be very taxing on the eyes during long exposure. If there is likely to be intensive use of the 386 PC for DTP work it may be advisable to have a second monitor able to display a full page with its own graphics expansion card. The software drivers for the second monitor would be loaded during the boot phase of the 386 PC.

With the DTP package occupying the second monitor it can serve a single task in the multi-tasking environment of the 386 PC. The other tasks can be accessed with the first monitor. These may include a word processor or a spreadsheet with outputs ready to import into the DTP task running on the second monitor. In this respect the 386 PC lends itself very favourably to the demands of DTP.

One important feature in DTP is the **What You See Is What You Get** (WYSIWYG) output to the printer. A true WYSIWYG will reproduce during the printing, exactly what appears in the working area on the monitor without any distortions or changes in the aspect ratio. Although many DTP software packages claim to have WYSIWYG the only proof is in the pudding – try it and see what you get with your printer.

There are several DTP packages on the market and the two most well known are Ventura and PageMaker – Sections 9.2.1 and 9.2.2 respectively. Another commendable DTP package known as Timeworks Publisher from GST Software Products, is distributed in the UK by Electric Distribution. Timeworks Publisher works from within the GEM window interface and can cope with text and graphics formats. The text and graphics files can be imported from a variety of sources and manipulated within one of the four work modes. Timeworks supports many graphics configurations and several printers. To add to its appeal, it also possesses a PostScript driver for use with laser printers (Section 6.1.2) and image setters (Section 9.2.4).

9.2.1 Ventura

Ventura Version 2.0, issued by Rank Xerox, is a widely used desktop publishing package aimed at a wide spectrum of users. It is hosted by either a GEM, Microsoft Windows or OS/2 Presentation Manager screen environment. It has therefore a strong window and mouse interface with a wealth of drop or pull-down menus.

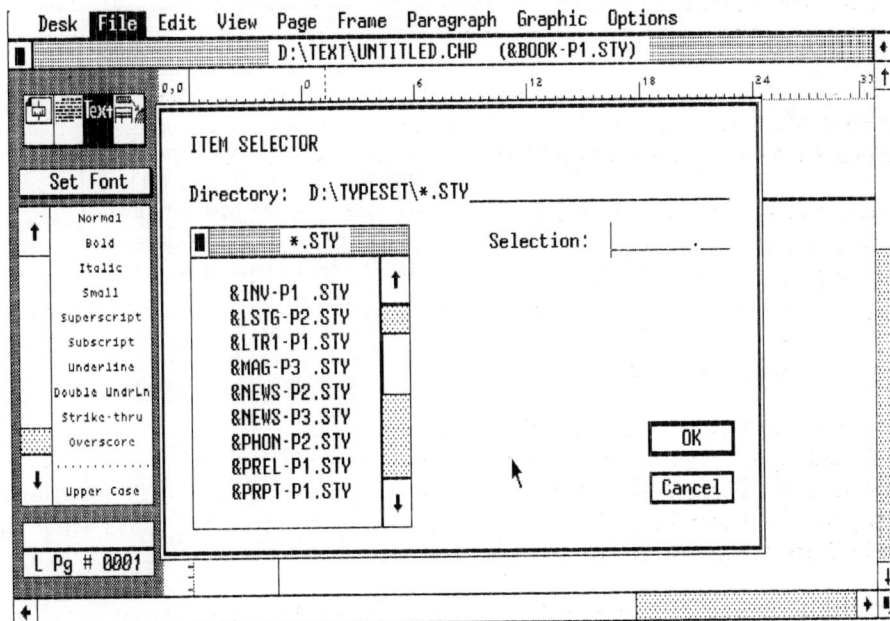

Figure 9.1 Menu of style options for Ventura

Figure 9.1 shows a typical Ventura screen display with a line menu along the top with the current assignment options and the function icons along the left-hand side. Each bar in the drop down menus opens up a dialogue box with further design options to enable the user to access the full facilities of the package. Many of the dialogue boxes have entries with question marks (?) which indicate that help information is available. Ventura 2.0 can produce **Camera Ready Copies** (CRCs) and if colour is required a separate page for every colour can be produced. Six colours from a palette of 62 million can be chosen. The flexibility of Ventura 2.0 is clearly evident from its ability to import files from different word processing packages using the Merge Text option. The files are then combined to form a unified chapter. Alternatively files from the standard word processors, MultiMate, Word Perfect, WordStar and Word can be directly imported.

Once a file has been loaded, it appears as continuous text flow and there are several layout text styles to choose from. The text can be laid out in multi-bcolumn styles.

Adjustments can easily be made to the text and heading size by first tagging the paragraph (or heading) and selecting, with the mouse, the appropriate option from the

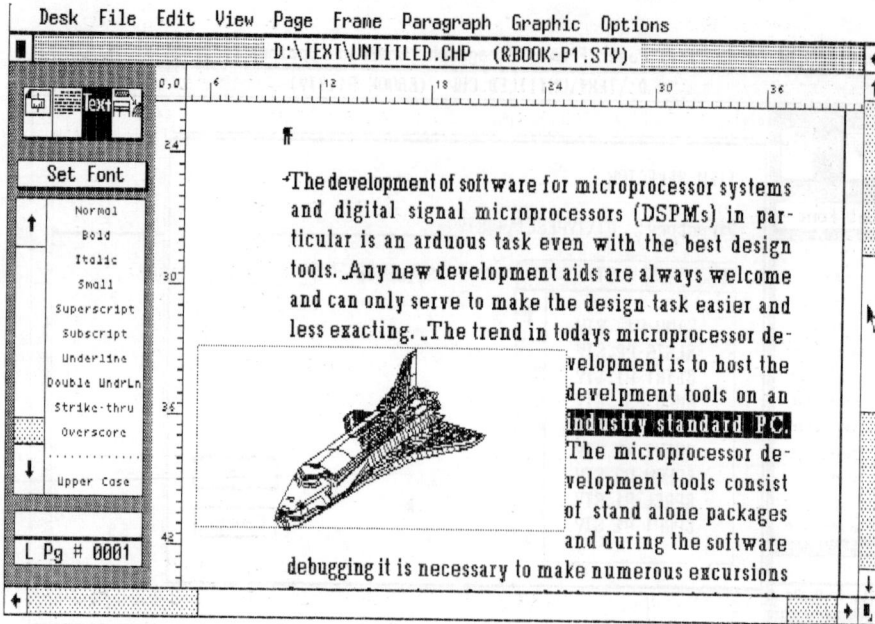

Figure 9.2 Text wrapping when an image is imported into Ventura

assignment list on the left hand side. These changes are automatically made to all other similar paragraphs in the document. Headings of different sizes can be defined and positioned on the page to the user's specification. Angular rotations of the text can also be effected at either 90, 180 or 270 degrees.

Ventura 2.0 can operate in one of four modes which are selected with the mouse from the icons on the top left hand side of the display. The modes are:

❑ Frame Function

❑ Paragraph Tagging Function

❑ Text Editing Function

❑ Graphics function

In the frame function mode the mouse can be used to implant a frame or box, of adjustable size, into the text. The frame has the effect of displacing the text as shown in Figure 9.2, which is referred to as text-wrapping. The frame can, at any time, be resized or moved anywhere within the document. Images can also be imported into Ventura 2.0 and these can be drawn from a number of different sources as shown in Table 9.1 opposite. Once an image has been imported it can be positioned within the active frame. Like the frame, the image can be resized and even have its aspect ratio adjusted (height to length ratio). Labels under each image can be automatically incremented or adjusted as more frames are added to the text.

AutoCAD	GEM Draw/Graph
Dr. Halo DPE (GEM output)	Macpaint Image
GP Video Show format	Lotus 1-2-3 Symphony(pict)
Macintosh PICT format	Mentor Graphics CAD
Publisher Paintbrush	PostScript files (EPS)
GEM Paint/PC Paintbrush	DXF file format
HPGL plotter files	WMF
CGM files (Lotus Freelance)	TIFF

Table 9.1 Direct file input sources for Ventura 2.0

The paragraph tagging mode is like a coarse version of the text editing mode where instead of dealing with single words or sentences whole paragraphs are manipulated. This is particularly useful for changing fonts or moving wholesale paragraphs around the document. The text editing mode allows the user to add additional text into the document and address each letter, word or sentence.

This enables the change in emphasis; examples of the typical operations of the edit mode are from normal to bold, italic, superscript, subscript and underline. The usual cut and paste options are also available which can be used on either text or diagrams. The graphics mode is useful for providing shading to areas of text as shown in Figure 9.3 overleaf. Various degrees of filling density can be chosen to attain the required level. There is a basic tool-box which enables the user to manipulate squares, circles, straight lines, text boxes and ellipses with various shading levels.

The choice of available screen fonts is determined by the selection of printers during the installation of Ventura 2.0. For example if two printers are connected to a 386 PC, a LaserJet Plus and an Epson FX-80, then the choice of fonts are Swiss, Dutch, Symbol and Courier. The user has a reasonable control over the font size and its emphasis and on returning to the document the tagged heading or paragraph will be restyled in the new font. There is an excellent range of printers to chose from during the installation procedure and this is reflected in the number of installation disks (23) which carry all the supporting font drivers.

Desk File Edit View Page Frame Paragraph Graphic Options

D:\TEXT\UNTITLED.CHP (&BOOK-P1.STY)

Set Font

Normal
Bold
Italic
Small
Superscript
Subscript
Underline
Double UndrLn
Strike-thru
Overscore

Upper Case

L Pg # 0008

note-pad which would take the form of an icon on the PC screen, thereby allowing the team members to communicate in a well organised and consistent manner.¶

The cost of a 80386 PC based development system is somewhat greater than the basic IBM clone equivalent. However the benefits gained by reducing the design cycle period will allow the additional investment to be clawed back through shorter product development times. ¶

Ref 1 Microprocessor Development and Development Systems Ed: V.Tseng. Granada (1982)¶

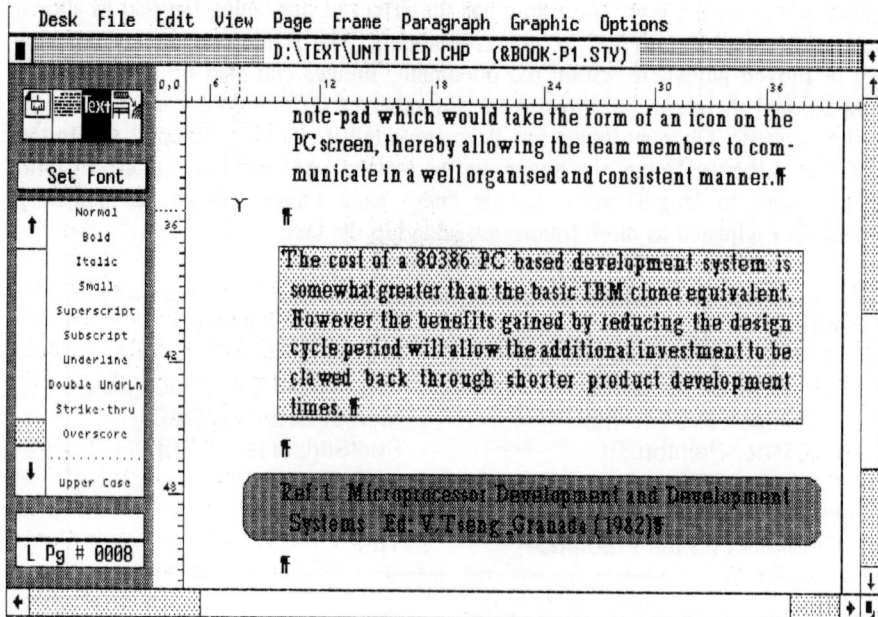

Figure 9.3 Areas of text can be highlighted with shading

Also available with Ventura 2.0 is the **Professional Extension** which is installed as an integrated package along with the main program. The Professional Extension allows expanded memory to be utilised to accommodate sizeable documents depending on the expanded memory. The Edco hyphenation dictionary can also be installed in expanded memory to provide a fast spell checker.

When the Professional Extension is installed it provides Ventura 2.0 with a fifth icon referred to as the Table Edit and offers a variety of additional options. This enables numerical Tables to be constructed in grid format to allow convenient lining up of columns with accompanying text.

Ventura 2.0 can import Lotus 1-2-3 files (.PRN) directly and these files can be implanted into the Table grid format. The grid structure is by no means rigid and each cell within the grid can be manipulated individually for the purpose of improving the display. For technical publications the WYSIWYG equation generator is a very attractive feature. A set of equation fonts, which includes most Greek and mathematical symbols, is provided and equations can be typed anywhere within the text. To balance the display, control can be exercised over vertical justification and this allows text to be inserted into defined vertical spaces.

Ventura 2.0 is a very attractive DTP package and is ideal for coping with large documents. For several users working on the same document, the 386 PC in its multi-user capacity can be employed. A networked version of Ventura 2.0 would be required and this would be resident on a 386 PC acting as a file server (Section 8.5.5). The file server, which would hold an image database and the necessary software for the DTP peripherals, could be accessed by all the users.

9.2.2 PageMaker

Released by Aldus, PageMaker 4 requires a windows environment in which to function (Windows/386 – Section 5.5.1) and once installed makes extensive use of the graphics facilities afforded by Windows/386 on the 386 PC. For the full freedom offered by PageMaker a mouse is essential as the options appear as menus and screen icons. Before a text document is loaded into PageMaker a group of pages (referred to as the template) are configured as columns by the user. As the document is then loaded the text fills up the defined columns. The auto-flow feature is evident as the text is justified within the columns and more pages are created to accommodate any outstanding text. PageMaker possesses a style-palette which enhances the auto-flow feature by allowing the user to create text defined styles (headline, alignment for example) and these can be stored as templates.

To help first time users PageMaker comes with a selection of style sheet templates which can be adapted by the users for their own design. The supplied style sheet files, with extension .PT3 include book layouts with one or two columns, newsletters (with variable columns) and presentation slides. When text is loaded into a sheet file template with image frames present, the auto text-wrap comes into play and fills the spaces around the frame with text. If the frame is moved or resized the text re-wraps itself around the new frame position.

One attractive aspect of PageMaker is its ability to import text files – through software devices known as filters – from a variety of word processors and these are shown in Table 9.2. The list of filters can be expanded provided they do not exceed 20. A file can be prepared before it is imported into PageMaker by enclosing paragraphs in corner brackets < > which is referred to as tagging.

Microsoft Word	MultiMate Advantage II
Windows Write	WordStar 2000
Word Perfect	XyWrite III
Display Write 3	Samna Word
IBM DCA Format	ASCII Text Files

Table 9.2 Some text sources which can be imported into PageMaker 3

When a paragraph is tagged in a word processor, it retains its tagging when it is imported into PageMaker. Also known as coding, the technique is a throwback to the typesetting era when these character extensions were required by the typesetter to emphasise the line. When tables are imported from a word processor, by using this tagging option, the table contents can be kept intact. This allows files to be imported directly from Lotus 1-2-3, dBase IV and other sources. PageMaker 3 uses a series of import filters for converting source information into a recognisable format.

For example when a Lotus 1-2-3 spreadsheet file is imported it is subjected to its respective filter and appears as an entire spreadsheet without being fragmented. The dBase IV filter is an advanced feature which can operate on the whole database and provides the user with a menu from which to select the required fields for presentation. As expected with a good desktop publishing system, the user can exercise considerable control over the layout of the text: line spacing, font changes, text facing, creating headings and access to various highlighting options.

Windows Paint	Windows Draw
In A Vision	PC Paint
PC Paintbrush	Publishers Paintbrush
AutoCAD	Lotus 1-2-3
Lotus Symphony Windows	GDI Metafiles
TIFF files	Scanned images

Table 9.3 Some graphics sources that can be imported into PageMaker 3

PageMaker is well equipped to cope with a large variety of imported graphics images (Table 9.3). It has the ability to recognise the format of an image file and perform the appropriate conversion as it is loaded in a document. Once an image has been entered into the working area it may be necessary to modify its appearance. The Image Control Sub-menu can be evoked to effect changes in the contrast, the screen pattern or the brightness. It is a straightforward operation to introduce horizontal and vertical lines around the image in order to improve its appearance.

In common with Ventura 2.0, PageMaker has a graphics tool-box for performing small-scale line drawings. Also included in the tool-box are circles, squares, soft cornered rectangles and various patterns with tints. The line width of the drawn figures can also be adjusted. Once a drawing is complete it can be situated anywhere within the document with the text justified left, right or centre.

With its WYSIWYG nature and extensive document handling provisions, PageMaker can reproduce a processed document on a wide range of matrix printers and other output devices which include:

❑ Printers with PostScript and DDT page description language

❑ HP LaserJet and LaserJet Plus

❑ Plus printers

❑ Linotronic 100 and 300 Imagesetters.

PageMaker is admirably suitable for the production of newsletters and brochures and is able to cope with up to 128-page documents.

9.2.3 DTP Monitors

Figure 9.4 A typical DTP monitor – the A4 MP5671. (Photo: Courtesy of Samsung)

Desktop publishing can be performed with low resolution graphics standards, EGA or Hercules, coupled to moderate resolution monitors. Using Ventura or PageMaker with either of these standards only allows a portion of the page to be visible at any one time. The graininess of the monitor gives poor legibility and clarity and can create eye strain. For intensive DTP work the Hercules and EGA standards are inadequate and it is advisable to use a minimum of a VGA (Section 4.3.3) with a corresponding high-resolution monitor and graphics card. High-resolution monitors allow whole pages to be viewed and they comes in A4 size, ie single page or dual page. On average the active size of the screen is 90% less than page sizes and most of the editing time is spent in a page reduced mode.

The resolution (pixel or dot density) for a DTP monitor will range from 720 x 728 to 1280 x 1240 for the more expensive version. The screen refresh rate (vertical scan frequency) is another important consideration not only for image update but also for the possible avoidance of screen flicker which is observable at rates less than 60 Hz. A refresh rate of 70 Hz or higher will provide comfortable long-term viewing. Many DTP monitors can also emulate other graphics standards – CGA, EGA and Hercules – and this is a useful feature if the 386 PC system is to be used for tasks other than DTP.

Many software packages can be tailored, during installation, to match the facilities on the 386 PC. To realise the full potential of a high-resolution monitor and graphics card, special drivers have to be loaded alongside the main software. Several monitor manufacturers supply software drivers for packages such as AutoCad, Windows, Lotus 1-2-3, Gem, PageMaker, Ventura and these must be considered when buying a suitable DTP monitor.

A typical monochrome DTP monitor is the 15 inch A4 Samsung MP5671 (Figure 9.4 overleaf) which has a resolution of 1006 pixels per inch by 1048 lines. It has a horizontal scan frequency of 62.75 kHz. Its refresh rate is 59.88 Hz and it is supplied with a full page driver card and a variety of software drivers. An example of a colour DTP monitor is the Supervision 980 Plus which is a 20-inch screen with a resolution of 1024 x 768 and refreshes at 60Hz. Again this monitor comes with a number of software drivers.

9.2.4 Imagesetters

If a high-quality finished product is needed it may be necessary to consider a suitable imagesetter. The print density of a good imagesetter should be at least 1200 dots per inch (dpi). This density provides a good grey scale with pleasing half-tones and this is adequate for most magazine publications. A requirement of any imagesetter is the ability to translate PostScript (much favoured by the Apple Macintosh), Ventura and PageMaker instructions into a series of dots which can be imaged onto bromide or film. This is referred to as the RIP and the majority of imagesetters have RIP units attachments or part of the integrated system. However, in general, imagesetters tend to be expensive and will represent a significant portion of a DTP investment plan.

An example of an imagesetter is the Linotronic 300 Imagesetter/RIP 3 which comes as two separate units, the intelligent RIP 3 and the imagesetter. The RIP 3, based on the Motorola 68020 microprocessor, has eight Mbytes of RAM storage and a

160-Mbyte hard disk which can cope with 2,000 fonts. The imagesetter can accommodate film, bromide and plate material. It is suitable for colour work and has printing rates ranging from 23 inches per minute for 635 dpi to 3.35 inches per minute for 2450 dpi.

Another example of an imagesetter is the Prism PS which has a similar RIP to the Linotronic 300 integrated into the imagesetter unit. The Prism PS uses semiconductor laser technology and accommodates film, bromide and plate material. The printing speed ranges from 25 inches per minute at 600 dpi to 6.25 inches per minute at 2400 dpi.

9.3 Computer-Aided Design

The growing importance of low-cost Computer-Aided Design (CAD) and Computer-Aided Manufacture (CAM), in all aspects of engineering, is clearly demonstrating the increasing role played by the personal computer. A 386 PC CAD facility will have to provide a number of functions. These will include a three dimensional (3-D) modeller for design and analysis activities; this is necessary to allow convenient engineering perspective to be realised quickly.

Another necessary requirement of a CAD system is a two dimensional (2-D) drafting facility for design and production of drawing work. With a CAD package, the user does not create an image directly, it is more of a set of drawing elements and their relative coordinates which are stored in a database. The image is therefore assembled from the combination of these elements which can be edited by scaling, rotation and translation. When there are many drawings in a multi-user system then a good record management facility will also be required to ensure fast access and safe storage.

The facilities offered by a network of 386 PCs can supply the needs for secure storage and common access. There are specific requirements for CAM which include **Graphical Numerical Control** (GNC) to permit interactive computer control part programming for CNC machining. To tackle the demands of this field, the 386 PC has a lot to offer with its impressive computation power, low cost data storage and powerful input/output expansion capability.

9.3.1 Requirements

From a hardware point of view a CAD system based on a 386 PC has a number of requirements which are best served with at least a 25-MHz machine with several additional features. CAD work is very demanding upon memory and the processor's resources which explains why the majority of early CAD packages were only functional on mainframe and mini computers. PCs were simply not up to the mark and the emphasis shifted from large computers to systems like Apollo and Sun benchtop work stations. However the advent of the 386 PC has extended the range of viable systems to include personal computers as suitable platforms for hosting CAD software.

The nature of CAD work is intrinsically very visual and this clearly points to a minimum of VGA graphics and matching monitor (Section 4.3.3) with its high-resolution colour graphics and fast refresh rate. This is especially important to allow fast two and three dimensional translations and rotations of screen figures which rely heavily on fast writing speeds. To support these functions a maths coprocessor 80387 or 83D87 (Section 3.1.2) is essential for the scaling and recalculation of coordinate positions which is mathematically very intensive. The user input is an aspect which also warrants close attention. The entry of a drawing into a CAD package can be accomplished in a number of ways. One of the more popular means is the digitising Tablet (Section 6.4) which enables very accurate (0.33 mm) line resolution to be achieved. The puck or movable cursor on the digitising Tablet has accurately aligned cross wires for positioning coordinate entry to a high precision.

Disk memory and fast access times are also essential features of a 386 PC based CAD system. Design drawings can be very complex and require considerable amounts of memory. It is therefore not surprising to find some drawings taking several Mbytes of data. Not all the drawing may accommodated by the 386 PC's memory which means that the system will have to depend on virtual memory (Section 2.2.3) to access other parts of the drawing. For this to be transparent to the user, the virtual memory fetch must be fast, which requires a high-performance disk drive.

9.3.2 AutoCAD/386

One of the most popular CAD software packages is AutoCAD and in text of this nature only a brief outline of its many options can be presented. For further reading, a set of AutoCAD references is given at the end of this chapter. AutoCAD is a flexible drawing platform which allows high-accuracy design definition coupled with features for correcting drawing errors. These are performed with ease without having to redraw the entire drawing. It does this by providing a set of entities or drawing elements which are used in the construction of the drawing.

AutoCAD/386 can accommodate 2-Dimensional and 3-Dimensional drawings and incorporates the PharLap DOS Extender (Section 2.3.4) which expands the working memory area to 16 Mbytes. By allowing the whole of AutoCAD/386 to be loaded into memory the need of paging overlays from the hard disk drive is minimised. For very complex drawings there will be a substantial demand for additional memory and minimum of eight Mbytes of Extended memory should be considered. Problems which would have appeared with terminate and stay resident (TSR) routines should no longer occur since they can be loaded into the Extended Memory area. This makes AutoCAD/386 more amenable to network applications where the network drivers are normally loaded as TSR routines during the power-up phase of the 386 PC.

Once AutoCAD is up and running there are a number of ways of executing commands. The **Advanced User Interface** (AUI) enables the user to enter commands via the pull-down menus (engaged with a mouse and click) and icon menus. Alternatively, drop-down menus (engaged when the mouse is on the menu header) or direct command line entry can be used. The user has direct access to display dialogue boxes which show the option and current settings. There is a substantial database of drawing shapes and an impressive array of manipulation options. As an example, the display area can be partitioned into a number of viewports to allow different perspectives of the drawing to be observed. Each viewport can be operated on individually. For coping with repetitive operations AutoCAD is provided with a programming language, called AutoLisp, which allows the user to create higher-level functions.

There are many AutoLisp applications programs available from third-party sources for creating 2-Dimensional and 3-Dimensional predefined objects and operations. The output files of AutoCAD readily interface with other application programs, Ventura 2 for example, because of the widespread acceptance of its .DXF file format. .DXF files have an ASCII format and can be edited with an ordinary text editor. However if required the .DXF files can be stored in binary format, thereby reducing the amount of disk storage.

AutoCAD/386 is compatible with AutoShade/386 from Autodesk which is compiled with the PharLap 386 DOS Extender. AutoShade provides solid modelling or rendering. It converts a wire-frame style AutoCAD 3-D model into a 3-D perspective image by colouring the facets and adding variations in shades and tones. AutoShade is, however, memory and computationally intensive which subsequently requires the full resources of the 386 PC.

After AutoShade/386 has been installed, a new menu appears in AutoCAD/386. The next step is to use AutoLISP to create a file which allows the user to place lights and camera in the drawing – similar to setting up a photographic session. AutoShade/386 then performs the task of calculating the intensity of light emitted from each surface from knowledge of the intensity and incident direction of the light. It then redraws the 3-Dimensional perspective model with all the appropriate shading. By having several AutoLISP files with different light and shade settings, a number of different perspective images can be produced. The saved output from AutoShade/386 is a FILMROLL file which no longer depends on the original AutoCAD drawing.

The additional hardware required to support AutoCAD on a 386 PC depends greatly on the scale of the task involved. To obtain the maximum benefit from the package, investment will be necessary in the graphics, the output plotting device, the digitising Tablet and networking if there is a need for a multi-user system. Although AutoCAD will run comfortably with a VGA configuration, for major tasks very high-resolution graphics standards will have to be used.

To make the most of AutoShade the graphics and monitor should have a 256 colours as the customary 16 colours with the enhanced graphics adaptor (EGA) are inadequate. A typical graphics attachment which allows the full facilities of AutoCAD to be realised is Xcellerator 1600 from Cambridge Computer Graphics (Section 4.3.4). This has a display resolution of 1600 x 1200 pixel (screen dots) and is powered from the Texas Instruments TMS 34010 Graphics Processor which is supported by up to eight Mbytes of video RAM.

9.3.3 VersaCAD/386

A CAD application program which exploits the full 32-bit potential of the 80386 CPU is VersaCAD/386 from Versacad Corp of California. This package runs the 80386 CPU in both Protected (Section 2.2.3) and Real Modes (Section 2.2.1) to obtain maximum performance. Very large tasks can be undertaken with VersaCAD/386 since it has provision to access 16 Mbytes of memory. To add to its throughput, it also supports the Weitek 3137 coprocessor (Section 3.1.3) or the 80387 (Section 3.1.2).

VersaCAD/386 has a 3-D design facility for surface model construction in addition to the normal 2-D drafting option. For 3-D design there is a library of solid objects which can be called on and this includes cones, spheres and cubes. The user's own wireframe primitives can also be defined and stored as standard objects. Within the 3-D design facility there is an option to allow drawings, created from 2-D drafting, to be imported and extruded into a solid model. The model can then be viewed from a variety of perspectives, isometrically, hidden line or with colour shading. An attractive feature of the VersaCAD/386 is the multiple viewports. A solid object can be featured in several viewports or windows showing its different perspectives. If a modification is made to the object in one of the viewports then equivalent modifications ripple through the remaining viewports. The 3-D model in each viewport is therefore updated with every amendment.

The 2-D drafting facility of VersaCAD/36 contains all the options that one would expect to find in a quality drafting package and this includes a readily accessible library for holding user-created symbols and standard drafting primitives. Objects can be fetched from the library and assembled according to the user's design. An automatic cut-away option is also available for any drawing which may have several levels of design.

For scaling and measurement purposes, VersaCAD/386 offers high-precision (16 decimal places) sizing with tolerance estimates. For repetitive operations, the primitive commands can be compiled into a record and play-back macro which can be featured and called from a menu. The more intricate operations of VersaCAD/386 can be accessed by using the **CAD Programming Language** (CPL) which permits the user to apply an expert system approach to CAD engineering.

To enhance the perception of the 3-D modelling, the module QuickRender can be used for colouring and shading. It works in a similar manner to AutoShade (Section 9.3.2) where the object can be viewed from a variety of perspectives with different lighting angles. It performs hidden line removal, fast colour shading and offers a degree of live animation, provided the graphics board has the computational power to cope.

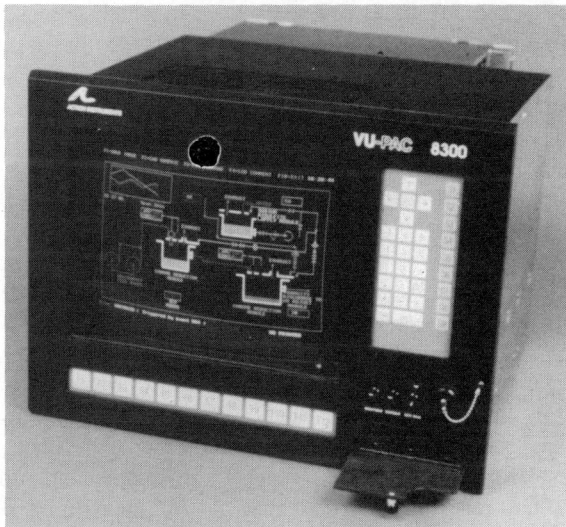

Figure 9.5 The VU-PAC830 industrial 386 PC from Action Instruments

Drawings from other CAD applications programs can be imported into VersaCAD/386 after they have been subjected to a suitable translator such as 2D/3D IGES. Equally drawings created in VersaCAD/386 can be exported and rendered suitable for other PC CAD systems using a **Drawing Exchange Format Translator.** As a design progresses it would be useful to estimate the cost of materials used and VersaCAD/386 has an option for performing this task. Information from parts lists of items used can be compiled together with labour charges and this can be helpful for assessing the overall cost of the project. Alternatively the item costing can be exported to a spreadsheet for a more complete analysis.

9.4 Industrial Process Control

There is substantial scope for the 386 PC in process control and data acquisition systems in a small-scale industrial unit. The essential elements for these tasks is reliability, fast data acquisition and processing facilities, generous mass storage and a highly responsive visual display. In this respect a 386 PC, furnished with suitable data acquisition expansion cards, a 80387 coprocessor, a sizeable hard disk drive and VGA graphics, has a great deal to offer.

Many industrial environments would be unsuitable for the conventionally packaged 386 PC, however there are number of 386 PC manufacturers who package their machines in rugged industrial enclosures which make them more resistant to the perils of the shop floor. The VU-PAC 830, from Action Instruments (Figure 9.5) is a typical example of a 386 PC industrial work station which comes with a 14 inch VGA colour monitor and a 50-Mbyte hard disk drive. It also has a protected NEMA 4.12 front panel key Section and room for 10 expansion cards in its card cage.

Process control by its very nature is an ensemble of concurrent processes and the opportunity of using the multi-tasking options on the 386 PC is therefore very attractive. For example, one task could be responsible for acquiring plant data while another would be performing the data analysis. The processing power of the 386 PC could be distributed over several tasks. An expansion card may be acquiring several channels of input plant data. If there is a need to analyse the data from each channel with the same application program, then the 386 PC could be multi-tasked.

In its multi-tasking mode, several Virtual 86 machines (VMs – Section 2.2.2) could be generated within the 386 PC and each VM could be running the analysis application program for the different input data channels. Since data is easily exchanged between VMs, account can be made of interdependent processes. Having briefly discussed a few possibilities where the 386 PC may find a place in process control it will be instructional to explore some of the finer aspects involved in these applications.

9.4.1 Data Acquisition

A 386 PC can be configured as a data acquisition platform by incorporating within its card cage a suitable expansion card (Section 9.4.4) and running an appropriate application program.

For most data acquisition tasks, the 386 PC would act as a passive instrument monitoring, storing and processing the input signals (Figure 9.6 opposite). What makes the 386 PC eminently suitable for this type of function is the fast Direct Memory Access (DMA – Section 2.3.5) facility which allows very rapid transfer of data to memory. The very large hard disk drive (HDD) capacity provides a very convenient, low-cost storage medium for digitised signals. This coupled with the wealth of signal analysis application programs and its computational power make the 386 PC a very attractive tool for data acquisition and processing.

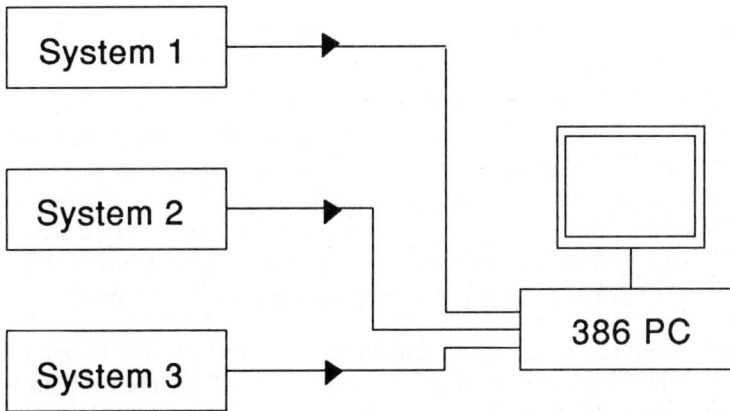

Figure 9.6 Arrangement of a 386 PC acting as a passive monitor for several systems

ASYST from Keithly Instruments is a good example of a comprehensive software package for data acquisition and processing. Alternatively, a spreadsheet approach for data analysis is the DADiSP software from the DPS Development Corporation and distributed in the UK by Adept. DADiSP allows several graphs to be displayed simultaneously – any change in one variable ripples through the other graphs like a normal spreadsheet (Figure 9.7). It can be used in conjunction with a number of proprietry I/O expansion cards or with the IEEE-488 interface (Section 7.3.1).

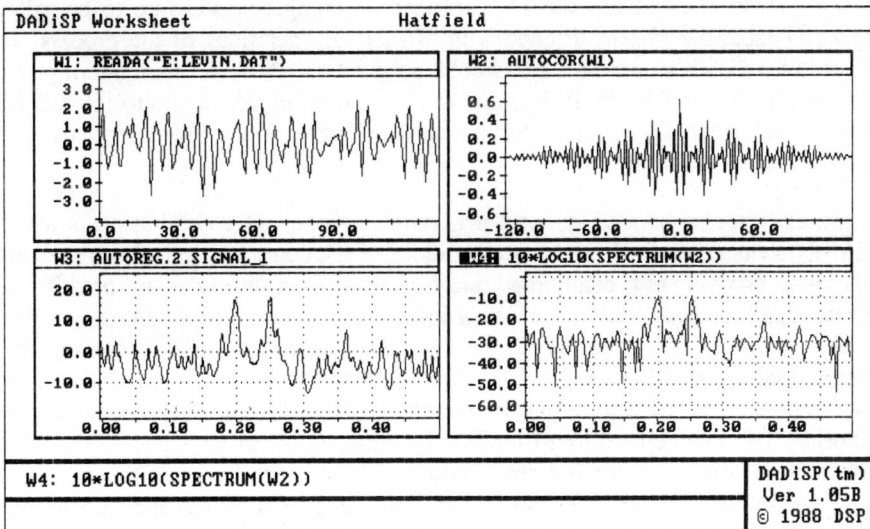

Figure 9.7 DADiSP – a convenient method of displaying data

9.4.2 Process Control

When using a 386 PC for process control, not only can it collect and process signals, but it can respond actively by producing signals. It can therefore become an active component in the control process and form part of the feed-back loop if required. The 386 PC will therefore be operating in real-time and must be configured to receive interrupts from the processes. In this context its performance will be critical and its speed of response will be a major factor in its function. The expansion cards must be chosen with care to ensure that interrupt mechanisms can be implemented.

Multi-tasking becomes an attractive feature to allow the 386 PC to control several processes and this will have the effect of easing software development for the plant control. Before with only one program running on the PC, all operations would have to performed from within the one program. With the 386 PC, each process can have its own program running concurrently with other process control programs. The task of software maintenance is therefore greatly eased and in principle existing software, written for the XT PCs, can be run directly without modification.

The reliability of a computer in process control applications is of great significance and a number of features of the 386 PC can be considered when addressing this issue. In the multi-tasking environment, if one of the process control programs goes down its damage will be confined within the 386 PC and the remaining processes will continue uninterrupted.

The high performance of the 386 PC can permit contingency software to be called rapidly to enable the system to cope with off-normal operations of the process. To enhance the reliability, the 386 PC would be powered through an uninterruptable power supply (UPS – Section 10.3.1) and in the event of power failure to the 386 PC supply special measures could be taken to ensure that the controlled processes are relaxed into safe conditions.

The 386 PC can also be used to construct complex models of control systems which effectively simulate the real operating conditions of the control system. With a model of the real process, test conditions can be constructed in order to predict the performance of the system. An example of an application program which can perform this task is PROG SIM from PCA Associates. By using the high-resolution, fast refresh graphics facility on the 386 PC, the user can also create a dynamic visual representation of the industrial process on the 386 PC monitor – ideal for process monitoring. This can be used to great effect by allowing the process operator a direct interface with the process. Industrial processes can therefore be schematically represented on the 386 PC display. By placing safeguards within the system, the process operator can introduce measured changes to the performance of the system.

The computational power of the 386 PC can be harnessed to perform a variety of functions required in control processing. This suggests that **Direct Digital Control** (DDC) can be applied directly and the familiar **Proportional Integral Derivative** (PID) control mode can be implemented in real time with multi-variable inputs. An example of the current software for process control is the LT/Control Software from Burr Brown. This performs real-time industrial control, process monitoring with real-time and customised process flow diagrams in full colour animation. Also included in the software are routines for open and closed loop PID control.

Many industrial processes are complex systems and an integral feature in the design of any process monitoring computer system will probably be a local area network (LAN – Chapter 8). It is often necessary for the localised controller to communicate with a master control which monitors the global progress of the industrial unit. The 386 PC is well matched for this task with the extensive range of LAN configurations which suit a small unit with only a few users, or a much larger unit with many tens of users. However the idea of having a central or master controller is giving way to distributed control designs, consisting of a network of local controllers able to pass and exchange information freely without the intervention of a master controller.

9.4.3 Distributed Control

Having discussed the need for data acquisition and process control, the scope of applications for the 386 PC can be broadened to include distributed control which encompasses data acquisition and process control to form a fully integrated system with management control. The essence of distributed control is to minimise the processing load of a central controller by allocating the processing functions to an array of localised intelligent controllers. This has the effect of removing the status of the central controller, as its functional role has been distributed to the intelligent local controllers. Each local controller will be responsible for controlling the activity within its own specified area.

This distributed architecture has a distinct advantage over the central controller design, namely reliability; if the central controller goes down it is very likely that the system will come to a grinding halt. However in a distributed system, if a local controller malfunctions, it is very likely that its function can be performed, remotely, by another local controller.

The requirements for local controllers which make up an effective distributed control system are:

❑ Good data acquisition facilities and self operated management

❑ Fast response processing for closed control switching logic to effect actuators

❑ Versatile user communication with other controllers.

What are the characteristics required of a personal computer system to satisfy the needs of a distributed control design? The answer must lie in a comprehensive open networking environment which can accommodate **programmable controllers, data acquisition systems** and a **Management Information System** (MIS). This requirement can be realised from several 386 PCs, hosting appropriate expansion cards, linked by means of a local area network (LAN). A particularly attractive feature of using a network of 386 PCs is the choice of operating systems – UNIX for the larger systems and DOS for more modest needs.

In a distributed control system there will be requirement for some form of data management. This will be responsible for batch receipt downloading of data, batch monitoring and batch report generation. Furthermore there may also be a need for statistical quality control (SQC) involving expert systems functions. The inclusion of MIS, to create a fully integrated processing environment, is important to enable resident application software to analyse the on-line performance of industrial processes. This permits resource costing to be considered for purposes of monitoring profit margins. One of the 386 PCs on the LAN can be dedicated to this task and it could function as a server for the management tasks.

A software product which embraces many of these management features is Onspec SAA, which has been issued by Heuristics and runs under IBM OS/2 (Section 5.6). This is part of a wider range of products designed to serve the needs of distributed control. Onspec SAA uses the Systems Application Architecture (SAA – Section 5.6.2) with a windows front-end display. In its basic form, Onspec SAA is multi-tasking for data acquisition and provides animated graphics, trend analysis, alarm monitoring and historical analysis. Furthermore, it has options for report issuing and can be expanded to include statistical quality control and real-time expert system operation.

The 386 PC in distributed control will hasten the introduction of low-cost real-time statistical quality and process control procedures. This is particularly attractive in processes where products emanate in a continuous stream – paper and steel for example. The computational power and multi-tasking aspects of the networked system of 386 PCs can cope with the demands of analysing hundreds of variables to provide instant quality reports. On a network of 386 PCs each machine can be configured as a server and this allows its resources to be accessed by other 386 PC on the network. As an example, with its multi-tasking ability, any 386 PC can not only access the data files of any other 386 PC, but load and run an application program remotely. If a number of users required some fresh data from a remote 386 PC controller, they could remotely load an acquisition program and input data from an I/O expansion card. This could be performed even if the expansion card is currently being used by the hosting 386 PC.

Needless to say security should be a very high priority and the UNIX System V/386

(Section 5.4.1) operating system goes some way to satisfy this need. Therefore coupled with its ability to provide concurrent transaction processing, which includes batch reporting, it is very likely that the 386 PC will have a significant impact upon distributed processing.

Many of the functions so far discussed form part of what has become known as **Supervisory Control And Data Acquisition** (SCADA). A SCADA system will have three basic hardware needs:

❏ Local controllers which function as acquisition and control units

❏ A communication network linking the controllers

❏ A convenient method for attaching workstations to the network.

What is required of SCADA software is the link between the plant operation and the Management Information System which requires acquisition data to be presentable as records for database software such as dBASE IV. Moreover the plant manager should have the option of interrogating the controllers to provide a wider scope of batch information such as manufacturing time, plant conditions and resource usage.

One software product which embraces these needs is Batchtrack from Di-An Micro Systems which employs a Structured Query Language (SQL) approach to integrate many of the functions required for flexible automation within a distributed control network.

Currently there is an abundance of SCADA software for the PC on the market from sources like Apricot Sigmex, Dowty Information Systems, Serck Controls, Dickingson's, Difa Measuring Systems, Modcomp, TCS Interface Products and ABB Kent Process Control. A comprehensive range of control processing products is available from the Industrial Computer Source. However there are relatively few software packages which have options for coping with transaction processing, which is understandable since the first and second generations of personal computer have only performed minor functions in control processing. It is envisaged that as the 386 PC becomes more widely used in process control, the appearance of application programs for performing transaction processing will be more frequent.

9.4.4 Input/Output Expansion Cards

For data acquisition and process control applications the 386 PC will have to be augmented with one or more I/O plug-in expansion cards which will be expected to perform a variety of functions. Typical requirements of the expansion cards are:

❏ Input and output of analogue signals

❏ Input and output of digital signals (serial and parallel)

❏ Switch relays and actuators

❏ On board timers and interrupts

Many signals derived from industrial systems will be in analogue form and these will have to be converted into digital equivalent signals before the 386 PC can process them. To achieve this, the expansion card will need a fast **Analogue to Digital Converter** (ADC) of at least 12-bits wide and if possible 16-bits with a conversion rate of not less than five microsecs.

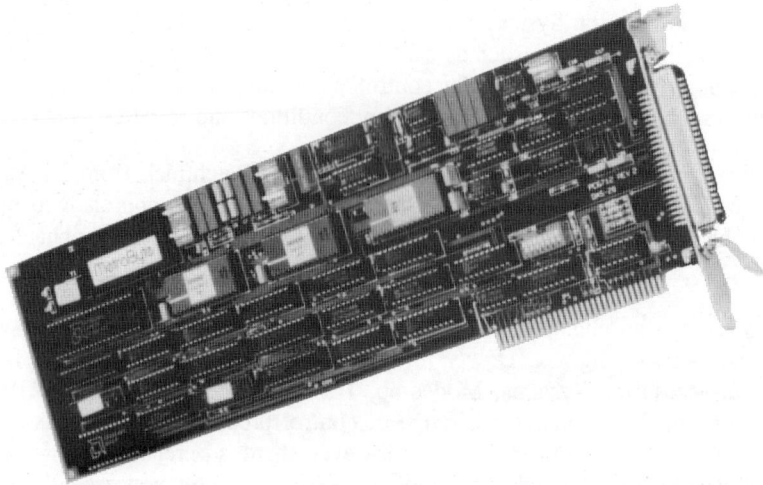

Figure 9.8 The DAS-20 analogue input/output expansion card from MetraByte. (Photo: Courtesy of Keithley Instruments)

There are many I/O expansion cards which have the AT-style Industry Standard Architecture (ISA) interface which fits into the 16-bit socket. On many of these cards the ADC is multiplexed between several analogue input channels, which allows the ADC to sample each input in succession. For data acquisition purposes a DMA facility should also be on the I/O expansion card. This will allow the samples of the input signal to be stored directly to either RAM or to the hard disk drive. This operation occurs without the intervention of the 80386 CPU and maximises the throughput of data.

In addition to sampling analogue input signals, the I/O expansion card should be able to produce two types of outputs – analogue signals which result from the computations and parallel digital signals. The I/O card will therefore be furnished with a Digital to Analogue converter (DAC) which should also operate at the same rate (if not faster) than the ADC. Again the DAC may be multiplexed to permit several analogue outputs from the 386 PC which is essential for multi-variable tasks which involve a number of signals. Some process control operations require digital outputs – stepper motors for example, and a number of digital ports on the I/O expansion card can serve this purpose.

Frequently the digital outputs from the card will be expected to switch relays for actuators which control high current devices and it may be necessary to have the digital inputs and outputs optically isolated to avoid spikes from entering the 386 PC circuitry. The I/O expansion cards will also need a timer to set the sampling period for the ADC, and interrupt lines from the process to request immediate attention from the 386 PC CPU.

A typical I/O expansion card is the DAS-20 (Figure 9.8 opposite), from the MetraByte Corporation and supplied in the UK by Keithley. It can accommodate 16 single-ended analogue inputs and 2 analogue outputs. With the DMA active, the maximum sampling rate can exceed 0.1 Msample/sec with a 12 bit precision. It comes with floppy disk which has call routines and provides information on configuring the interrupts and DMA channel.

9.5 Image Processing

Image processing (IP), until the introduction of the special purpose imaging expansion cards for the PC, has very much remained in the domain of mainframe and mini computers costing many thousands of pounds. The reality of the 386 PC, hosting an imaging expansion card, has opened up the many exciting possibilities that IP has to offer, at very reasonable costs.

IP is an esoteric subject which deals with the manipulation of images for the purposes of improving quality and revealing hidden detail. Contrasts between features can be adjusted to emphasise character differences and this is a major requirement in many medical imaging systems. Features in the original image, which cannot be distinguished by the human eye, can be brought into sharp vision. Poor quality pictures can be greatly improved by using the methods of image enhancement which are mathematically very intensive.

To illustrate this a colour image on a VGA monitor with a picture resolution of 720 x 480 pixels represents over one Mbyte of data, with each pixel requiring individual processing. Several IP algorithms require a calculation to be performed on each pixel relative to its eight surrounding neighbours. This in itself will require over eight million floating point calculations to be performed on a single picture.

In IP, at least five fundamental attributes are required:

❏ A high-quality colour graphics monitor

❏ A powerful mathematical processor

❏ Lots of fast access memory

❏ An image capturing system

❏ Proven software

All five of these requirements are now available for the 386 PC and this presents many promising opportunities for the widespread commercial application of IP.

9.5.1 Basic Requirements

There are at least two methods of performing IP operations on a 386 PC. The first is to use the computational power of the 80386 CPU and its coprocessor and the second is to employ a image capturing expansion card with its own processing intelligence. With either method, it is highly desirable to have high-resolution graphics to display the images and for this the minimum option is a colour VGA. The screen refresh rate should be at least 70 Hz and it will probably be necessary to copy the BIOS ROM into shadow RAM to ensure that the screen writing is maximised (Section 2.8.1).

The intensive numerical operations required to realise many IP functions can be performed by using the 80386 CPU coupled to a Weitek 3167 coprocessor (Section 3.1.3). This combination can provide impressive, high-performance floating point calculations which are fundamental in IP algorithms. A great deal of IP software has been written for mainframe and mini computers in FORTRAN-77, with much of this source code available in the public domain. In principle the FORTRAN-77 source code can be ported directly into the 386 PC and compiled for the Intel 80386 – Weitek 3167 coprocessor (Section 3.1.3) combination. Additional code however would have to be written to enable access to the bit image of the VGA graphics card.

If the 386 PC is to be used extensively for IP applications, then a large hard disk drive (HDD) will be required. Each image can take up in excess of one Mbyte and it is advisable to keep the IP code and the images on separate HDDs. To maximise the transfer of images between VAG and the HDD, it is preferable to have a direct memory access (DMA – Section 2.3.5) option on the VGA card otherwise a lot of time can be spent waiting for the screen refresh to finish. Alternatively, a specialist imaging expansion card can be used and a number of these will be mentioned in the next section. Integral in many of these cards is the circuitry required for digitising and capturing the image from a suitable imaging device.

9.5.2 Imaging Hardware

The availability of low-cost imaging systems and scanners provides a convenient method for importing images into the 386 PC. Many of these imaging systems are easily interfaced to a 386 PC and can be used just as easily for loading images for desktop publishing applications. Some commercial image capturing systems come with their own graphics processor and an example of this is the Microeye TC Transputer Image Processing expansion card from Digithurst (Figure 9.9) which has 3 Mbytes of RAM (1 Mbyte for each colour) and a resolution of 668 x 480 pixels. With the three bytes per pixel it is able to provide 16.7 million colours but not all of these though are discernable by the human eye. The card is interfaced directly to a Panasonic **Charge Coupled TV** (CCTV) camera, which comes with software, for performing rudimentary IP functions and for windows control.

Figure 9.9 The Microeye TC transputer image processing expansion card. (Photo: Courtesy of Digithurst)

Alternatively if intensive processing is required the IAS25 from Joyce-Loebl is a possible option. This is an image analysis board featuring the Texas Instruments TMS320C25 digital signal microprocessor (DSMP) which is very efficient at performing many IP algorithms. It has a pixel resolution of 512 x 512 and a frame store of 512 x 512 x 8 bits for the three primary colours. A software package, called Genias, is available for this board, which performs a variety of operations including arithmetic geometry, object detection, convolutions and colour calibration.

IBM has recognised the importance of IP by releasing its own package, Audio Visual Connection, which comes as two I/O expansion cards: the Audio Capture and Play-back Adaptor and the Video Capture Adaptor. These two adaptor cards are available in the Micro Channel Architecture (MCA – Section 3.8.1) format. Image data for the system can be sourced from a video camera, video disk or video tape. Sound input on the other hand can be sourced from a tape cassette player or CD player and both image and sound data can be stored on Write Once Read Many (WORM – Section 7.4.2) optical disks. Play back can achieved by either head phones or audio amplifier for the sound or direct to a television for the images. To support the Audio Visual Connection, Microsoft and Intel have adopted a standard disk compression technique which permits the optimum storage of its data on WORMs.

9.5.3 Imaging Functions

Having briefly reviewed some of the imaging systems on the market for 386 PCs, we can discuss the range of operations which can be performed on the captured images in order to render them more visually useful. This will require a numerical process (a calculation) to be performed on each pixel in the image. To effect this processing, a technique involving **Look Up Tables** (LUTs) is sometimes used. Each pixel is represented by one byte of memory and this can have one of 256 values ($2^8 = 256$). If a calculation is performed on a pixel value, the result must also be one of 256 values. Therefore, as an alternative to performing a calculation, a LUT containing all possible results is used. Normally as the image is digitised, the captured data is stored as pixel values. Alternatively the pixel value from the digitised image can be used to address the LUT and the result from the LUT is stored as the pixel value. A complete numerical process can be stored in a LUT and can be put into effect as the image is digitised. A whole range of numerical processes can be performed in this way and some of these are listed here:

❑ Addition of two images (sum)

❑ Subtraction of images (difference)

❑ Frame averaging, through addition and division

❑ Multiplication of images (product)

❑ Division of images

❑ Logical operations, AND, OR XOR

❑ Arithmetic operations on each pixel (mult, division, addition and subtraction of constants)

❑ Signature calculations (sum of pixel brightness)

❑ 3 by 3 convolutions

❑ Edge detection through pixel differences

❑ Noise reduction by 3 by 3 pixel averaging

As an example, consider adding the stored image of 256 x 256 pixels to an incoming freshly digitised image. If there are 256 LUTs, each of depth 256 bytes then the current image can be stored in the LUTs. An internal address generator would normally assign the pixel address for the incoming data byte to be stored. However this address generator addresses the appropriate LUT location and the contents of the addressed LUT is then added to the incoming data byte and the sum stored in the proper pixel memory. This mechanism is available on the Oculus-300 Imaging Board, supplied by Perdix Components, and can cope with 120 images per second at a resolution of 256 x 256 pixels.

A method of enhancing the quality of an image is by means of **histogram equalisation**. The intensity of one of the prime colours, held by a pixel in an 8-bit image, will be represented by the one of 256 levels ($2^8 = 256$). The darkest possible shade of the pixel will be 0 and the brightest possible shade will be 255. What frequently happens in images is that the shades of a colour, within a localised region of the image, all bunch around a small range of colours. If there is image region which is very dark then the pixel values are low and vice versa for bright regions. Histogram equalisation allows the shade values, within a defined region, to be broadened out by rescaling and this results in greater detail becoming visible, enhancing the image contrast. Histogram equalisation routines or options are usually found in IP applications and represent a simple method of improving image quality.

Having discussed a few IP functions it will be constructive to consider a number of commercial products which provide IP facilities. Data Translation of Marlboro, Massachusetts manufactures an impressive range of IP products, under its interface specification DT-Connect, ranging from expansion frame grabbing cards to advanced IP software. For example, the DT2851 frame grabber expansion card accommodates 512 x 512 x 8-bit images and has two on-board memory buffers. The image input rate is 30 images per second and a range of real-time processing options are available which include frame addition, subtraction, division, multiplication and a number of logical operations. These are accomplished by means of LUT processing and the DT2851 lends itself to industrial inspection requirements such as robotic vision.

When linked to the DT2859 8-channel video multiplexer, the DT2851 can process images from up to eight separate video sources.

There are a number of software products from Data Transation which can be used in conjunction with image grabbing expansion cards and form part of the DT-Connect standard. DT IRIS is a subroutine library which can be used in the development of IP application programs for the DT2851. There are routines in DT IRIS for performing frame averaging, image reduction and text, line and circle overlays. The routines from DT IRIS are coded for the Intel 80287 microprocessor and consequently do not employ the full computational resources of the 80386 CPU found in the 386 PC.

However, they can be called from Microsoft's high-level languages Pascal, C and FORTRAN. Alternatively, DT/Image-Pro is an interactive mouse-driven, standalone application program. It allows a range of image manipulation operations including localised histogram equalisation. Localised processing is permitted by means of defining window areas and up to 13 windows can be defined simultaneously. This type of processing is very attractive for graphic art, image archiving and general business information presentation requirements.

For advanced IP needs, the PC Semper is an operational environment which supports an extensive array of algorithms which rely on numerical intensive operations. However it was designed to run on the IBM AT (and clones) hosting the 80286 and at the time of writing a dedicated version for the 386 PC was not available.

9.5.4 Image Processing Applications

The range of applications for IP is quite vast and it is beyond the scope of this book to enter into a full discussion of this area. However a couple of areas will be briefly reviewed to serve as illustrative examples.

A field that is currently receiving considerable attention is robotic vision which requires an image recognition facility. The intelligence of the robot can be implemented in a 386 PC fitted with the following:

❑ A suitable image capturing expansion card

❑ One or more expansion cards for controlling the stepper motors of the robot system

❑ Expansion cards for receiving analogue signals from the robot's touch and position sensors

❑ A software development facility for algorithm development.

There is a variety of tasks that the 80386 CPU would perform in addition to the image or pattern recognition. In an intelligent robot system, it is quite probable that its design would have a number of multi-variable control functions to perform concurrently with the imaging tasks. Both types of operation require considerable numerical processing capability and the 80386 CPU, along with its coprocessor, would be suitably taxed. Developing appropriate algorithms for pattern recognition is still a keen research area and FORTRAN and C are two high-level languages favoured for this purpose.

An area receiving a great deal of attention is Image Processing Documentation (IPD) which involves the capturing of images from a suitable source such as video or camcorders. The images are then subjected to appropriate processing and refinement before they are imoported to a desktop publishing package. This is a keen application area for the 386 PC since all stages of IPD can be performed on a single machine. If there are several users the tasks could be shared among a small network.

Many medical systems rely heavily on visual image information and improvements to medical images can be achieved by the application of IP techniques. For example, the quality of an X-ray image can be greatly enhanced by using image noise reduction techniques along with histogram equalisation methods. During the 1990s the 386 PC equipped with imaging enhancement hardware will be used more and more in medical practice. Not so much to replace existing techniques but to compliment them in the search for better pictures.

Further Reading:

Software Development on the Intel 80386 Microprocessor
1. 80386 A Programming & Design Handbook, P Brumm & D Brumm, Tab Professional & Reference Books (1989).

2. Programming the 80386, J H Crawford & P P Gelsinger, Sybex.

3. Advanced 80386 Programming Techniques, J L Turley, McGraw-Hill (1988).

4. 80386/80286 Assembly Language Programming, W Murry & C Pappas, Mc Graw-Hill (1986).

5. 80386 Assembly Language Primer, M Edelhardt & S Kanzler, Prentice-Hall (1987).

6. 80386 Programming Guide, L A Leventhal, Bantam (1988).

7. Programming the Intel 80386, B E Smith, Foresman Scott (1987).

8. Dr Dobb's Toolbox of 80286/80386 Programming, P Robinson, M & T Publishing (1988).

9. 80386 Book: Assembly Language Programmer's Guide for the 80386, R P Nelson, Microsoft (1989).

10. Assembly Language Programming for the 80386, J Fernandez & R Ashley, McGraw-Hill (1898).

11. 80386 Macro Assembler and Toolkit, P Brumm & D Brumm, TAB Professional Reference Books (1989).

12. 80386 Hardware Reference Manual, Intel (1989).

13. 80386 Programmers Reference Manual, Intel (1989).

14. 80386 Systems Software Writers Guide, Intel (1989).

15. Microsoft Macro Assembler 5.1: Programming in the 80386 Environment, J Mueller & W Wang, Windcrest (1990).

FORTRAN
1. Introduction to FORTRAN 77 and the Personal Computer, R H Hammond, W B Rogers & J B Crittenden, McGraw-Hill (1987).

Desktop Publishing
1. Desktop Publishing Today, (Monthly), Industrial Media Ltd, Blair House, 184 High Street, Tonbridge.

Ventura
1. Ventura Publishing, QUANTA Learning Systems, 1987.

2. Ventura Instant Reference, M Holtz, Sybex.

3. The ABCs of Ventura, R Cowart, Sybex.

4. Instant Ventura Publisher, T Pompili, K H Thompson & S J Bennett, Brady.

5. Mastering Ventura 2, M Holts, (second edition), Sybex.

6. Ventura Power Tools With Software, R Altman, Sybex.

PageMaker
1. Instant PageMaker, T Pompili, K H Thompson & S J Bennett, Brady.

AutoCAD
1. Mastering AutoCAD, G Omura, (third edition – Release 10), Sybex

2. The ABCs of AutoCAD, A R Miller, (second edition – Release 10), Sybex.

3. Advanced Techniques in AutoCAD, R M Thomas, (second edition – release 10), Sybex.

4. AutoCAD Desktop Companion, R M Thomas (Release 10), Sybex.

5. AutoCAD Instant Reference, G Omura, Sybex.

Process Control
1. Control Systems, (Monthly), Industrial Media Ltd, Blair House, 184 High Street, Tonbridge, Kent.

2. Control and Instrumentation, (Monthly), Morgan Grampian plc, Calderwood Street, London SE18.

Image Processing
1. Image Processing, (Quarterly), Reed Business Publishing Group, Quadrant House, The Quadrant, Sutton, Surrey.

2. Digital Image Processing, C Gonzalez & P Wintz, Addison-Wesley (1987).

3. Digital Image Processing and Computer Vision, R J Schalkoff, John Wiley (1989).

10

386 PC Design and Management

Having established some of the capabilities of the 386 PC and ways of enhancing its functionality, it will be of interest to the user to consider some of the aspects which relate to maintaining it as a reliable system. Selecting the appropriate 386 PC design to match a particular workplace or environment is also an important aspect of its application. Fortunately there are several design options available which may be considered to ensure that a 386 PC will be best suited to meet the needs of the user(s). 386 PCs are delicate pieces of equipment and cannot sustain periods of prolonged rough treatment. Attention should always be paid to the operating conditions in which the 386 PC is expected to function, as hostile environments will greatly reduce its reliability and serve only to aggravate the user. Not only can this lead to a serious degradation in the performance of the facility, but it will also increase, unnecessarily, the investment costs of the computer.

10.1 Design

The design format of the personal computer was established with the early IBM PCs and basically it has remained unchanged. Although there are slight variations on the original design, the 386 PC is still housed in a single unit with separate monitor and keyboard attachments. The 386 PC is available is basically four design formats:

❑ the standard desktop

❑ the tower system

❑ the lap-top

❑ the special purpose industrial unit to operate in the shop floor environment.

The size, or footprint, of early desktop PCs tended to be rather large. The standard style, measuring approximately 24 by 15 by 6 inches was, by any stretch of the imagination, big for a desktop utility. One of these on your desk left very little room for much else. Office space is always at a premium and PC designers have eventually become aware of this fact and have realised that users no longer want half their desk occupied by a computer. To alleviate this problem, the 386 PC was accommodated on a rigid, purpose-built PC trolley.

With the development of dedicated chip sets (Section 2.1) and improved manufacturing tecniques for printed circuit boards, there emerged a reduced style or small footprint PC. The small footprint has gone some way in resolving the problem of limited desk space. On average, measuring 15 x 15 inches, the reduced style is relatively compact. One possible casualty of a reduced style 386 PC may be the loss of space to accommodate I/O expansion cards, however this feature is dependent upon the make of the machine.

If the 386 PC has only one accessible drive, it is acceptable to lay it on its side, supported by angle stands, and have it tucked away under the desk. However there should be easy access to the floppy disk drive and the power switch. If there are other types of accessible drives in the 386 PC, WORM drive or tape streamer for example, then it may be impracticable to have the 386 PC out of arm's length. If the 386 PC is furnished with a CD-ROM drive then it should be mounted in a horizontal position. Having the 386 PC under the desk also increases the chances of it being kicked when a hard disk access is in progress and this may result in undesirable consequences.

10.1.1 Tower Systems

The tower system design has now become an accepted format for 386 PCs which are required to support many enhancements. It is attractive for accommodating high-capacity hard disk drive units (> 300 Mbytes) and the necessary I/O expansion cards required for a LAN where the 386 PC tower would act as a file server (Section 8.5.5).

Standing as an upright system, a 386 PC tower occupies surprisingly little room and has the ergonomic feature of having the accessible drives positioned at the top of the system. The key feature of the 386 PC tower is the heavy-duty rating of the power supply which will be subjected to sizeable loads during normal operation. If the 386 PC tower is hosting as a network file server, it will be accommodating a large hard disk drive of a few hundred Mbytes and possibly a number of network expansion cards. These facilities are power hungry and it is essential, in order to maintain smooth running of the network, that the power supply is adequately rated with a comfortable power safety margin.

In a multi-user system a 386 PC tower will probably require an integral tape streamer

(Section 3.7) as backups constitute a major feature in the management policy of a computer system. Again it must be emphasised, that in the event of all the 386 PC tower enhancements and disk drives operating simultaneously, the rating of the power supply must be able to comfortably support the loading. Typical power supply ratings for a tower system will be of the order of 400 VA.

Since 386 PC power systems are primarily bought for their ability to support enhancement features, it is important to specify the I/O expansion bus standard. If possible, provided the 386 PC tower is not an IBM machine, the user should try to obtain the Enhanced Industry Standard Architecture (EISA – Section 7.3.4). This will ensure that the 386 PC tower will be compatible with future I/O expansion cards and the cards that are currently being manufactured. An example of a quality tower system is the SYSTEMPRO from Compaq which is available with the EISA expansion bus and has 11 expansion slots. SYSTEMPRO can be supplied with a variety of hard disk sizes and has four Mbytes of system RAM as standard.

10.1.2 Portables and Lap-tops

Portables or transportable 386 PCs, which they are sometimes referred to because they form an all-in-one system unit with integrated keyboard and display, are especially useful for field applications where the user is likely to be away from the office and needs to access data quickly. Typically, entire site maintenance schedules can be held on the hard disk unit and accessed by personnel who require this type of information. Alternatively the portable 386 PC could be used as a source for diagnostic data, inventory information and even as a storage of service manual information. The advent of the CD-ROM allows this last requirement to be realised.

One area where the 386 PC is likely to find substantial applications is for users working from home. The demand for this option is likely to grow in the 1990s in reaction to ever mounting traffic congestion. When the portable 386 PC is fitted with a suitable modem (Section 7.1), all the resources of the office network can be at the user's disposal. The portable 386 PC becomes a service on a Local Area Network (LAN) for other users to access if needs be. The option of working from home is only one step removed from the current practice where many users may spend 80% of any working day in front of a PC.

A major requirement with a portable 386 PC is the ease with which it can be moved from location to location with a minimum of disruption. One of the design features, which all portable 386 PCs have in common, is their high degree of compactness and ease of operation.

The fundamental differences between the ordinary desktop 386 PC and the portable will be the display unit, the reduced size keyboard and a smaller volume in the card cage. The display will either be liquid crystal (LCD – Section 4.4) or a gas plasma

(Section 4.5). Not only are these displays more compact than CRT monitors but they also consume very much less power. The operational performance of the a portable 386 PC will be comparable to that of the desktop; hard disk drives in portable 386 PCs should have access times less than 28 msecs and offer everything that the desktop equivalent has.

An example of this class of 386 PC is the Compaq Portable 386 (Figure 10.1) which has a 20 Mhz 80386 CPU, 1 Mbyte of RAM and a 640 x 400 resolution gas plasma display. It comes with a standard high-density 5.25 inch floppy disk drive and a choice of hard disk drives, 40 or 100 Mbytes. The card cage is large enough to accommodate two expansion cards and there is a socket for the 80387 coprocessor (Section 3.1.2).

Figure 10.1 The Compaq Portable 386 PC. (Photo: Courtesy of Compaq)

Lap-top 386 PCs are generally smaller than the portable variety but still offer a comparable performance. Some lap-top 386 PCs are battery powered and this feature renders them suitable for users who work during long haul travelling periods. The distinguishing feature of the lap-top PC is the very high degree of compactness which has been realised through advanced manufacturing techniques for high-density printed circuit boards. One of the original purposes for the reduced 80386SX CPU (Section

2.2.5) was for lap-top and portable 386 PCs but their adoption for these classes of machines is by no means widespread.

An example of a lap-top 386 PC is the Toshiba T3200SX which uses a 80386SX microprocessor. Despite its lap-top design, it requires a mains power and weighs 17 lbs. Among the 92 keys on its reduced size keyboard are 12 function keys and a separate numeric key pad. The screen is a high-quality orange on black plasma display (Section 4.5) and is built to the VGA graphics standard with 640 x 480 pixel resolution, or 80 columns by 25 lines of text. Since the display is VGA, it offers 16 levels of orange shades. However it does have a VGA port (along with two RS-232 ports) for driving a CRT VGA monitor.

The T3200SX can accommodate up to 13 Mbytes of RAM; the RAM expansion modules are attached directly to the motherboard. There is also a socket for the 80387SX maths coprocessor. Internally, there is room for two expansion cards or alternatively the Toshiba Hayes compatible modem which adds to its functionality. The disk storage comes as either a 25 ms access time 40-Mbyte or 80-Mbyte hard disk drive and a 3.5 inch floppy disk drive.

10.1.3 Multi-user

A number of manufacturers make 386 PCs specifically as multi-user systems where the 386 PC motherboard and its resources are housed in a central unit. Each user would access the services of the 386 PC via one of several terminals which would be interfaced to the central unit. A multi-user system will be furnished with a suitable operating system (Section 5.5) which can support several users and allow each to access the services of the 386 PC.

In general the more users on a system the more memory, both hard disk space (Section 2.5) and RAM (Section 2.3), will be required. There should be a minimum of 60 Mbytes of hard disk storage and eight Mbytes of RAM. A tape streamer (Section 3.7) is also recommended to back-up the data files, which acts as a useful security feature in the event of the hard disk drive(s) malfunctioning.

It is important to ascertain, from the supplier, whether the memory capacity of a multi-user system can be upgraded to accommodate more users. It is also important to plan ahead for future needs before making a commitment for a particular system. On deciding that a multi-user system is the best solution, ensure that the appropriate application programs can successfully run in a multi-user environment. Information regarding file locking, security and access priority should be sought from the supplier of both the application programs and the 386 PC hardware.

An example of a dedicated multi-user system is the family of QC-386 systems from Bromcom Computers of Bromley. Four systems are available: QC-386/SX supporting three users to the QC-386/HP supporting 32 users with the option of UNIX (Section 5.4). The terminals are interfaced to the central units via RS-232 serial links (Section 3.3.2) and each system has the option of running under Concurrent DOS/386 (Section 5.5.3).

10.2 Maintenance and Warranty

As a general rule, 386 PC hardware will be supplied with a 12-month warranty; in the event of a fault developing the supplier will repair or replace the offending item. Some manufacturers offer an extended warranty to cover the second and subsequent years and the cost of this will be calculated on a percentage basis of the net value of the system.

Although the warranty covers the hardware, the security of the accumulated data is the responsibility of the buyer (or user) and depending on its value, provision should be made to back-up the data on a regular basis (Section 3.7). The components of a 386 PC which require maintenance include the cooling fan, the keyboard, the mouse and the tape streamer (if there is one). The hard disk drives are sealed units, but since they are rotating continuously while the PC is on, they will show signs of wear after a few years of operation. An early indication is an increase in background noise from them and it is advisable to have the hard disk drives covered by the maintenance agreement.

Dust is one of the major plagues of personal computers and although there will be a dust mesh in front of the cooling fan, small dust particles will enter the PC unit and deposit themselves on the electronic components. It is worthwhile every few months to clean the dust mesh on the cooling fan as this will improve its effectiveness. During routine maintenance the dust deposit should be removed to prevent possible short circuit tracking occurring. One potential problem are the strip connectors in the card cage (Section 3.2). If a fine deposit of dust does gather in these connectors then it may impede the operation of an expansion board inserted into the cage.

The mechanism in the ball-designed mouse (Section 3.5) tends to attract dust and this can limit its performance. Normally the ball can be easily removed and cleaned with a minimum amount of fuss. The keyboard can suffer depending on the user; grime and dust can accumulate, not only on the surface of the keys but also under the keys with the effect of increasing contact resistance.

Heavy-handed users can expect keyboard problems with the contact membrane under the keys softening to give mushy response and possible key failure. Under these circumstances it is advisable to have a number of spare keyboards available and ensure that they are covered in the maintenance.

10.2.1 Corporate Maintenance

The value of contract service or customer support will be largely dependent upon the nature of the application for the 386 PC. For a company installing a networked system of 386 PCs there are two possible methods for providing a maintenance service. After sales customer support, from the equipment suppliers, or service from a third-party contract company. The importance of a maintenance service for a network of 386 PCs cannot be over emphasised. For example, a financial institution simply cannot afford to allow its networked system to fail. In the event of malfunction there must be contingency measures to isolate the fault and yet maintain at least a partially working system. The ability to minimise the damage to the whole system from a single device failure is a very important design requirement.

When designing a network system, contingency plans should be drawn up to account for possible device failure and the ability to redistribute resources if necessary. If the system develops a fault then a fast and responsive maintenance service should be in place to cope with the customer's needs. In a networked system, where not only maintenance will be expected but possible upgrades of additional resources to the system will be required, then good, competent services are needed. Networking technology is not easy to understand or implement. The user must satisfy himself that the contractor of the maintenance service has adequate experience and manpower resources to provide a viable service.

A number of maintenance service companies provide a portfolio of services which include consultancy, staff training, installation, software support and system upgrading. Networks tend to be organic and their growth, through hardware and software upgrades, must be carefully nurtured otherwise they will cease to provide the expected service. Although the majority of suppliers of 386 PC provide a degree of customer support, other third-party companies have regional centres and provide specified time call out contracts for their customers. However establishing an agreement through a maintenance contract is no easy task.

10.2.2 Maintenance Contracts

The whole question of maintenance contracts for personal computers has no clear-cut solutions and in many respects depends on the goodwill of the supplier and the customer. Although maintenance contracts do not feature strongly with the purchase of a single 386 PC, a contract for several 386 PCs, for a critical network system, warrants particular attention. It is not unusual to find some suppliers using maintenance contracts which contain clauses and conditions drawn from a variety of different sources which may not be relevant to personal computers. Since so much of the PC technology was developed in the USA, it is not surprising to find, in some contracts, clauses only acceptable in the American legal system.

For example, exclusion clauses are valid in English law and unless they are described as conditions, the clauses will not be valid in American law. Although there have been attempts by the Institute of Purchasing and Supply to establish a set of model conditions, these have not met with too much success. This is partly due to the rapid developments in computer technology which outpace the model conditions. To compound this limitation, there is difficulty in providing a comprehensive set of model conditions to encompass the many possible services and products offered by a supplier.

With these potential problems in mind, a contract may exist between the two parties, the customer and the supplier. To avoid additional difficulties, in the contract it should be clearly defined which party is responsible for setting out the customer's specification and these specifications should be listed. It is advisable to make this clear and nothing should be left unwritten if it is considered important. Because the contract exists between two parties, it is important that the division of risk is clearly mapped out; legal advice may have to be sought to achieve this. In the contract, it should be made clear to customers what their obligations are and how much it is going to cost them.

Many 386 PCs come with a free one or two-year warranty and although this may be satisfactory for a single user, a warranty for a networked system will require, as previously stated, careful attention. Some provision should be made for on-site cover and a rapid response to equipment malfunction. If this is considered important by the customer, it should be listed in the maintenance contract. It is always advisable for the supplier to make visible, to customers, a serial number catalogue of their equipment and it should be made clear, in the maintenance contract, the obligations of the supplier in the provision of replacement equipment.

10.3 Component Reliability

A 386 PC is a multi-component system and each component has its own measure of reliability. A failure or a malfunction of any one component does not necessarily render the whole system inoperative. It is instructive to gain an appreciation of the degree of reliability of the various components. The highest reliability will be found with the electronic components resident on the motherboard. However their performance can be jeopardised if the cooling fan in the main unit is not working properly. The cooling fan is normally situated to maintain a constant air flow across the integrated circuits to prevent overheating. It is important that air flow is not obstructed or diverted. The PC should not be run for long periods with the cover off and the unused expansion slots should always have their end cover plates in position.

The fan also provides cooling for the expansion cards which are positioned longitudinally to the air stream. The reliability of the expansion cards will be compromised if they are inserted and removed frequently. The edge connectors of each board can only withstand a finite number of insertions; each time a board is removed there will be a decrease in its reliability. The same applies to the insertion slots for the cards; each time they are used the quality of the contact diminishes. It should be standard policy not to regularly remove the expansion cards.

The power supply unit (PSU) within the 386 PC will usually have a high reliability provided the loading from the system is not excessive. There should always be a comfortable margin between the average power consumption of the system and the rating on the PSU. Care must always be taken, if additional expansion cards are inserted into the 386 PC, to ensure that the PSU can cope with the extra loading. PSUs have been known to go down without any apparent reason; however they can be replaced easily.

Many applications for the 386 PC involve the storage of large amounts of information. Current hard disk drive sizes reflect this storage capacity with 500 Mbyte drives being commonplace. With this large data storage, reliability is crucial, since a head crash or total access failure can be very expensive to recover from. Unfortunately the hard disk drive, by virtue of its mechanical moving parts, will have a relatively low reliability rating. Although a HDD itself can be replaced, the data contained on it will probably become irretrievable. However the probability of a HDD failure is very low, provided it is treated properly, although one cause can be a sudden powe failure when data is being transferred to the disk. Every effort shoulld be made to ensure this does not happen inadvertently. Various contingency measures can be adopted in the event of a failure to allow a partial recovery at least. The inclusion of a tape streamer (Section 3.7) is one measure, and active methods such as disk mirroring can also be used to safeguard against disk failure.

The monitor can also suffer from reduced reliability which can arise from phosphor burning. If the same image is kept on the screen for a great length of time then the image becomes permanently burnt into the phosphor. This effect is especially prevalent with terminals which are attached to mainframes running a single software operation. Phosphor burning not only leads to the unsightly burn image but also destroys the monitor's ability to produce the proper range of colours. It is therefore important to prevent phosphor burning by keeping the screen brightness to a comfortable minimum. It also helps not to have the 386 PC close to a window with bright sunlight pouring in, as this reduces the screen contrast and sets up irritating reflections. To prolong the life of the CRT it is possible to install a terminate and stay resident routine to turn the graphics off after a period of 10 minutes if there is no screen or mouse activity. This option is found in Windows/386.

When the 386 PC is switched on, it is normal for a memory diagnostic check to be carried out and this is sometimes followed by an optional system component diagnostic check. It is certainly worthwhile, from time to time, to go though this exercise. If a fault is suspected then the first measure is to soft boot (Ctrl-Alt-Del) and enter the diagnostics menu. The diagnostic check will include an examination of System Memory, Graphics Card, Disk Controller(s), Parallel Ports, RS-232 Ports and Coprocessor.

If a failure is recorded then a telephone call to your friendly authorised 386 PC dealer is in order. The market leaders in the sale of 386 PCs pride themselves on the quality and reliability of their well engineered products. Generally, part of the price difference between an unknown model and an up-market Compaq or Dell 386 PC is the expected long-term reliability. For 386 PCs operating in commercially sensitive areas where task scheduling is critical then reliability must be a prime consideration and should form part of the costings in the initial system design.

10.3.1 The Uninterruptable Power Supply

A number of problems can arise with the mains power supply which can unduly effect the reliability of a 386 PC system. The most common are power surges or fluctuations in the mains voltage or mains frequency. These surges, which propagate along the grid from various sources, can effect the performance of the delicate integrated circuits within the 386 PC. The outcome is an unpredictable event in the operation of the system and possible data loss. Blackouts occur when there is a total loss of power and if this should occur the currently processed data will be lost. Although national grid failures are quite rare events in most European countries, there is however no guarantee that someone in the basement will not pull the wrong fuse out by mistake. Brownouts (severe voltage drops caused by localised high power demands) are more frequent and these can have an adverse effect on the system performance.

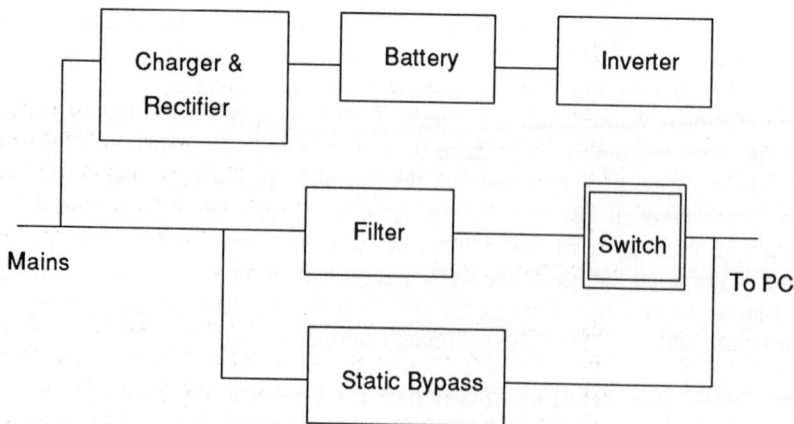

Figure 10.2 Schematic of offline Uninterruptable Power Supply

One way of minimising the effects of mains power interruptions is to use an Uninterruptable Power Supply (UPS) which resides between the mains supply and the computer system. The main function of a UPS is to provide a clean, safe power supply by filtering the mains and to offer protection against power failure by providing a power back-up from a battery.

UPSs are available in three basic designs: the offline unit, the online unit and the interactive unit. In the offline design there is a filter, a charger/rectifier, an inverter and a battery back-up (Figure 10.2 opposite).

The computer is connected to the mains via a filter unit which removes the fluctuations and cleans up the supply. The charger/rectifier produces a DC output which keeps the battery topped-up. If there is a blackout or brownout the inverter (which acts as a DC to AC converter) comes into play and draws power from the battery and maintains a constant power supply for the computer. The response of the inverter is no more than a few msecs. The online design has the same components as the offline version except the charger/rectifier (which charges the battery) and inverter are in series (Figure 10.3).

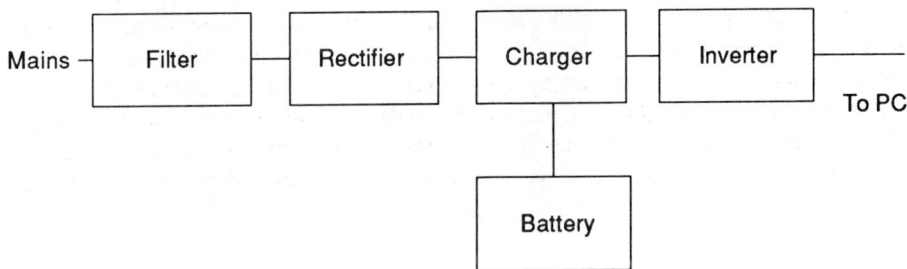

Figure 10.3 Schematic of Online UPS

All the input power from the mains passes through the charger/rectifier to become intermediate DC. The inverter then converts the DC back to AC which is fed directly to the computer. The double conversion process acts as an effective mains filter and when there is mains drop the battery automatically compensates for the shortfall. In the event of a computer(s) overloading the UPS a static bypass switches into operation and connects the computer direct to the mains supply.

The static bypass should also come into operation if the UPS malfunctions or should fail to operate properly. This will give the user sufficient time to find a replacement UPS. The DC to AC conversion is normally carried out using one of two techniques, linear or pulse width modulation (PWM). Linear conversion has the advantage of not producing high levels of electromagnetic interference which is sometimes the case with PWM.

In the design of the interactive unit, the power for the computer is normally drawn through a filter unit direct from the mains. If there is a brownout in the mains supply, the inverter becomes partially active and, like the online design, compensates for the shortfall by drawing power from the battery.

When there is a wholesale blackout the inverter becomes totally active and provides the power back-up for the computer from the battery. Interactive units are normally cheaper than the other designs but their ability to cope with mains frequency variations is not as good. The highest reliability is found with the online UPSs, but for a single 386 PC system the offline UPS is normally quite adequate provided it can supply over 200 VA.

Figure 10.4 The Pioneer Online 1KVA UPS. (Photo: Courtesy of Quadshield)

When looking for a UPS it is advisable to determine the power back-up period of the battery and whether it can be augmented with additional batteries in order to extend the back-up period. Several large UPSs have three-phase outputs but this is not required for 386 PCs. There are many manufacturers of UPSs and a typical example is the Pioneer 1KVA from Quadshield (Figure 10.4) which has a front panel display for indicating its current status. Alternatively Sola-Banner makes an extensive range including the online Mini UPS. This can deliver an output power of 600 VA and has a battery back-up of four hours.

10.4 80486-based Systems

The release of the very high-performance 80486 (also known as the i486) 32-bit microprocessor by Intel in the second quarter of 1989 ushered in a new processor which will find applications in workstations as well the up-market PCs.

The 80486, fabricated from the Intel CMOS IV process, has integrated on a single piece of silicon an enhanced CPU, a numerical coprocessor, a cache controller (Section 2.3.2) and 8K of cache memory. It is therefore not radically different from the 80386 family of chips, but does represent a reduced number of chips.

Having this high degree of integration has lead to an impressive performance and some 486 PCs have Landmark ratings (Section 1.2) of over 100. A schematic diagram showing the functional elements of the 80486 is shown in Figure 10.5 overleaf. The main characteristics of the 80486 microprocessor are:

❏ Binary compatibility with the previous range of Intel microprocessors which means that it can run MS-DOS, OS/2, Windows/386 and UNIX System V/386 based software

❏ High level of component integration which includes the floating point unit, cache memory and pages, virtual memory management

❏ High performance 32-bit data throughput with a clock speed at either 25 Mhz or 33 Mhz accommodating a burst data rate of 106 Mbytes/sec.

If a system hosting the 80486 is to be used for numerically intensive applications, there is the option of coupling the 80486 with the Wietek WTL 4167 floating point coprocessor. As with the WTL 3167 (Section 3.1.3) only code compiled for the WTL 4167 will actually use the coprocessor. As 486 PCs emerge many of them will have a socket to accommodate the optional WTL 4167 coprocessor.

Among the commercial systems that have adopted the 80486 is the Apricot VX FTserver (Figure 10.6 overleaf) which offers a 15 million instructions per second (MIPs) computing power. It is primarily intended to function as a network server and is able to accommodate MS-DOS and MS-NET, UNIX System V/386, LAN Server, OS/2 and LAN Manager.

The FTserver is available in two configurations, the 400 series for network functions and the 800 for multi-user UNIX systems. The cache memory sizes range from 64K to 128K depending on the model and the expansion ports are based on Micro Channel Technology (MCA). The hard disk drives use the Small Computer System Interface (SCSI – Section 7.3.3) design which is well matched for disk intensive activity found in network systems. The motherboard has many integrated features including an

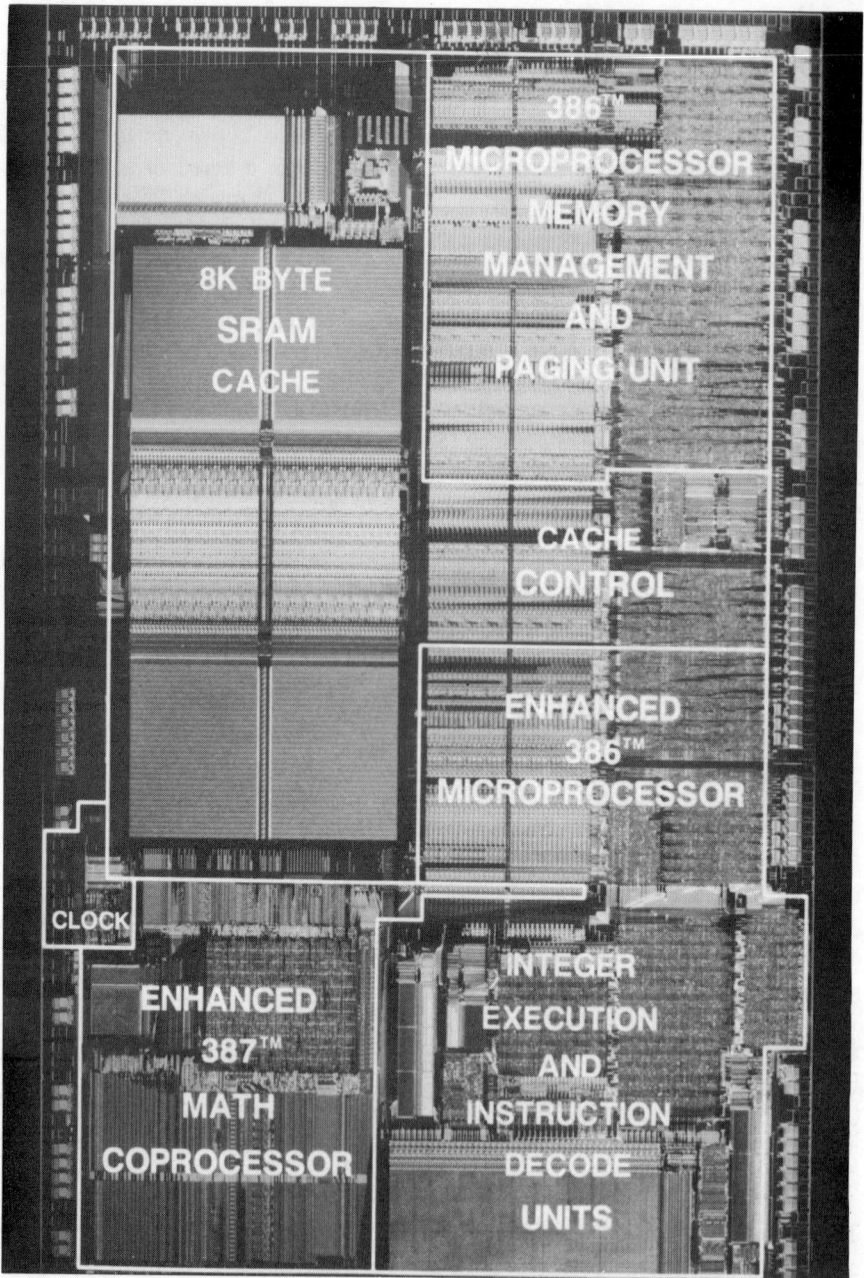

Figure 10.5 The 80486 die showing the positions of the functional units. (Photo: Courtesy of Intel)

analogue VGA connector, an Ethernet interface, a mouse port and a number of serial and parallel ports. FTserver incorporates several security features and fault tolerant networking communications.

Figure 10.6 The Apricot VX FTserver based on the 80486 microprocessor

A question often asked is: What is the future of the 386 PC with the emergence of the 486 PC? Although several 486 PCs have appeared, the greatest threat they pose is to the sector of the market currently enjoyed by the minicomputer and the workstation. To exploit the full multi-user and networking potential of the 486 PC, it must be served by a suitable operating system and one of the best candidates for this task is UNIX.

There will be a steady erosion by the 486 PC of the territory held by minicomputers in the commercial sectors. Being able to offer the processing power required by large financial packages, the 486 PC will become a very attractive alternative to the minicomputer.

The 386 PC, on the other hand, is still the best machine for running DOS application programs because of the economical advantage it offers over the 486 PC. DOS programs still enjoy considerable popularity and will continue to do so for the time being. 386 PCs have well and truly established their market position and will remain dominant as a single user computing platform and as a network workstation for the foreseeable future.

The 386 PC will continue to serve as the most suitable starting platform for UNIX program development. The low-cost and inherent flexibility of the 386 PC for adapting to specific design configurations will ensure its continuing support for at least the first half of this decade.

Some of the Vendors and Distributors cited in the text

Action Instruments, St. James Works, St. Pancras, Chichester, West Sussex. 0243-774-022. or 8601 Aero Drive, San Diego, CA-92123. (619) 279-5726.

Alloy Computer Products, Alloy House, Mercian Close, Cirencester, Gloucestershire, GL7 1LT. 0285-659571.

Analog Devices Inc, One Technology Way, P.O. 9106, Norwood, MA 02062-9106 USA. or **Analog Devices,** Oakwood House, South Road, Harlow, Essex, CM20 2BY. 0279-418611.

Apricot Computers Ltd, Apricot House, 11 Hagley Road, Edgbaston, Birmingham, B16 8LB. 021-456-1234.

Aramante, Unit 6, Bittacy Business Centre, Bittacy Hill, London, NW7 1BA. 081-349-1111.

Autodesk, South Bank Technopark, 90 London Road, London SE1 6LN. 071-928-7868.

Bayan, 115 Flanders Rd., Westboro, MA 01581. (508) 898-1000. (Amarante is a UK distributor.)

Box DRI, Monterey, CA 93942, USA. (408)-649-3896.

Burr Brown International Ltd, 1 Millfield House, Woodshots, Meadow, Watford, Herts, WD1 8WX. 0923-33837.

Cablines Ltd, Unit 4, Orchard Business Park, Sandiacre, Notts, NG10 5BP. 0602-491010.

Cambridge Computer Graphics, Graphics House, Convent Drive, Waterbeach, Cambridge, CB5 9QT. 0223-863311.

Cristie Electronics Ltd, Bonds Mill, Stonehouse, Gloucester, GL10 3RG. 0453-823611

Cherry Electrical Products Ltd, Coldharbour Lane, Harpenden, Herts, AL5 4UN. 05827-63100.

Comcen Technology Ltd, 45/51 Wychtree Street, Morriston, Swansea, SA6 8EX.

Compaq Computer Ltd, Hothan House, 1 Heron Square, Richmond, Surrey, TW9 1EJ. 081-332-3000.

Computer Marketing plc, Yorktown House, 8 Frimley Road, Camberley, Surrey. GU15 3HS. 0276-691122.

Ctrl-Alt-Del, 32 North 13th Street, Central Milton Keynes, Buckinghamshire, MK9 3BP. 0908-662759.

Cyrix Corporation, P.O. Box 850118, Richardson, TX 75085. (214)-234-8387. (Micro Call Solutions is a UK distributor.)

Data Translation Ltd, The Mulberry Business Park, Berkshire, RG11 2QJ. 0734-793838.

Di-an Micro Systems, Mersey House, Battersea Rd, Heaton Mersey, Stockport, Cheshire, SK6 2SD. 061-494-9001.

Dickinson Computer Systems, Winchester, Hants.

Digital Research Inc, Oxford House, Oxford St., Newbury, RG13 1JB. 0635-35304.

Digithurst Ltd, Church Lane, Royston, Herts, SG8 9LG. 0763-242955.

Dilog, Brackmills Business Park, Caswell Road, Brackmill, Northampton, NN4 0PW. 0604-767636.

Dram Electronics, Latham Close, Bredbury Industrial Park, Stockport, SK6 2SD. 061-494-9001.

DSC Nestar Systems, 1 Brooklands Road, Weybridge, Surrey, KT13 0RU. 09323-53911.

Electric Distribution, Meadow Lane, St Ives, Cambs, PE17 4GL. 0480-496666.

Epson (UK), Campus 100, Maylands Avenue, Hemel Hempstead, Herts, HP2 7EZ. 0442-61144.

Firdata, Research House, Fraser Road, Perivale, Middlesex, UB6 7AQ. 081-997-6750.

First Nation Sales, 70 High Street, Wallingford, Oxford, OX10 0BX. 0491-34383.

Graphic Sciences, 17 The Green, Richmond, Surrey, TW9 1PX. 081-940-9480.

Hewlett Packard Ltd, King Street Lane, Winnersh, Wokingham, Berks, RG11 5AR.

Hitachi UK, Trafalgar House, Hammersmith International Centre, 2 Chalk Hill Road, Hammersmith W6 8DW. 081-748-2001.

Howtek (Technex) Digithurst Ltd, Church Lane, Royston, Herts, SG8 9LG. 0763-242955.

IBM National Response Centre, 414 Chiswick High Road, London, W4 5TF. 081-995-7700.

IGC, 4800 Great America Parkway, Santa Clear, CA 95054, USA. (404)-986-8373. (Phasestrong is a UK distributor).

Irwin, Cipher House, Ashville Way, Wokingham, Berkshire, RG11 2PL. 0734-775757.

INTERACTIVE Systems, St Johns Court, Easton St, High Wycombe, Buckinghamshire, HP11 1JX. 0494-472900.

Industrial Computer Source Ltd, PO Box 81, Chichester, West Sussex, PO21 7SD. 0243-533900.

INMAC Ltd, 16 Silver Road, London, W12 7SG. 081-740-9450.

Intel Corporation (UK) Ltd, Pipers Way, Swindon, Wiltshire, SN3 1RJ. 0793-696000.

Joyce-Loebl, Dukesway, Team Valley, Gateshead, Tyne & Wear, NE11 0PZ.

Keithley Instruments Ltd, The Minster, 58 Portman Road, Reading, Berkshire, RG3 1EA. 0743-861287.

KPG Comm Net, Tolworth Tower, Ewell Road, Tolworth, Surrey, KT6 7EL.

Level V Distribution Ltd, Ashford House, Dale Road South, Darley Dale, Matlock, Derbyshire, DE4 2EU. 0619-733141.

Megastore Ltd, Unit B, Progress House, Albert Road, Aldershot, Hampshire, GU11 1SZ. 0252-344355.

MetraByte Corp, 440 Myles Standish Blvd., Taunton, MA 02780, USA. (0508)-880-3000. (Keithley is a UK distributor.)

Micro Call Solutions, 17 Park Road, Thame, Oxford, OX9 3XD. 0844-261500.

Myriad Solutions Ltd, St John's Innovation Centre, Cowley Road, Cambridge, CB4 4WS. 0223-421181.

National Instruments (UK), 21 Kingfisher Court, Hambridge Road, Newbury, Berks, RG14 5SJ. 0635-523545.

Nestar Systems, 1 Brooklands Road, Weybridge, Surrey, KT13 0RU. 09323-53911.

Nighthawk Electronics Ltd, PO Box 44, Saffron Walden, Essex, CB11 3ND. 0799-40881.

Novell Ltd, Avon House, Sweetwell Road, Off Longshot Lane, Bracknell, Berks, RG12 1HH. 0344-860400.

Onelan Ltd, PO Box 107, Henley-on-Thames, Oxfordshire, RG9 3NQ. 0734-404859.

Pacific Data Products, 6404 Namcy Ridge Drive, San Diego, CA 92121, USA(619) 552-0880. (Protek is a UK distributor.)

Panasonic Business Systems, Panasonic House, Willoughby Road, Bracknell, Berks, RG12 4FP. 0344-853915.

Perdix Components Ltd, Unit 4, Airport Trading Estate, Biggin Hill, Kent, TN16 3BW. 0959-71011.

Phasestrong Ltd, The Sanderson Centre, Unit A21, Lees Lane, Gosport, Hants, PO12 3UL. 0705-511673.

Plasmon Data Systems, Whiting Way, Melbourn, Herts, SG8 6EN. 0763-61466.

Protek, Unit 2, Horton Industrial Park, Horton Road, West Drayton, Middlesex, UB7 8JD. 0895-446000.

Quadshield Ltd, 21 Alston Drive, Bradwell Abbey, Milton Keynes, MK13 9HA. 0908-320350.

Qume, Qume House, Park Way, Newbury, Berkshire, RG12 1EE. 0635-523200.

Roland Digital Group, Amalgamated Drive, West Cross Centre, Brentwood, Middlesex, TW8 9EZ. 081-847-5665.

Samsung Electronics Ltd, Unit 1, Hook Rise Business and Industrial Centre, 225 Hook Rise South, Surbiton, Surrey, KT6 7LD. 081-391-0168.

Seagate Technology, Angler Court, Spittal Street, Marlow, Bucks, SL7 1DB. 0628-890656.

Sharp Electronics Corp, Sharp Plaza, Mahway, NJ 07430. (201)-529-8757 or Sharp House, Thorpe Road, Newton Heath, M10 9BE. 061-833-0226.

SMIS, Alen Turing Road, Surrey Research Park, Guidlford, Surrey, GU2 5YF. 0483-506611

Software Paradise, Avenue House, King Edward Avenue, Caerphilly, Mid Glamorgan 0222-887521.

Summit Board Computing Ltd, Summit House, 11 Grange Way, Colchester, CO2 8HF. 0206-761922.

The Santa Cruz Operation Inc, 400 Encinal Street, P.O. Box 1900, Santa Cruz, California 95061 (800)-726-8649. (Level V Distribution is a UK distributor.)

Transtech Devices Ltd, Summit House, 11 Grange Way, Colchester, CO2 8HF.

Torus Network Products (TNP), Science Park, Milton Rd, Cambridge, CB4 4GZ. 0223-423131.

Vernon Microsystems, The White House, Church Street, Hungerford, Berkshire, RG17 0JH. 0488-8477.

Versacad UK Ltd, The Creative Workshop, Lovel Road, Winkfield, Berkshire, SL4 2ES. 0344-886421

Weitek, Greyhound House, 23/24 George Street, Richmond, Surrey, TW9 1JY. 0549-0164.

Index

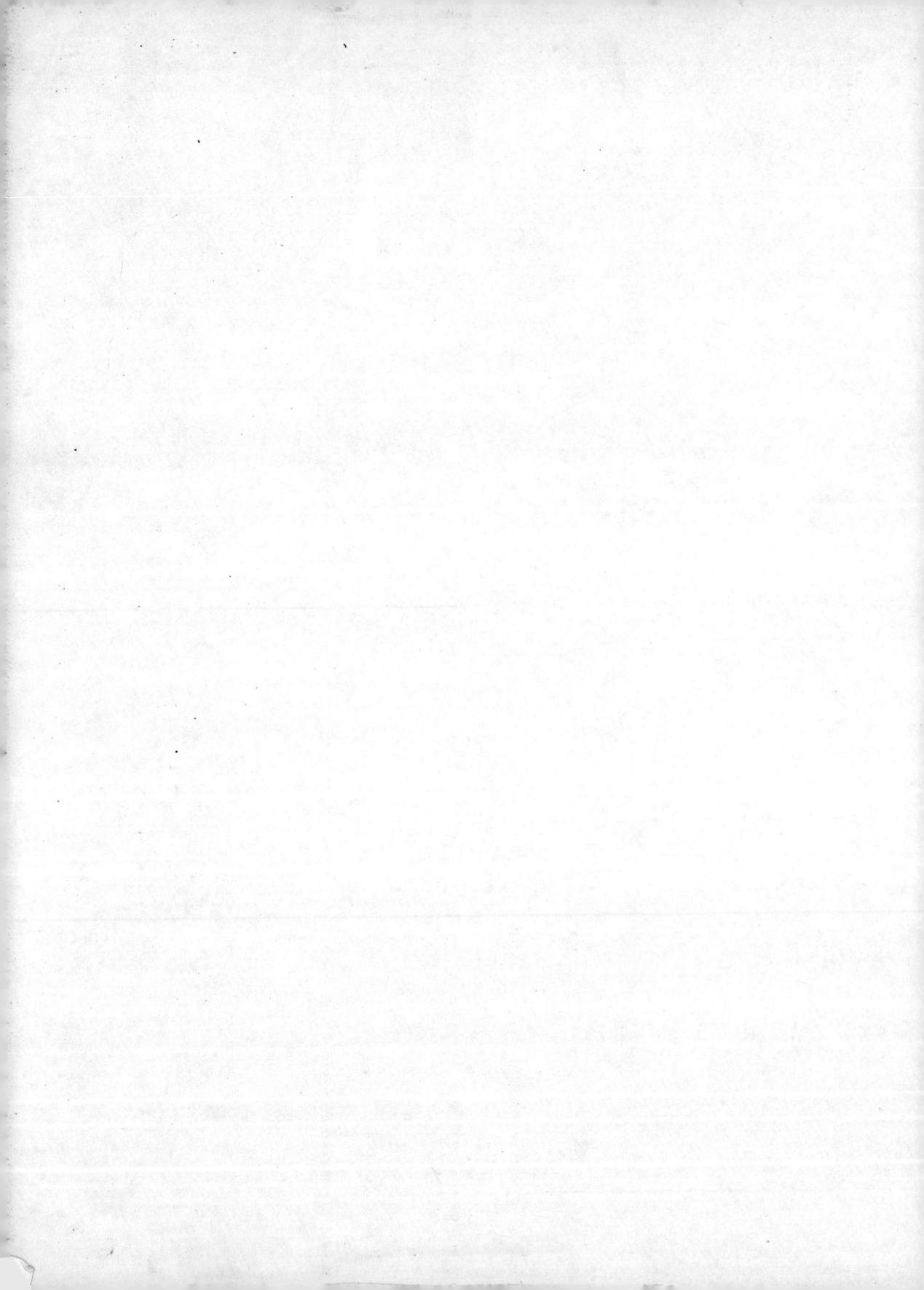